TWAYNE'S WORLD AUTHORS SERIES

A Survey of the World's Literature

Sylvia E. Bowman, Indiana University
GENERAL EDITOR

RUSSIA

Nicholas P. Vaslef, U. S. Air Force Academy
EDITOR

Nikolay Gogol

(TWAS 299)

TWAYNE'S WORLD AUTHORS SERIES (TWAS)

The purpose of TWAS is to survey the major writers —novelists, dramatists, historians, poets, philosophers, and critics—of the nations of the world. Among the national literatures covered are those of Australia, Canada, China, Eastern Europe, France, Germany, Greece, India, Italy, Japan, Latin America, the Netherlands, New Zealand, Poland, Russia, Scandinavia, Spain, and the African nations, as well as Hebrew, Yiddish, and Latin Classical literatures. This survey is complemented by Twayne's United States Authors Series and English Authors Series.

The intent of each volume in these series is to present a critical-analytical study of the works of the writer; to include biographical and historical material that may be necessary for understanding, appreciation, and critical appraisal of the writer; and to present all material in clear, concise English—but not to vitiate the scholarly content of the work by doing so.

Nikolay Gogol

By THAÏS S. LINDSTROM

Scripps College

Twayne Publishers, Inc.   ::   New York

Library of Congress Cataloging in Publication Data

Lindstrom, Thaïs S
  Nikolay Gogol.

  (Twayne's world author series, TWAS 299. Russia)
  Bibliography: p.
  1. Gogol', Nikolaĭ Vasīl' evich, 1809–1852.
PG3335.L52   891.7'8'309   73–17457
ISBN 0–8057–2377–3

To Elena Mogilat

Preface

Gogol is a writer who seems to justify by himself alone the very existence of literary criticism. His commentators have been baffled about how to approach this intractable and difficult genius, whose fruitfulness has stimulated diverse and at times mutually exclusive theories in the interpretations of his works.

Gogol's world contains multitudes. One purpose of the present study is to touch upon the many contradictory and complex features of his art at each point of its development and, through a careful examination of the major works, give reason and plausibility to the multiple facets of cumulative Gogolian scholarship. Among a host of interpreters, socially minded Realists, Romantics, Symbolists, and Formalists have all claimed Gogol for their own. Critical opinion has included such disparate views on the significance of his writings as that of the militant liberals of his own day who dubbed him the father of Russian Realism and denunciator of the tsarist regime, that of the Russian Symbolists who saw his work as a wild poet's fantasy peopled with improbable monsters, or the early twentieth-century technicians of style for whom Gogol—as the first real master of Russian prose—was an innovator of language whose manipulations of verbal devices appeared as the essence of his art.

The central problem that arose from this "whirlwind of misunderstandings," as Gogol himself called the controversy which raged around him during his lifetime and for several generations of critics, was the propensity to place his work within a known literary tradition. Despite repetitive Soviet adjurations to the contrary, of all the major Russian writers Gogol alone stands apart from the mainstream of political and social ferment that gives continuity to Russian literature. Almost by an accident of time his writing can be considered with that of the Realists who followed him. And yet, because his fiction has the look of the feudal Russia of his day, crammed as it is with minutely observed *Kleinmalerei*, he has been frequently labeled as a founder of the Natural school that includes such Realists as Grigorovich, Turgenev, Goncharov, and Ostrovsky. In accordance with this view, his influence was uncovered in the humanitarianism and pathology of Dostoevsky, the descriptions of bucolic existence in Turgenev, in Chekhov's somber humor, and in Leskov's adroitly bizarre storytelling techniques. By now this familiar tendency of singling out certain typical Gogolian traits pointing to a close relationship with the psychological and historical climate which is the hallmark of the nineteenth-century Russian novel has contributed to a confusion among Gogolian scholars as to the writer's position and importance in European literature.

Perhaps only now that the chaos and fragmentation of the twentieth-century experience have become commonplaces in our literature can the essential modernity of Gogol be properly understood. In his brief writer's life, remarkably free of other than professional incident, he produced for his unsuspecting countrymen a miracle of prophecy in evoking with an intuitive rightness of genius an image that was to haunt the Western European artistic imagination a hundred years later. His intensely subjective, inner-directed vision predicts the deliberate estrangement and withdrawal of the modern artist from an increasingly conformist and mass-minded society. Anticipating the modern artist, Gogol plotted in his private life and in his fiction escapes from a vulgar, trivialized, soulless world that imaginatively he found uninhabitable. He saw the evil spreading everywhere and he adopted the watchful marginal strategy of the writer who is on the ramparts of his city, reflecting the turmoil and looking out at the advancing lines of the enemy. With his hyperbolic binoculars he spotted and diagnosed it as a supremely outrageous assault on the consciousness of man. His anger at the dehumanizing effects of city life, the reduction of the individual to a faceless robot by the ruthless impersonality of the bureaucratic machine, the soul-leveling power of moneyed enterprise might have served to spark present-day apprehensions. The meaninglessness of existence drained of spiritual resources verges in his stories on what the existentialists of our time have described as the vacuum of boredom and despair.

Gogol's answer to the cosmic solitude and homelessness that

was also his personal situation was a violent one: his heroes escape into sexual fantasy, hallucinating dreams, madness where free juxtaposition of the conscious and the unconscious with unpredictable juxtaposition of unrelated thoughts and images is the rule, and there emerges an alogical irreality to which the surrealist poets were to provide a final expression. There is also the satirist's revenge on the venal indulgences of the "establishment" which deforms the offenders into huge caricatures, comic or demonic, to whom Gogol denies humanity just as the Cubists in their disfiguration of the human form rejected its traditionally revered beauty of symmetry and proportion. Here, again, the quality of excess and contained savagery in the Gogolian grotesque meets the metaphor of contemporary literature that favors sensational and extreme situations.

Within the limits of this brief introduction to Gogol, what the writer has in common with our age has been specifically discussed in connection with the significance of his major heroes, his theater, and the construction of his comic grotesque. No attempt has been made to treat the complexity and scope of this theme beyond the inferences, implicit in the interpretation of his works, that the writer's vision outdistanced his epoch and reached to our own time.

THAÏS S. LINDSTROM

Contents

Chronology

1809   Born March 20 in Sorochinets, in Ukraine.

1821   Enters Nezhin Secondary School.

1825   Father dies.

1828   Graduates with low civil service grade. Leaves for St. Petersburg.

1829   Seeks job in capital. Publishes *Hanz Küchelgarten* under pseudonym at his own expense. Burns all copies of *Hanz*. Sails to Lübeck, Germany, where he remains one month. Returns to St. Petersburg.

1830   Obtains minor post in Department of Public Works. "St. John's Eve" without the author's name appears in *Notes of the Fatherland*. In *Northern Flowers,* under pseudonym, chapter from "a historical novel" also appears.

1831   In Delvig's *Literary Gazette* two articles under pseudonyms published: two chapters from "A Ukrainian Tale," "The Terrible Boar," and one signed by Gogol—the essay "Woman." Delvig recommends him to Zhukovsky who introduces him to Pushkin, Pletnyov, and Alexandra Smirnova. Through Pletnyov, appointed as history teacher at The Patriotic Institute. Leaves Civil Service. Publishes first volume of *Evenings on a Farm near Dikanka*.

1832   Spends summer at Vasilevka. In Moscow meets Pogodin, Shchepkin, and Sergey Aksakov. Publishes second volume of the Ukrainian tales.

1834   Appointed adjunct professor of history at St. Petersburg University.

1835   Reads *The Wedding* at Pogodin's house. Publishes *Mirgorod* and *Arabesques*. Dismissed from University.

1836   Reads *The Inspector General* at one of Zhukovsky's "Saturdays." *The Carriage* and "The Morning of a Government Official" appear in *The Contemporary*. Première of

The Inspector General at St. Petersburg. Composes *After the Theater*. Leaves Russia. Visits German resort towns and Swiss cities. *The Nose* and "St. Petersburg Notes" appear in *The Contemporary*. Spends winter in Paris.

1837   Settles in Rome, spending summers at German spas.

1839   Returns to Russia for an eight-month stay. In Moscow reads first chapters of *Dead Souls* to friends.

1840   Becomes seriously ill in Vienna. Back in Rome completes *The Overcoat*.

1841   Returns to Moscow with manuscript of *Dead Souls*. Has difficulties with the censor. *Rome*, under the title "Fragment," published in *Muscovite*.

1842   Publishes *Dead Souls*. For next six years wanders all over Western Europe from spa to spa, seeking cure for increasing physical ailments. Revised version of *The Portrait* appears in *The Contemporary*.

1845   Burns all drafts of Part II, *Dead Souls*.

1847   Publishes *Selected Passages from Correspondence with Friends*.

1848   Makes pilgrimage to Jerusalem. Returns to Russia: Vasilevka, Moscow, Odessa, Moscow again. Continues writing Part II of *Dead Souls*.

1852

Feb.   4–Starts severe regime of fasting and prayer.

Feb. 11–Burns Part II manuscript of *Dead Souls*. Weakened by extreme and continuous fasting. Becomes very ill.

Feb. 21–Dies.

CHAPTER 1

Establishment of Identity

I *Childhood in the Ukraine*

NIKOLAY Vasilievich Gogol was born into a family of Ukrainian landowners. Their estate of some three thousand acres and two hundred fifty serfs was situated in the district of Poltava, the very heart of the Ukraine, where the fertile black earth and gentle climate made possible an easy and plentiful life. In his first Ukrainian stories Gogol was to recall the countryside of his childhood, the verdure of its gardens and the sun-drenched beauty of the landscape beyond:

How languishingly warm the hours when midday shines in the stillness and sultry heat and the blue fathomless ocean, a cupola bending voluptuously over the earth, seems to be sleeping, sunk in languor, holding the beautiful earth close in its ethereal embrace . . . the broad branches of cherry, plum, and apple trees are bent under their fruit; the sky, and its clear mirror, the river in its green, proudly erect frame . . . how full of languor and delight is the Ukrainian summer! [1]

In this magnificent natural setting, the household led a comfortable manorial existence, their needs and wishes reaching no further than the main town of their district, Mirgorod. A trip to this town, made only a few times a year in their spacious, old-fashioned carriage, was a great event. Local and more frequent entertainment was provided by folk singers and dancers at their own village fairs. Innumerable neighbors and friends were received with wide unpretentious hospitality made effortless by the presence of many house serfs and an abundant ever ready table of home delicacies and home brews that were the bounty of the estate.

At the time of Nickolay's birth, his extraordinarily pretty mother was only 18 and her husband, Vasily, 29. Although duly registered as a member of the Ukrainian landowning nobility,

Vasily Gogol-Yanovsky, for that was his full name, had dubious claim to the peerage. His ancestry traced back to Ostap Gogol, a colonel in the Cossack army who had been rewarded with a piece of land in 1674 after service with the Polish king, Casimir. It is unlikely that any of his descendants were ennobled, as they were all priests. The writer's great-grandfather, Demyan, also a priest, added the Polish version of his father's Christian name, Yan, to the family name which thus became Gogol-Yanovsky. The writer's grandfather, Afanasy, became a major in the army, but he was also a seminarian who taught the children of wealthy neighbors Greek, German, and Polish. He fell in love with one of his pupils, Tatyana Lizogub, daughter of an important Ukrainian nobleman, and as family tradition has it, first sent her a fervent declaration in the shell of a nut, then abducted and married her. Her father agreed reluctantly to this mésalliance and endowed the young bridegroom with a piece of property on condition that he exchange the less esteemed clerical vocation for the status of landowner. Lizogub was probably influential in having a document forged that accredited Afanasy with the title to nobility, recorded in 1794 in the peerage book of the province of Kiev. The writer himself referred vaguely and grandiloquently to his "Cossack ancestors," and upon his arrival in St. Petersburg dropped the second part of his surname, considering its origins as "something that the Poles must have invented."

Gogol's father was a gentle, unambitious man, best remembered for his ardent and persistent courtship of thirteen-year-old Maria Kosyarovskaya, a neighbor's daughter whom he wooed with daily letters for over a year, imploring her to keep secret the "passionate declarations of my lovesick heart." The little girl, however, showed them to her father, admitting that she was very fond of her admirer, as fond as she was of her dear aunts. Her father solemnly read the letters out loud to the assembled family and dictated suitable replies. When Maria was fourteen, her parents permitted her to be led to the altar, stipulating that she return home for at least a year, but her husband claimed her within six months. Until the husband's death twenty years later, they were deeply happy and produced twelve children. Only four of these survived beyond infancy.

In his approach to life, Vasily Gogol alternated between an indulgence in dreamy sentimentality and the exercise of a sharp and mocking wit. This oscillation was also markedly present in the character of his famous son. The elder Gogol had a taste for writing and liked to pen rhetorical verses, but he also wrote two lively comedies, based on Ukrainian puppet shows featuring traditional figures such as the comic devil, an impudent country woman, and a deacon in an oversized coat. These plays were produced on the Kibintsy estate which belonged to Dmitry Troshchinsky, a distant relative who was immensely wealthy. Troshchinsky was a prominent personage in the province; he considered himself a patron of the arts and liked to dazzle the local gentry with his serf orchestra and theater. Here, Vasily Gogol would at times be pressed into the duties of secretary and master of ceremonies and could be counted on to entertain the guests with his accomplished telling and acting out of humorous stories.

In contrast, back home on his own modest property he would spend many solitary hours in the garden, clearing paths, building grottoes and arbors that he labeled with highly poetic names such as the "Temple of Meditation" and the "Vale of Peace." As passionately fond of birds as he was of flowers and plants, he did not allow the serf girls to use the pond near the house for washing clothes for fear of disturbing the nightingales. Impractical and easygoing, Gogol's father was essentially a dilettante; an indifferent farmer, a hobbyist gardener, amateur playwright, an amiable and gregarious host, he seemed content to pursue his many undemanding interests in the indolent atmosphere of humdrum rural life. Despite this, he was subject to fits of unaccountable black melancholia and suffered from a nagging hypochondria. Any symptom of physical illness, his own or that of members of his family, brought on an exaggerated anxiety and fear of death. His son was to resemble him in these psychological disturbances.

Actually, Nikolay Gogol had little personal contact with his father. His childhood passed in the permissive atmosphere of the feminine household of overindulgent relatives and servants, dominated by Maria Gogol who loved her third child—her first son—blindly and compulsively. Her first two children were stillborn. Nikolay was a sickly boy and was cosseted, spoiled and pampered.

His naïve and emotionally unstable mother, who retained the mentality of a girl of fifteen, granted her son's every caprice,

gloried in his every action, and praised him volubly and inde-
fatigably to anyone who would listen. Later, across the distance
of years and geography, she continued to enlarge the pantheon
of his achievements, reading and rereading his letters to her
entourage and acclaiming him, to his irritation and embarrass-
ment, the greatest writer in the world and even attributing to
him the invention of the steamship and the railroad engine![2]

This immoderate demonstration of love bordering on idolatry
inflated the importance of his own ideas in the boy's mind and
encouraged him to become egotistical and self-centered. In uncharacteristically trenchant lines written to his mother when he
was twenty-four, he recalled his early years at home: "I looked
upon everything as if it had been created only to gratify me. I
loved no one in particular except you and I loved you only because Nature inspired me to do so."[3] In the same letter he reveals
another aspect of his mother's influence upon him: "I went to
church only because I was ordered to do so or because I was
carried there. . . . I crossed myself only because I saw others
crossing themselves. But once—I remember it vividly—I asked
you to describe The Last Judgment, and you told me, a child, so
clearly and movingly about the happiness that is waiting for
virtuous people; you pictured so graphically the eternal misery
of sinners that it awakened my sensibilities and later evoked in
me the most lofty thoughts."[4]

This avowal may explain in part Gogol's recurring panic at
the thought of death, his apprehensions concerning life after
death, and the presence in some of his writings of a real and
hated devil. His mother's surface piety, evidenced in the conventional observance of religious ritual, uncritically accepted the
lurid details of a medieval hell and absorbed the superstitions of
demoniacal folklore. All Apochrypha fed her credulous and neurotic mind. She impressed upon her children a primitive belief
in an actual physical link between the world of heaven and that
of earth, which young Gogol drank in and which remained entrenched in his imagination.

He was a thoughtful child inclined to withdraw into a dreamy
silent contemplation of his own. At other moments, such as the
one he described many years later to his friend Alexandra Rosset-
Smirnova, he would attain a high state of nervousness and be
gripped by morbid fears:

Establishment of Identity

I was 5 years old. I was alone at Vasilevka. Father and Mother had gone out. My old nurse was with me, but she had gone off somewhere. I had squeezed myself into a corner of the sofa and listened to the ticking of the pendulum in the old-fashioned wall clock. There was a rush of sound in my ears, something was moving toward me and then drawing away. Would you believe it—it seemed to me even then that the ticking of the pendulum was the ticking of time, receding into eternity. Suddenly the faint meowing of the cat broke the oppressive silence. I saw it creeping carefully toward me as it meowed. I shall never forget how it crept along, stretching itself, its soft-pawed claws scratching faintly on the floor and its eyes gleaming evilly. I became frightened. "Kitty, kitty," I muttered, and to give myself courage, jumped off the sofa, grabbed the cat that was easy to get hold of, ran into the garden and threw it into the pond, and several times when it tried to scramble out, I pushed it further away with a pole. I was afraid, I was trembling, and yet at the same time, I felt a kind of satisfaction, that may have been the feeling of revenge for the way it had frightened me.[5]

II School Years

At the age of nine, when he was ready for formal instruction, his father was unable to afford a private tutor and sent Nikolay and the younger son, Ivan, to school in Poltava. This first plunge into a world where he was no longer the principal personage was a traumatic experience for Nikolay. During the first summer vacation he became seriously ill; his illness may have been aggravated by the death of his little brother, Ivan, to whom he was greatly attached. His parents decided to place Nikolay at the newly established residential High School of Advanced Studies in Nezhin; with Troshchinsky's influence he obtained a state scholarship and remained at that school for the next seven years.

Men distinguished for their intellectual achievement are often known to have been wretched students during their schooldays. Gogol was no exception. Of the great Russian writers, he was most probably the one who profited least from formal education. By temperament and upbringing he was completely unprepared for a systematic intake of knowledge. Despite the fact that the laxity of the administration equalled the inadequate academic background of the teaching staff, most of Gogol's instructors remembered him as a stubborn, inattentive boy, difficult to discipline, who managed to learn almost nothing. Young Gogol was not lazy; rather he was bored by the drudgery of classroom drill and became very quickly expert at distracting himself in a far corner of the room, where shielded by the half-open lid of his desk, he would scribble, read from literary magazines or paint and draw tiny landscapes and figures. Individual course records show that he knew no mathematics, very little Latin and French, was unable to learn German, and evinced interest only in Russian history and literature.

If the sojourn at Nezhin gave little to Gogol in the way of formal education, it did provide him with what is perhaps a boarding school's most important function to a nonconforming adolescent—the time and shelter from the outside world in which to find and assess himself. Moreover, the school environment taught Gogol a great deal, expanded and strengthened him, and he may have resented the intrusion of conventional academic study, because instinctively, he sensed that there were too many other challenges in his new situation that he had to face, fight, and understand.

From Gogol's letters to his parents one can reconstruct the changing pattern of the extracurricular activities that absorbed him. A plea for money with which to buy books is a recurring one. In his third year, the students' literary club began to subscribe to St. Petersburg periodicals that published avant-garde writers, Nikolay Karamzin, Vasily Zhukovsky, Alexander Pushkin, and the German Romantics, who were undermining the Classical canon rigidly adhered to by the literature instructor, Nikolsky, and therefore excluded from his courses. One of Gogol's typical hoaxes had been to submit Pushkin's poem, *Prorok* (*The Prophet*), for a homework assignment as one of his own, and when Nikolsky corrected it in class as an example of bad syntax, Gogol could not resist naming the real author. The teacher's imperturbable reply was that it only proved the worthlessness of Pushkin's verse!

With the uncritical enthusiasm of the young and the provincial, the boys devoured the latest examples of Gothic fantasy, lyrical Romanticism, and Sentimental sensibility. Gogol took charge of the student library, where he made the readers wear paper gloves of his own design that would keep the treasured stock from becoming grease-stained. At Saturday night meetings, the "literati" read aloud their own creative attempts at poetry and prose, and decided whether they were worthy of inclusion in the handwritten school magazine, *Dung of Parnassus.* These occasions were the first circumstances testing Gogol's writings; only two poems have survived from these works submitted to this early public.

Unreliable, time-blurred recollections by his former school-fellows inform us that one of Gogol's compositions was a tragedy in iambic pentameter. Its title *Razbouniki* (*The Brigands*), suggests a borrowing from Schiller; another, *Dve Rybki* (*Two Little Fishes*), was a ballad that commemorated—touchingly—the sad fate of Gogol himself and his younger brother; a third was an unfinished satire in five parts called *Nechto o Nezhine* (*Something About Nezhin*);* the only prose effort, *Bratya Tverdisla-vichi* (*The Brothers Tverdislavich*), a narrative based on Slavic history, was rejected out of hand by the young critics. Gogol, with apparent calm, at once tore up the manuscript and burned it. This was the first of his many literary autos-da-fé.

Although he was little appreciated as a potential man of letters, Gogol's acting ability earned him unreserved praise and a brilliant stage career was predicted for him. This withdrawn, evasive schoolboy, given to fantasies and exaggerated attitudes, suddenly lighted up at the very idea of theater with a spontaneous ardor and serious dedication. He wrote home in ebullient detail about school performances in which he was costume designer, stage hand, set painter, director, and actor. It was as if the staging of a greater pretense released an inner tension in him and allowed him to drop his own posturings. In creating a role, he transformed himself into another person with a mimetic and verbal assurance rare for one his age. He excelled in the portrayal of prototypal old men and women. As Harpagon in Molière's *L'Avare,* he managed to touch his chin with his nose to affect a miser's mask and in *The Minor,* Fonvizin's Classical comedy, he masterfully projected the monstrously stupid and tyrannical Mme. Prostakova and her sickening overindulgence for her lout of a son.

Another type of pleasure that made the summer holidays a landmark for Gogol was the excitement and lure of the open

---

* The full title is: *Nechto o Nezhine, ili durakam zakon ne pisan* (Something about Nezhin, or the Law is Not Written for Fools).

road. Many a time in later life he was to shake off a fit of depression with its help. Riding in a cart from Nezhin to Vasilevka—a two-hundred-mile trip which took several days—a glorious sense of well-being and detachment took hold of him. It was an escape from school routine and a heady draught of fresh impressions that he might use later. Eagerly and keenly observant, the boy grafted on his mind the most minute details of the rural landscape, while his travelling companion, Alexander Danilevsky, snored at his side.

Danilevsky was a neighbor's son and classmate, and one of Gogol's few close friends at Nezhin. Two others, Konstantin Basili and Nikolay Prokopovich, both leaders of the "literati" group, remained closely associated with Gogol afterwards. His boon companion, however, was Gerasim Vysotsky, known for a blistering wit that rivalled Gogol's own. Both excelled in comical turns of speech and in inventing mocking epithets with which to brand teachers whom they despised. Vysotsky suffered from an eye ailment and was confined for long periods in the infirmary where sitting under an umbrella he gathered around him his fellow wags. A story has it that when Gogol was about to be severely disciplined, he simulated such a brilliant fit of madness that he was isolated in the infirmary near Vysotsky's umbrella and managed to spend two enjoyable months there, gnashing his teeth, howling fearfully, and attempting to smash chairs whenever a teacher or the visiting doctor appeared.

Gogol's anti-social exhibitionism found other outlets; he would walk, head held low, on the wrong side of the school corridor and jostle oncomers, or pace up and down in his room producing fortissimo imitations of an owl's screech, a pig's grunt, and the croaking of a frog. When asked why he made such noises, he replied that he preferred the company of animals to that of human beings. There is little doubt that such freakish conduct was compensatory behavior for humiliations he had endured upon his arrival in Nezhin.

When the undersized, gauche, scrofulous, and scrawny boy with a face made birdlike by an inordinately long and pointed nose had been deposited in the school vestibule, bundled in his mother's many shawls, he was instantly surrounded by a mob of jeering boys. Gogol could not shake off the memory of this first onslaught and did not settle down into a *modus vivendi* with his schoolfellows. Something in his highstrung and complex organism resisted the normalcy of relaxed relationships with other people.

To make up for the difference that he felt existed between himself and the other boys, Gogol resorted to posturing in a bid for attention; he even exploited and exaggerated his own physical shortcomings. His self-caricature was so successful that he naturally extended his repertoire by caricaturing others. He discovered within himself an unsuspected strength: the ability to put his finger on the most unflattering imperfection of the subject he mocked and magnify it out of all proportion. The Mysterious Dwarf, as Gogol had been nicknamed for his eccentric behavior, was feared by his fellow students and teachers alike.

Evidence that Gogol was not displeased by his reputation emerges in a rather pretentious and complacent self-analysis written to his mother at the age of nineteen:

Everyone considers me to be an enigma; no one understands me completely. At home I am supposed to be a kind of wayward, insufferable pedant who deems himself more intelligent than everyone else and different from the rest. Would you believe that inwardly I have laughed at myself along with you? Here I am called meek, an ideal of humility and patience. In one place I am the quietest, the most modest and well-mannered person; elsewhere I am morose, pensive, uncouth etc.; on other occasions garrulous and boring in the extreme, considered by some clever and by others stupid. Only when I enter upon my real career will you discover what my true character is.[6]

What was his career to be? According to one biographer he was at first impressed by the opulence of Troshchinsky's mansion and by the obsequious respect paid to its owner, who had served as Minister of Justice and had been decorated by two Russian sovereigns.[7] He wished to emulate Troshchinsky. But soon Gogol wanted still more than that. He was convinced that a superior destiny awaited him in a wider field of endeavor, that he would "even be useful to the world at large."[8] What he dreaded most was that he might become a mere "exister," as he wrote despairingly to Vysotsky during his last school year when his friend was already in St. Petersburg.[9] Gogol feared that he would be an "exister" in the future planned for him by his mother: after graduation he was to return to Vasilevka to help her manage the family estate.

As a result of this fear, his uncle received the following page of impassioned rhetoric in which Gogol describes his ambitions, probably in the hope of enlisting support:

I have considered all the posts and types of public service and have decided upon—jurisprudence. I know that more is needed to be done in this than in any other field and that here I can be a real benefactor and be of greatest use to humanity. Injustice is the world's greatest evil and it tears at my heart. I have sworn not to waste a moment of my short life without accomplishing some good. During the last two years I have been constantly studying international and national law which is the basis of all law and now I am devoting my time to the laws of my country. . . .[10]

Perhaps Gogol had read some books on jurisprudence, but there is nothing to prove that he had ever studied it nor did he refer to it ever again. This was typical of the fabrications that Gogol was to indulge in so frequently; he expressed plans or desires that became concrete images in his mind as rapidly as he gave expression to them. In another instance, he informed his mother that he had spent his allowance on a complete set of Schiller's works and was now rewarded by reading them several hours each day;[11] Gogol had undoubtedly persuaded himself at the time of writing that he had indeed read the works upon his shelf, although he was barely able to decipher the most elementary German.

A few months before graduation he began to make a tremendous effort in order to pass the final examinations. His school certificate shows uniformly good grades in all subjects, but this must have been pure formality, for when he left the school he could enter the civil service only at the fourteenth rank—the lowest level.

After graduation, discouraged by the low civil service grade that was bound to delay a swift climb up the bureaucratic ladder, Gogol wrote his uncle in a more subdued tone: "I shall always be able to support myself somehow. I am skilled at some trades. I tailor well, am pretty good at painting frescoes on walls and have learned something about cooking. . . ."[12]

III   Hanz Küchelgarten

Had Gogol considered a writer's career? Although he had told no one about it, he had composed a poem in seventeen parts, entitled *Hanz Küchelgarten*. His longest creative experiment to date, he took it with him to St. Petersburg.

The long poem has little intrinsic literary value. It abounds in borrowings and imitations. The plot is based on a sentimental idyll, *Luise*, by the German poet Johann Heinrich Voss, available to Gogol in Ivan Teryaev's translation. It is centered around a restless Romantic hero who echoes the torment of Werther, has the wanderlust of Chateaubriand's *René*, rebels against materialistic society in the manner of Aleko in Pushkin's *Gypsies*, and is filled with the idealistic aspirations of the poet Lensky in *Eugene Onegin*. The poetic structure alternates unevenly and unsurely between iambic pentameter and a four-foot rhymed line; and many of the stylistic devices are taken from Pushkin and Zhukovsky. In the lyrical passages Gogol overloaded his language with archaisms and conventional epithets, and occasionally resorted to Ukrainian colloquialisms to complete a rhyme. The description of familial settings, however, is simpler and livelier. Realistic images of the house, the domestic interior, and the fields are strong, convincingly drawn, and anticipate the easy flow of later writing.

The autobiographical flavor of this immature work makes it interesting. The story of Hanz—a stereotyped Romantic episode of escape from a gentle fiancée and from the serenity of the native village to distant lands that promise the fulfillment of vague but glorious dreams—is a formalized version of Gogol's own ambitions. The resemblance between Hanz and his creator apparently ends here; the young German, disillusioned and wearied by "odious and mercenary" reality, returns home from his wanderings, content to settle down with his faithful Luise to the bliss of the commonplace. According to Gogol, his hero lacked the "will of iron" to endure the onslaught of the world and was therefore easily drawn back to the shelter of rustic existence. At the time when he was writing the poem, probably in the summer of 1827, Gogol had a similar choice to make. Unlike his less stalwart hero, he opted to launch his life's program on a perilously insecure, unchartered course far away from home. Gogol could not know that the fate he had decreed Hanz was an unconscious prophecy about himself. Just as Hanz nostalgically yearned for his ancestral home, so did Gogol continue to treasure memories of the Ukraine and, also like Hanz, remained true to the traditions of the landowning class.

At the Nezhin high school, the only academic institution he ever attended, the traditions of extreme political conservatism, adherence to the dogma and ritual of the Russian Orthodox Church, and a conventional ethic were entrenched and enforced. When Belousov, a progressive-minded instructor, humanized his lectures with open discussion and introduced the hitherto-unheard-of doctrines of the natural rights of man and individual freedom, his Philistine and pedantic colleagues were shocked and outraged. Gogol, who was to recreate Belousov's portrait in the second part of *Dead Souls*, found him extremely stimulating and came to his defense when an official inquiry into the new teacher's methods was instigated by the school authorities. Belousov had been careful not to dislodge from his pupils' minds the fundamental credo of Russian autocracy, that is the inviolability of the Tsar, the justice of the institution of serfdom, the sacrosanct authority of the state religion. Gogol reached maturity with these concepts intact, and they permanently shaped his social and moral orientation.

His psychological organization was in complete antithesis to this coherent ideology. It was fluid, contradictory, chaotic; his temperament was essentially unstable, inclined to polarity and excess. He was prey to nervous tensions and when, like a coiled spring, they were suddenly released, alternating moods of boisterous gaiety and depression would take possession of him in swift succession. His sensibilities were equally divided between a heart overflowing with effusive sentiment and a sarcastic rapier-like mind quick to note and flay the incongruous and the absurd. It was a secretive, introverted mind given neither to laughter nor openness in the relaxation of easy companionship. In Nezhin and elsewhere later in his life, he remained solitary for the most part and an outsider. Gogol felt his apartness and his complexity. He wrote to his mother: "Often I think about myself: I ask why, in creating a heart like mine, perhaps the only one of its kind in the world, at any rate rare in the world, a heart pure and avidly aspiring to love all that is lofty and beautiful, why God has placed this heart into such a coarse envelope? Why has he invested it with such a complex of contradictions, obstinacy, insolent vanity, and profound humility?"[13]

For six impatient months, after leaving school, Gogol lived at Vasilevka with his mother and his two younger sisters. Since his father's death in 1825, three years previously, the revenue from the estate had been dwindling due to Maria Gogol's incompetence in managing the property and her unfortunate propensity for investing capital in risky enterprises. With difficulty she finally raised the sum needed for her son's departure by means of a personal loan and an additional mortgage, and in midwinter Gogol set off to the capital with a twenty-five-year-old servant and Danilevsky. He preferred to take the longer route to St. Petersburg—avoiding the shorter and more travelled one because it passed through Moscow—for he wanted his first impressions of a metropolis to be those of the city of his dreams.

IV Early Setbacks

St. Petersburg gave Gogol a very chilly welcome indeed. To begin with, he caught a severe cold from leaning out the window in his excitement as the carriage approached the city. And by the time the young men found a tiny, dark, two-room apartment off a backstairs passageway on the fourth floor—the only lodging they could afford—Gogol's nose was frostbitten and he had to stay four days in bed. Disillusion followed upon disillusion. The edifice of his dreams crumbled catastrophically before the bureaucratic megapolis set in snow and ice. The symmetrically laid out streets along which countless preoccupied officials hurried, their chins and noses muffled in scarfs and turned-up collars, made the young provincial feel depressed and forlorn, and he complained in his first letter home that he thought "the city would be more handsome and magnificent than it is, and all the rumors that one hears about it are just a pack of lies."[14] It was also, he added, terribly expensive. In the first few days he had spent a third of all his money on a new dress-coat, trousers, boots, and hat. When Danilevsky joined the Cadet Corps, Gogol, with his servant Yakim, moved to even smaller quarters and rationed themselves to three logs of firewood, a few candles, and one hot meal a day. Letters of recommendation from home gained him entrance to the houses of several persons of affluence who invited him to dinner, promised vaguely to help him find a good position, and then forgot all about him.

Remembering his stage laurels in school, he attempted to obtain an acting part in one of the companies of the Imperial Theaters. The audition was a failure. Gogol had to give a dramatic monologue replete with circumlocutions that he hardly understood and that he was expected to recite in the bombastically declamatory manner fashionable at the time. Instead, in his nervousness he stammered, read haltingly in a barely audible voice, and was so mortified by his performance that he did not return to find out the director's verdict.

In March 1829, an important St. Petersburg magazine, *Syn otechestva* (*Son of the Fatherland*) accepted a poem in six eight-line stanzas from Gogol. Entitled "Italy" and sent in unsigned, it was a conventional evocation of the land beloved by the Romantics, strongly reminiscent of Pushkin's verses on the same subject. It was Gogol's first appearance in print. This may have encouraged him to publish at his own expense *Hanz Küchelgarten,* which he had been revising during his first months in Petersburg and which he cautiously signed with the pseudonym V. Alov. He prefaced it with a comment from the editors "who were proud to present to the public the work of a new young talent."

Despite Gogol's anxious queries among his friends about "Alov's" poem, it remained unnoticed until two critics—one from *Moskovsky telegraf* (*Moscow Telegraph*), the other from *Severnaya pchela* (*Northern Bee*)—reacted to it with slighting irony, judging the theme unoriginal and the verse awkward and immature. Gogol took it very hard. He made the rounds of all the city bookstores, bought up the unsold copies of *Hanz*, which almost amounted to the entire edition, and with Yakim's help burned them in the wood stove of the hotel room that he took for that day.

His immediate reaction to an environment that would not recognize his worth was to leave it. Earlier, writing to Vysotsky, he had expressed the hope of visiting other countries, even distant America,[15] and now on the rebound of his humiliation, he decided to go abroad. But how was he to raise the funds needed for such a journey?

By lucky coincidence the money became available when his mother sent him 1,400 rubles to pay into the bank as interest on their mortgaged estate. Having appropriated this sum, an action that could have led to the financial ruin of his family, Gogol wrote about it to his mother only when he was ready to leave St. Petersburg. The letter is a masterpiece of Gogolian fabrication, and fascinated biographers have been inclined to reproduce it in full.

He wrote it in the pompous overheated style to which he usually resorted in addressing his mother even when he was most sincere. He begs "his rare and magnanimous mother to forgive her ever unworthy son! . . ." He had made every effort to find a foothold in the city, but he had been pursued by every kind of ill luck and then, at last . . .

such terrible punishment! . . . You know how unusually steadfast I am for a young man . . . who would have expected such weakness from me? But I have seen her . . . no, I will not name her . . . she is too lofty for everyone, not only for me . . . She is a goddess but lightly clad in human passions . . . the tortures of hell surged in my breast . . . everything in the world was alien to me, death and life equally unbearable . . . I understood that I had to run away from myself . . . and I recognized . . . the Invisible Hand that came to my aid and blessed the way that He pointed out to me . . . and so I decided to go away . . . everything went smoothly, even to obtaining a passport . . . only the money was lacking.[16]

Whereupon in a few concise lines Gogol tells the poor woman how he appropriated the interest money for which he obtained a four month period of grace from the bank and solemnly promises never to ask her for money again. The letter concludes with a reminder that the monthly penalty is five rubles for each thousand and a further request that if possible she send Danilevsky a hundred rubles to pay for some linen and a coat that he had given Gogol.

Gogol sailed to Lübeck and from there gave his mother yet another reason for his departure that was as much a fiction as the "goddess" from whom he had fled. All that spring, he wrote, he had been ill, a rash had broken over his face and hands, and the doctors had advised him to take the waters at a small town near Lübeck. This additional completely gratuitous invention only confirmed his mother's worst fears, for she was already distraught by the idea of the "goddess," to her mind a wicked woman, who had hurt her boy. Now she became convinced that "Nikolenka" had been ensnared by a prostitute who had transmitted a venereal disease to him.

During his six weeks' stay in Germany, Gogol flitted about from one seaside town to another, but remained indifferent to his new surroundings. In Hamburg, only the Gothic cathedral and the architecture caught his imagination. This was his first step into the Middle Ages, a period of history that continued to enchant him until he discovered in Rome the art of the ancient world.

Back in St. Petersburg, penniless, desperate, and not daring to write home for help, he appealed for help to Faddey Bulgarin, a prolific and infamous journalist, who was paid by the secret police for informing on suspected liberals among artists and writers. Gogol presented him with some fulsomely eulogistic verses, and the strategy worked. Bulgarin was flattered and secured for Gogol a small post at the Imperial Chancery. Shortly afterwards, Andrey Troshchinsky, nephew and heir of Dmitry Troshchinsky, who had recently died, came to Gogol's aid. He agreed, somewhat grudgingly, to replace the interest money that Gogol had subverted for his freakish voyage, paid his young relative's rent, even gave him a winter overcoat, and obtained for him a more lucrative job in the Department of Imperial Domains. Gogol asserted later that during the fourteen months that he was attached to the civil service, he learned only one skill, that of sewing copy paper into permanent folders.

V First Publications

Meanwhile, he continued to write. The *Hanz* fiasco persuaded him to abandon poetry, and he succeeded in placing an unsigned story, set in the Ukraine, entitled *Bisavriuk, ili Vecher nakanune Ivana Kupala* (*Bisavriuk, or St. John's Eve*) in the *Otechestvennye Zapiski* (*Notes of the Fatherland*). A chapter from a historical novel, signed OOOO (one of Gogol's pseudonyms), appeared in an almanac edited by Pushkin's close friend, the poet Baron Anton Delvig. By the end of 1830 several of Gogol's pieces appeared in rapid succession in *Literaturnaya Gazeta* (*The Literary Gazette*), which Delvig edited in collaboration with Pushkin. Among them were two chapters from *Strashny kaban* (*The Terrible Boar*), a Ukrainian tale, entitled "Uchitel"

(The Teacher) and "Rezultaty Porucheniya" (The Results of the Errand), which describe the efforts of a middle-aged and somewhat dim-witted seminarian, tutor in a landowning family, to win the love of a beautiful young girl with the cook's collaboration. The verve of the style hints at the future Gogol—outlandish comparisons, an easy interplay of the lofty and the burlesque. The deftly handled splattering of gossipy interest in the teacher's suspected machinations in managing the estate adumbrates the role of rumor in *Dead Souls*; the hilarious incompetence of both the cook and the teacher when wooing the girl they both adore gives promise of the numerous occasions in Gogol's later fiction when supposedly romantic encounters disintegrate into farce. "Mysli o geografii" (Some Thoughts about Geography) followed, and in January 1831, an article called "Woman" appeared to which, for the first time, Gogol signed his own name.

Before Delvig died in 1831, he introduced Gogol to the immensely influential Vasily Zhukovsky who was both poet laureate and tutor to the crown prince. In turn, Zhukovsky recommended the young provincial to Peter Pletnyov, poet, critic, and superintendent of the Patriotic Institute for Girls.* In 1833 Pletnyov was appointed professor of Russian Literature at St. Petersburg University; after Pushkin's death, four years later, he took the poet's place as editor of *Sovremennik* (*The Contemporary*) and became Gogol's literary agent. Through his influence Gogol obtained the post of history teacher at the Patriotic Institute, and was introduced to various rich families where he was employed as a private tutor. This freed him from the detestable and menial drudgery of employment at the Ministry. He now had more spare time and he used it to study painting. That was a new interest. He frequented the Academy of Arts and met struggling young artists.

Some twenty of his former schoolfellows were now in the city; these young Ukrainians would gather at each other's apartments or bedrooms and assuage their homesickness with native folk songs, impromtu Cossack dancing, tall stories narrated in dialect, and suppers of curd and boiled dumplings—a popular Ukrainian dish which Gogol could cook like a master.

* (Patriotichesky Institut) was a school for daughters of officers of noble birth.

VI *Alexander Pushkin*

Although money was still scarce, his income barely meeting his needs, life became more animated and took on a deeper coloration. An event of decisive importance occurred at this time: he met Alexander Pushkin.

Just before his first meeting with Russia's greatest poet, Gogol had read Pushkin's *Boris Godunov* and had written a lyrical, near ecstatic impression of the drama.[15] He touched upon the greatness and intangibility of art and the role it played in the lives of men. These themes obsessed him, and in his solitude he was striving to develop and clarify his thoughts about them. In Pushkin's immediate circle these ideas were frequently and lucidly discussed. When Gogol found himself in the company of Vasily Zhukovsky, the novelist Vladimir Odoevsky, Peter Pletnyov, and Alexandra Rosset, their brilliant twenty-two-year-old patron and intermediary at court, and listened to Pushkin speaking about the problems of creativity, the complexities of literary esthetics, and the difficulty of bridging the gap between the artist and his public, the fledgling author felt transported, inspired, and at the same time at peace, because he was intellectually at home.

Pushkin was perhaps the only human being whom Gogol unreservedly admired and respected. It is difficult to overrate the influence of the older writer upon the younger one; their association from 1831 to 1836 was significantly Gogol's most productive period. Gogol literally thawed in Pushkin's sunny, spontaneous, and direct presence. "Kind Pushkin has tamed the stubborn, secretive little Ukrainian,"[17] wrote Alexandra Smirnova in her diary.

Gogol's knowledge of the Classics was steadied and strengthened when Pushkin introduced him to Dante, Cervantes, and Shakespeare. He was granted that rare and thrilling student's privilege of unstinted attention and critical consideration from a supremely intelligent and mature mind. Pushkin unerringly sensed Gogol's satirical powers and, in Maxim Gorky's words, "Gogol, guided by Pushkin, chose the right road, and while he was on it, firmly and powerfully, created his greatest works." [18]

It is not clear whether Gogol started to write about the Ukraine because he was homesick or because he was capitalizing on the current vogue for Ukrainian folklore and Ukrainian literary motifs. In one of his first letters home, he stated that "here every-thing Ukrainian catches the public's attention" [19] and without disclosing his plan, he began to bombard his mother with re-quests for all available material pertaining to Ukrainian folk art, legends, superstitions, songs, sayings, copies of his father's plays, information about dress, food, wedding and funeral ceremonies, and descriptions of fairs. He had already experimented with *Bisavriuk or St. John's Eve* which was later included in his col-lection of Ukrainian tales, and although this story roused no comment, Gogol persevered. Two years later, in 1831, he brought out the first volume of *Vechera na khutore bliz Dikanki* (*Eve-nings on a Farm near Dikanka*), and within twelve months the second volume appeared, the entire work comprising eight stories placed in the Ukraine.

Suddenly the *Evenings* became popular. Pushkin praised them for their gaiety and freshness; other critics in Moscow and St. Petersburg wondered who the author was and acclaimed an exciting new talent.

CHAPTER 2

First Creative Realizations

I Ukrainian Images

THE first part of the *Evenings on a Farm near Dikanka* includes *Sorochinskaya Yarmarka* (*The Sorochinsky Fair*), *Vecher nakanune Ivana Kupala* (*St. John's Eve*), *Mayskaya noch, ili Utoplennitsa* (*A May Night or The Drowned Maiden*), and *Propavshaya gramota* (*The Lost Letter*); the second part includes *Noch' pered Rozhdestvom* (*Christmas Eve*), *Strashnaya mest'* (*Terrible Vengeance*), *Ivan Fyodorovich Shpon'ka i ego tyotushka* (*Ivan Fyodorovich Shponka and His Aunt*), and *Zakoldovannoe mesto* (*The Enchanted Spot*).

With the exception of *Ivan Shponka*, these stories depict a rural Ukraine that never existed except in the imagination of its people. It is the mythical world of the vigorous, carefree Cossack peasant whose traits, beliefs, and everyday life are commemorated in the folklore, folk song, and puppet theater of this region. Gogol's pen, inspired by this oral tradition and happily submissive to its mixture of fact and fantasy, rearranges it into a picturesque, polyphonic extravaganza.

The episodic narrative of each story is packed with swiftly changing scenes that range in colorful succession from romantic trysts and spookish adventure to pure buffoonery and farce. Against the magnificent décor of the Ukrainian landscape, Gogol dexterously manipulates prototypal figures of the Ukrainian "Punch-and-Judy show:" the lazy peasant and his shrewish wife; the cunning gypsy; the omnipresent devil; the pompous local official; a pair of young lovers. As their animator, arranger, and stage director, the author exploits them in related incidents which turn on situation rather than character. Gogol invents little. He uses his imagination to intensify the folk memories of his native region and provides in his fictional rearrangement of them an appearance of reality by means of a profusion of concrete details from the daily life of the Ukrainian peasant.

In the variety of artistic components that build up the structure of the *Evenings*, the unifying principle is movement. *The Sorochinsky Fair*, which opens the collection, provides a good example. In the din, bustle, heat, and carnival excitement of a country fair, the action that starts with a kiss and twenty-four hours later terminates in a wedding, grows from a trite private episode of young love triumphant over a wicked and wanton stepmother into a crescendo of general pandemonium. In his attempt to win the girl, the village lad seeks the aid of a resourceful gypsy, who throws the superstitious peasants into a panic with his revival of an old wives' tale of the devil in the shape of a pig, who searches for the red shirt he had once sold at the fair for a drink. When a pig's snout appears at a darkened window where the traders are revelling, fear reigns. A young seminarian, the stepmother's paramour, who had been hidden from the company, falls off the stove in fright, while a farmer rushes out clamping an oversized earthen pot instead of his cap on his head. The story's tempo reaches its apogee at the wedding when everyone begins to dance to the fiddler's bow.

What gives literary distinction to the tale is Gogol's structural control of his material through a persistent interplay of deliberate affinities and contrasts. Every salient part has its counterpart. The devil is represented by the red shirt (Gogol's color for the demoniac motif) while the young lover, Grytsko, wears a white one. The love at first sight in the open air between Grytsko and the beautiful young girl is juxtaposed to the furtive and carnal tryst of the ugly stepmother and her seminarian paramour in the hut, which becomes burlesque when they are interrupted in their lovemaking by the returning guests, and the seminarian is pushed out of sight. The wicked old woman and her stepdaughter are, of course, opposites in looks, age, and character. Still, Gogol relates them and does so in the most natural, yet ironical way. Left alone, the young bride-to-be, thinking about her impending marriage, tries on the stepmother's cap in order to imagine herself as a married woman. Bending her head to the floor, she sees reflected in the hand-mirror the loose boards behind which the seminarian was hidden. That instant is a forward flash into her future: will she not become, Gogol seems to ask, like her stepmother, wearing the same kind of headdress and possibly indulging in similar illicit pleasures?

The sense of youth heading for the disintegration of age, barely hinted at in this scene, is amplified to a macabre crescendo at the end of the story when old women join the wedding dance: "Upon their aged faces breathed the indifference of the grave. . . . They pushed their way among the young, laughing, living human beings. Caring for nothing, far removed from the joys of childhood, without a glimmer of compassion, it was only drink that like a puppeteer tugging at the strings made them move as if they were human; they slowly wagged their drunken heads, keeping in step with the merrymakers, not casting one glance at the young couple." [1]

In a gradual reversal of feeling as the sounds of the revelling fade away, Gogol voices his melancholy as he is left alone with the receding echo of gaiety that cannot be recaptured. He regrets that "joy, that lovely fleeting guest, flies away from us." Gogol's tone in this digression is conventionally sentimental, but the last image of the ancient crones has impact and significance beyond the typical Romantic's apprehensiveness toward the mechanization of life. With their entrance Gogol appears to foreshadow the fate of the young dancers and to complete the circle.

Superhuman power is again evoked in *A May Night*, this time in the guise of a water nymph. According to a legend that young Levko relates to his beloved at their midnight rendezvous by a moonlit pond, the nymph was driven by the stepmother witch to suicide in that pond, which "like a frail old man, held the dark, far-away sky in its cold embrace, covering with its icy kisses the bright stars, which gleamed in the warm ocean of the night air as though they felt the approach of the brilliant monarch of the night." [2]

In similar passages, saturated with verbal music and nocturnal imagery, Gogol recreates the fairy tale's magic which permeates Levko's dream. In the dream he meets the nymph, helps her, and receives supernatural aid from her in winning his father's consent to marry the girl he loves. On another level, in a vigorous assertion of fact over fantasy, Levko, angered by his father's undue attention to his fiancée, engages a boisterous band of village ruffians to bring his pompous father to ridicule, resulting in a brawling buffoonery.

The interplay of contrasts is developed further in *Christmas Eve*. Within the cycle of adventures that befall the main characters, Gogol brings together the most respected citizens of the village who have been secretly enjoying the favors of the seductive witch, Solokha. As they visit her in succession, she hides one from the other in coal sacks that are carried out into the street. The predicament of the portly lovers disintegrates into pure farce. The complicated action vacillates between the mundane and the fantastic, as for example when the witch who had just slid down the chimney," crept out of the oven, threw off her warm cloak, straightened her clothing, and no one could have known that she had been riding a broom a moment ago." [3] The incidents that texture the narrative are sharply tangible, extraordinarily vivid. There is something for everyone: a breath-taking flight across the winter sky to St. Petersburg, rustic lovemaking in the witch's hut, grotesque discomfiture of the local worthies, the sensuous dream of a young girl, and the brilliant reception at Catherine's court.

As in *The Fair*, there is abundant borrowing from popular folklore (the ride on the devil's back, the theft of the moon, the witch's transformation) and from the puppet theater (lovers hidden in sacks, dumplings flying into an open mouth, a wife beating her spouse with a poker).

A festive mood permeates the tale. Following Christmas tradition, the young people of the village go from house to house, collecting small gifts, singing carols, and dancing in the crisp winter air. Their laughter, scuffling in the snow, and scampering after the booty recall the carnival spirit of the Sorochinsky fair. The description of the moving throng is a deft piling-up of colorful, animated detail into taut phrases; Gogol catches individual gestures and snatches of talk and song, scatters and regroups the crowd in masterful choreography, infecting the reader with the spontaneous excitement of the holiday-makers. A sharper delineation of character gives *Christmas Eve* more fictional allure than was found in the earlier stories. Young Gogol was beginning to master his fictional craft. Vakula steps out of the young lover stereotype to dominate several situations as hero. A skillful blacksmith, he is also a religious painter known throughout the region for his representation of the Last Judgment on the village church wall. Gauche, tongue-tied, and generally miserable in the presence of the mocking and irresistible Oksana, Vakula shows stubborn resolution in pursuing his aims. In his skirmish with the devil, he outwits him and manages to bring him to heel, forcing him to execute his orders.

Supernatural involvement in the everyday life of the Cossack peasants is even more prominent in *The Lost Letter* and *The Enchanted Spot*. Their plots are linear, focusing on one particular situation from which all romantic element is absent. In the first, a tough old Cossack is entrusted by his chief to take a letter to the Empress. He sews it into his cap, loses the cap during a night's drinking, but finally wins it back in a card game with witches.

In *The Enchanted Spot*, an old Cossack grandfather is enticed by unholy spirits to dig up his field in search for gold which turns out to be dung. Both tales have a comic-ironic flavor. Gogol is obviously making fun of the naïveté of the two peasants.

The demoniac principle which dominates Ukrainian folk art is a major theme in the above five stories. But the ubiquitous devil of the puppet theater reproduced in them is mischievous rather than frightening. He is frequently unsuccessful in trying to raise havoc in human affairs. At times, he becomes a comical figure reduced to mortal size by his addiction to human vices—he is thievish, lecherous, and a drunkard. Besides, there is assurance that whatever harm is wrought by devilry may be undone if a Christian usage is brought to bear: The peasant trader makes a sign of the cross over his hatchet when he hacks the devil's red shirt to pieces (*The Fair*); Vakula holds his fingers in the shape of a cross over the devil's head during the ride to the capital (*Christmas Eve*); the Cossack wins the cap back from the evil spirits when he makes a sign over the cards dealt to him (*The Lost Letter*). This guarantee of victory over "unclean" beings, defined by Vasily Gippius as a fusion of Church canon with pagan legend,[4] was firmly embedded in the peasant mind. Gippius cautiously adds that although there is no proof of it, Gogol probably held the same superstitions.

The satanic power at play in *St. John's Eve* and *Terrible Vengeance* is quite different. The order of the world is reversed; man succumbs to monstrously evil powers beyond his comprehension. The cheerful village where peasants live in accord with nature is transformed into a macabre Gothic fantasy.

All comic ballast drops away. *St. John's Eve* concentrates on the disintegration of the farm hand, Petro, with the intensity and sense of doom of a Greek tragedy. He makes an unholy alliance with a Mephistophelean character in order to obtain in marriage wealthy young Pidorka whom he loves. In an orgiastic midnight scene in the depths of the forest, his lust for gold overpowers him. In return for the cursed gold, a bloodthirsty witch orders him to chop off the head of Pidorka's six-year-old brother. When Petro wakes up in his hut with the treasure beside him, the scene is erased from his mind, but he is racked by the compulsion to remember it. He is now free to marry, but his bride, made desperate by his depression and fits of insanity, summons a forest witch. Upon seeing her, Petro remembers his crime. Both he and the gold go up in flames.

The literary antecedents of the lavish use of supernatural horrors in this tale are found in *Faust*, in Johann Ludwig Tieck's story *Liebeszäuber* (translated into Russian in 1827), and especially in the French "Furious Fiction" school of literature.[5] The leitmotif of innocent blood shed in payment for dishonestly obtained wealth is a recurrent theme among early nineteenth-century Romantics of the West.

Even further removed from the gaily inconsequential climate of the village of Dikanka is the conflict between human valor and cosmic force in *The Terrible Vengeance*. This entangled tale, inspired by the metaphysical concepts of the German Romantics, moves in an atmosphere of imminent disaster along the ascending scale of gruesome visions drawn from the underworld of folklore. The taunting stillness of the sorcerer's castle, graveyard imagery, phantoms that come to life, all are intensified into hyperbole until any semblance of reality disappears.

The sorcerer, a suitable hero for this overly zealous exercise in the macabre, is the last descendant of a family accursed by a malediction reaching back to the beginning of time. More tormented than tormenting, he is in the grip of his own monstrous deeds that destroy everyone around him. Gogol places this malefic figure in dramatic contrast to his lovely young daughter married to a Cossack chieftain. In her innocence and charity she becomes the pawn between the two men competing for her love. She and her infant are murdered by her father who also betrays her husband to the Polish army. The impetuously brave chieftain Danilo, with his unbridled energy and fierce patriotism, is the prototypal hero of Cossack balladry. Gogol appropriately tells his story in language that emulates heroic Cossack poetry. Alliteration, repetitive refrain, and epic metaphor saturate passages relating to the life of the Cossack household. The young wife's despair at the sight of Danilo's dead body has the dirge-like quality of the traditional lament of Ukrainian peasant women: "You have turned blue as the Black Sea. . . . Why are you so cold, my lord? It seems that my tears are not scalding enough, they cannot warm you! It seems that my weeping is not loud enough, it will not awaken you! Who will lead your army now? Who will gallop on your black stallion, loudly calling, and lead the Cossacks, brandishing your sword? . . . Bury me, bury me with him! Throw earth over my eyes! Press the maple boards on my white breasts!" [6]

The sonorous, impassioned cadence of the style accords with the emotional intensity of the content that swings from a eulogy of human courage and freedom to a furious indictment of man's spiritual infamy. The lyrical digressions on the beauty of the Ukrainian landscape that decorated the preceding stories attain here, in the exuberant, chanting rhythm of the language, a hypnotic effect. The apostrophe to the Dnieper river in its various moods, for example, has the sound of a lover's rapturous eroticism. In a surreal fusion of form, sound, and movement, the river acquires a personalized beauty that Gogol withheld from his mortal heroines:

Marvelous is the Dnieper in quiet weather . . . one looks and cannot tell whether its majestic expanse is moving or not moving and it seems that it is made of glass, and its blue road that is like a mirror, immeasurably wide, endlessly long, twines and twists around the green world. . . . Marvelous too, is the Dnieper . . . when deep blue clouds soar like hills against the sky; the black forest quivers to its very roots, the oak trees creak, and lightning breaking through the heavy clouds suddenly illuminates the entire world—fearful then is the Dnieper! Its mountains of water roar, flinging themselves against the hilly banks, flashing and moaning rush back again and weep and wail in the distance.[7]

II   *An Experiment in Comic Grotesque*

The figure of Rudy Panko provides a unifying framework for the *Evenings*. He is the beekeeper at Dikanka and a garrulous host who entertains the rustic company in his hut with a rambling introduction to the stories that follow. Gogol may have borrowed the device from Walter Scott who started the *Waverly Novels* with relaxed, conversational prologues. But Panko himself as the alleged storyteller was probably created to give an air of authenticity to the tales and to root them even more firmly in the countryside of the Ukraine. For this, Gogol had a ready-made model in Pushkin's *Povesti Belkina* (*Tales of Belkin*) published in 1830, whose putative narrator, Ivan Belkin, was supposed to have recorded for his own pleasure interesting local happenings that had been told to him as true stories by real people.

In the course of the narration, there is no mention of the bee-keeper nor of the other teller of stories, the local sexton—Foma Grigorievich—whose personal comment prefaces *St. John's Eve, The Lost Letter,* and *The Enchanted Spot.* By introducing the sexton as the grandson of the old Cossack whose adventures are told in the last two stories, Gogol makes an additional attempt to add verisimilitude to the work. But he uses the prefatory device in yet another way: *Ivan Fyodorovich Shponka and His Aunt* is strikingly unlike the other tales, and to stress its distinctiveness, Gogol has Rudy Panko disclaim all responsibility for it, since it was related by an outsider, a man from a neighboring town who wrote it down in a notebook and left it at the beekeeper's hut.

Within the context of the *Evenings, Ivan Shponka* appears to be out of place. It is divested of all the props of folk-loric art. From the make-believe world of adventure and the robust farce of the puppet theater, we are transported to the humdrum life of a small landowner, forty-year-old Shponka, who at the request of his aunt retires from military service, returns to his estate and visits a neighbor's house where he meets a girl whom his aunt would like him to marry.

From the raw material of this prosaic reality, working outside of popular and Romantic tradition, Gogol produces his first piece of original writing. It is immediately clear that he is exploring new ways of presenting characters beyond the stereotypes of the

Ukrainian puppet theater that would produce a comic effect, and that his propensity for satire overrides the novelist's concern for the development of plot.

In the delineation of the main protagonists, Gogol retains the folkloric custom of defining personality by one dominant trait. But the method he uses to establish the portrayal is his own, and speaks for the originality and inventiveness of his satirical gift. His aim is to exaggerate one aspect of the individual until he becomes a caricature of himself, not unlike a cartoon sketch where the face becomes all nose, or all ears or all bushy eyebrows. But distinct from the cartoonist's art which projects distortion in a few quick, decisive strokes, Gogol's description of his heroes is slow and studied; it is constructed out of a gradual compilation and intensification of realistic, trite, seemingly irrelevant, habitually unnoticed, and slyly disparaging details. Occasionally, an obliquely damning comment or incident serves to outrage the familiar even further and heighten the comicality of the exaggeration. Shponka's neighbor, Grigory Grigorievich Storchenko, a petty despot who browbeats his household into terrorized servility, reaches at his dinner party the height of arbitrary caprice when he orders his butler to get on his knees and implore a guest to take a second helping from the platter. Shponka's aunt is "of a huge stature. . . . It seemed that nature made an unforgivable mistake in obliging her to wear a dark brown dress with tiny flounces on weekdays and a red cashmere shawl on Sundays and on her name day when she would have looked very much better with a dragoon's moustache and high boots." [8]

Ivan Fyodorovich Shponka is the first of Gogol's meek characters and perhaps one of his most memorable creations. He is at once too naïve, too receptive, too submissive to his aunt's ministrations, and too dull-witted. Gogol reserves his most refined irony for his hero's lack of mental equipment: " 'What are you talking about, Ivan Fyodorovich?', asked Grigory Grigorievich from the other end of the table. 'I, that is, I had the occasion to remark, that there are many far-away lands in the world,' said Ivan Fyodorovich, heartily pleased that he had managed to bring out such a long and complicated sentence. . . . When he heard that a book was being discussed, he assiduously started to help himself to gravy." [9]

Within the Gogolian satirical scheme, Shponka is an exaggeration in reverse and achieves a hyperbolic glow of importance by his very unimportance to himself and to others. His demands upon life are ludicrously minute. Attached to a regiment of hard-drinking and heavily gambling officers, he is content to spend his time alone polishing buttons, setting mousetraps, or simply lying on his bed. When travelling he is never bored. If there was nothing else to do, he would unpack his trunk, fold and refold his underwear, and repack it all again. Only once does he rebel against fate and even then only in a dream. When his aunt expresses her wish to marry him off, his terror of women becomes the terror of having a wife. His anxieties are unleashed in a nightmare which for sheer exuberant grotesque has few peers in Gogolian fiction. Shponka dreams that he is pursued by ubiquitous goose-faced wives whom he finds in his pocket, on the cotton wool that he takes out of his ear, and even as a piece of material from which the tailor is about to cut him a fashionable jacket.

In this story Gogol opens a window into a reality that is "thing" dominated. Ideas have no place in it; people are shut in a dense, physically cluttered environment, being merely one-dimensional versions of their own dominant and most unappealing characteristics. Hemmed in by objects that reduce all their needs and wishes to a material level, they move on restricted courses; the very nature of their world dehumanizes them, and breeds a lack of communication between them. A sense of confusion and disorder is projected further, building up the ambiance of the grotesque. For example, to his aunt's letter about five pairs of socks, some fine linen shirts, and a turnip that looks more like a potato, Ivan regretfully answers that he cannot find the wheat seed and Siberian grain. Instead of greeting the young man who has just been presented to her, the neighbor's mother wants to know how many cucumbers had been pickled that winter in his house. The only verbal exchange between a young couple left alone is about summer flies that can be killed with swatters made out of old felt slippers. Their conversation dies after that—as do all the others in the story—for lack of anything to say, even though one chatty guest perseveres at a dinner with accounts of huge watermelons and a trip to holy places, in the face of devastating inattentiveness on the part of the rest.

As an experiment in comic grotesque, the story is only partially successful. Despite the hilarious scenes (Shponka's tête-à-tête with the neighbor's daughter; his dream) and a number of ironic shafts directed at the mental and spiritual torpor, triviality, and complacent egotism of the "existers" in Shponka's milieu, the comicality of the narrative is weakened by the overcharged intensity of character portrayals. The final impression of dehumanized heroes moving in a vacuum of their own making is one of apprehension and dread. Gogol is still too involved with building up hyperboles for which he has a natural predilection; he has not yet learned to use his satirical talent in such a way as to create human aberrations that are both comic and grotesque.

But the future Gogol is already discernible in the seminal caricatures of the Shponka story which, like a preliminary sketch of a great painting, suggest in outline shapes what will reappear much strengthened in *Dead Souls*. Storchenko anticipates the magnificent brazenness and boorishness of Nozdrev, one of the main characters in the novel, and the vapid and ever aimiable Manilov may claim Shponka for a predecessor. Some of the stylistic devices of Gogol's mature art appear in this fragment of a story: an individual's low mental level is revealed by the paucity and dullness of his conversation, the dehumanized quality of human beings is emphasized by the mutability of people and things when, for example Storchenko's mother is described as "a coffeepot in a bonnet" and a man in a frock coat and an immense stand-up collar, so large that it covers the entire back of his head, has his head sitting in that collar "as though it were a small carriage."

III *In Search of a Vocation*

The second volume of the *Evenings on a Farm near Dikanka* was published in 1832, and during that late spring Gogol experienced the feeling of deflation that not infrequently comes upon the heels of success. He needed distraction. He was out of funds and he decided to spend the summer at his mother's estate. On his way to the Ukraine he broke the journey with a two-week stay in Moscow, where he was introduced to many prominent Muscovites eager to meet in person the author of the best-selling *Evenings*. Among others, Gogol made the acquaintance of Mikhail Maximovich, a collector of Ukrainian folk songs, Mikhail

Shchepkin the famous actor, and Mikhail Pogodin, the historian who took Gogol to pay a call on the Aksakov family.

Sergey Aksakov, who later wrote an important prose work, *Semeynaya Khronika,* (*The Family Chronicle*), was a typical Russian *barin** of the old school, Slavophile to the core, spontaneous, warm-hearted, generous, and rich. His large and hospitable house was the meeting place of well-known personalities from academic and literary milieux. The patriarchial *barin* was at first taken aback by the dandified appearance of the young man who wore a pale blue frock coat and multi-colored waistcoat with a long and heavy watch chain and high stiff white collar, and whose blonde hair was curled and brushed up into a quiff in front framed by carefully trimmed sideburns. He noted Gogol's extremely long nose, mocking eyes, and sly smile that fitted over his face giving it a slightly contemptuous and haughty expression.

Despite this unfortunate first impression, Gogol was soon surrounded by admiration and kindness. He remained diffident and evasive during this first visit, accepting the compliments that Sergey Aksakov and his fifteen-year-old son Konstantin heaped upon the Dikanka stories, with no obvious sign of pleasure. Temperamentally, his timidity and innate distrust of people stood in the way of a straightforward response to the open-mannered friendliness of the Aksakov family. He felt more at home with Mikhail Zagoskin, the playwright, whom he correctly assessed within the first few minutes of his visit as a compulsive chatterer and braggart while he was being shown Zagoskin's entire collection of books, caskets, and snuffboxes to the accompaniment of a description of his mainly fictitious travels. He was even more at ease with the well-known actor, Mikhail Shchepkin, upon whom he called unannounced and with whom he spent a relaxed evening swapping Ukrainian anecdotes, singing humorous Ukrainian songs, and talking about the theater.

Nonetheless, "dear Nikolay Vasilievich" became a permanent member of the Aksakov entourage and the object of the family's affectionate interest and concern. This relationship, in which Gogol received very much more than he offered, endured to the very end of his life.

At Vasilevka, Gogol discovered that as a result of some of his

* *Barin*—a gentleman; often, a landowner.

mother's foolhardy investments, the estate was verging on bankruptcy. But this did not prevent him from "vegetating" luxuriously for the next three months in the plenitude and sunshine of the Ukrainian summer, stuffing himself with fruit, corn, and delectable Ukrainian dishes. He also busied himself contentedly with the operation of the farm, painted arabesques on the walls of the living room, and gave history and geography lessons to his two younger sisters whom he planned to enroll at the institute where he taught.

When Gogol finally decided to return to the capital accompanied by his sisters, his mother objected to her daughters going on such a long journey without a maid. In a typical serf-owner's manner the problem was solved by marrying off one of the village girls to Gogol's manservant, Yakim, without a thought of considering the wishes of the young peasant couple. Despite the fact that Gogol was two months' overdue at his teaching post, the journey was pleasantly interrupted by a stopover in Moscow, so that Gogol could visit his new friends.

Back in St. Petersburg, Gogol moved to a larger although still poorly-heated apartment and felt ready after his long vacation to explore new territory. Shchepkin had him read several scenes from a comedy, *Vladimir tretiy stepeni* (*The Order of Vladimir, Third Class*) that Gogol had started during the summer, and although the actor had become excited over the play's potential Gogol knew that it would not pass the censor and gave it up. Two new stories, which were later included in the *Mirgorod* collection after having been reworked several times, were crowding his desk, but at this point remained unfinished. The writing process was fraught with difficulty. Inspiration eluded him, he complained of "creative constipation," and he felt that he had become unrecognizably cold, prosaic, and hard. He began to distrust his creative ability; writing was far from the fulfillment of his dreams. There had to be another outlet for his ambitions, and now that service to the state had lost its allure, Gogol turned to another field in his search for a suitable profession—history.

He had become sufficiently engrossed in his history and geography lessons at the Patriotic Institute to envisage writing a text, entitled *The Land and the People*, which was to be composed of pupils' notes taken during his lectures. Ukrainian history continued to fascinate him, and he wrote to his Ukrainian friend

Mikhail Maximovich, who was then teaching the history of Russian literature at the newly-founded University of Kiev, that he had begun a history of the Ukraine and it seemed to him that he could say a great deal about it that had not yet been said. When he learned from Maximovich that there was an opening in Kiev for a professor of Western history, he was lured by the academic sinecure and the chance to escape from the "wretched Northern climate." So he solicited the aid of all influential acquaintances, including Pushkin and Zhukovsky, to recommend him for the post. He also prepared an extensive report for S. S. Uvarov, Minister of Public Instruction, outlining his approach to general history in cannily patriotic tones and his own manner of teaching it, which, he stated, would be "an eloquent and intuitive presentation, both lofty and exalted, and yet simple and understandable to everyone." [10] Although the Kiev offer did not materialize, Gogol did obtain an appointment as adjunct-professor of history at the University of St. Petersburg through the good services of his friends.

For sixteen months, Gogol tried obstinately to perform his teaching duties, but he lacked the primary qualifications of trained scholarship and the habit of disciplined study necessary to the organization and preparation of regularly scheduled lectures. After a brilliant introduction on "Europe of the Middle Ages" which Gogol had written and memorized, he gave up all pretense at erudition and teaching. In his recollections Ivan Turgenev, who had been an auditor in the course, described the fiasco of that pedagogical performance:

His lecturing(!), to tell the truth, was highly original. In the first place, Gogol missed two lectures out of three; secondly, even when he appeared in the lecture room, he did not so much speak as whisper something incoherently and showed us small engravings of views of Palestine and other Eastern countries, looking terribly embarrassed all the while. We were all convinced that he knew nothing of history (and we were hardly wrong) and that Mr. Gogol-Janovsky, our professor, (he appeared under that name on the list of lectures) had nothing in common with the writer Gogol, already familiar to us as the author of *Evenings on a Farm near Dikanka*. At the final examination on his subject he sat with his face tied up in a handkerchief, as though suffering from a toothache, looking terribly depressed,—and never opened his mouth.[11]

It is common to regard the episode of Gogol the historian disparagingly and to have it serve as yet another illustration of his powers of self-delusion and the constant gaps between promise and fulfillment that existed in his life. *The Land and the People* did not advance beyond the planning stage. *The History of the Ukraine* that Gogol had envisioned as comprising four to six large volumes and for which he inserted an announcement in the *Northern Bee* in January 1834, requesting readers to send him historical material, dwindled to an introductory article as an excerpt from Volume I, Book I, Chapter I and was included in the *Arabesques* miscellany under the title of "An Aspect of the Formation of the Ukraine."

The public and relatively long-lasting, fiasco of his university career was probably a deeply humiliating experience for Gogol who was fully aware of the professional incompetence of his teaching. He needed little more than a bird's eye view of any past epoch to catch its tone, flavor, and what seemed to him its essence within his own hyperbolic vision. Gogol was in that way an ardent student of the past, a subjective historian, that is a Romantic, who shared with many of his contemporaries an idealized version of the past. A past that he would re-create, imaginatively and intuitively, as a glamorous panorama of mankind. But in the classroom situation he was irremediably flawed by his disorderly presentation of material, and hampered by an indifference and even hostility to objective analysis of facts.

When the university administration forced Gogol to resign by stipulating that he pass a doctoral examination in his subject, he wrote in unbounded relief to Pogodin that he was a free Cossack again and "that during the sixteen inglorious months of my mortification I have profited greatly and added to the beauty of my soul." [12] What he meant was that the setback in one field had spurred him on in another which he now claimed as his own. By April 1835, Gogol brought out two new collections: *Arabesques* and *Mirgorod*.

IV Arabesques (Arabeski)

Arabesques is an anthology of articles, some of them published previously, on history, literature, education, and the arts, written between 1831 and 1834. In it also are three new short stories— *Portret* (*The Portrait*), *Nevsky prospekt* (*Nevsky Prospect*),

Zapiski sumasshedshego (*The Diary of a Madman*)—which will be considered separately within the cycle of St. Petersburg stories.

Gogol apologized to Pogodin for the volume's hodgepodge character, the result of "clearing my desk of all the old stuff, some of it childish, to make room for a new life." [13] Still, in the introduction he claimed that despite the imperfections of the work, he had no right to deprive the reader of two or three new truths that he had advanced in it.

In fact, however, the "scholarly" essays that Gogol may have composed to enhance his academic prestige contributed little that was new. Those on history are verbatim reprints of his two successful university lectures; the first one introducing the Middle Ages, the second an analysis of the impact of al-Mamun on the fall of the Arab Empire, a dazzling display of rhetorical fireworks that the young professor had prepared for the occasion of the visit of Zhukovsky and Pushkin to his class.

Gogol's flight into art criticism in "Introduction to Modern Architecture" and "Sculpture, Painting, and Music," is little more than an effusive restatement of the prevalent Russian understanding of German Romantic esthetic theory. He eulogizes the "sacred trinity" of the arts, borrowing from the poet Dmitry Venevitinov a definition for sculpture that suggests the presence of the divine and from Schelling the idea that music has the power to draw the heart away into unknown distances. Like Novalis he deplores the flat, low design of nineteenth-century city buildings and turns nostalgically to the beauty of the Gothic cathedral "when fervent Christian faith compelled everyone to look heavenward" including the architect, "who sought to thrust his spires further and further into the sky." [14]

One literary commentary from the anthology deserves to be singled out. In "A Few Words about Pushkin," Gogol analyzes the poet's work with professional astuteness, emphasizing the typically Russian character of Pushkin's art in that it is quiet, unsensational, and finds its material in daily events. Perhaps inadvertently, Gogol is throwing a light on his own creative process. Even more interesting is the next statement in which he takes up the cudgels for the coexistence of Realism and Romanticism in literature. A writer need not pledge allegiance to either school; he may create two types of hero: "A wild mountaineer who has cut down an enemy lurking in a cave or has burned down an entire village" and oppose to this typically Romantic figure "the image of a courtroom judge in a threadbare frock coat covered with tobacco stains who has vindicated a large number of men in the ordinary process of interrogation and trial." [15]

But eventually, as Gogol must have known, the writer had to make a choice. Pushkin made it in the early 1830's when he realized that the public was becoming prosaically minded and composed *The Tales of Belkin* around contemporary events in a sober, laconic style. It is evident from his new collection of short stories, *Mirgorod*, that Gogol was still torn between his predilection for the world of adventure and fantasy and the stuff of daily reality upon which he could sharpen his satirical pen.

CHAPTER 3

Mirgorod Stories

I *A Historical Romance*

OF the four stories in the Mirgorod collection—*Starosvetskie pomeshchiki* (*Old-World Landowners*), *Viy, Povest' o tom, kak possorilsya Ivan Ivanovich s Ivanom Nikiforovichem* (*The Tale of How Ivan Ivanovich Quarreled with Ivan Nikiforovich*) and *Taras Bulba*—bearing the subtitle, *tales that serve as a sequel to Evenings on a Farm near Dikanka,*" only the fantastic *Viy* and *Taras Bulba* can be linked with the *Evenings* . . . cycle.

The military expeditions of the Dnieper Cossack, Taras Bulba, recall the struggles of the other Cossack chieftain, Danilo, against the Poles in *The Terrible Vengeance*. The pivotal movement of the earlier story, however, is charged with demoniac energies, its historical moment barely indicated, while *Taras Bulba* firmly rooted in the reality of war is abundantly furbished with graphic details of a besieged Polish town, individual feats of valor in open combat, and the carousing of the Dnieper Cossacks in their military camp in between campaigns.

Inspired by the heroic period of the Ukrainian War of Liberation against the Poles in the sixteenth and the seventeenth centuries, Gogol pieces together a composite picture of that epoch with no specifics as to dates or places, centering the story around the Dnieper Cossack leader, Taras Bulba, his two sons, and his band of Cossack warriors.

Here, as in Gogol's earlier abandoned attempt to compose a historical novel, he had trouble in constructing a sustained and plausibly motivated plot.[1] The love episode between Bulba's youngest son Andrey and the Polish governor's beautiful daughter, which inevitably leads to Andrey's betrayal of his own people, is completely conventional in the Walter Scott manner. The humorous scenes between the Cossacks and a Jewish merchant (a type who figures largely in Cossack humor) occur less as an integral part of the story than as a device to introduce comic relief.

The principal characters show little development. Both brothers are lifeless stereotypes, one a weakling who cannot resist a woman's guile, the other a paragon of courage, fortitude, and honor. Taras Bulba himself is more interesting and comes fully alive. His presence is felt in every scene; he embodies all the tough, casually brutal, virile, and gregarious qualities of his men. Even in their immense appetite for eating, drinking, and courting danger they are only pale replicas of the crusty old Bulba whom Gogol projects as the idealized image of a nationalistic, Orthodox Ukraine, and as a symbol of its glorious past. But with his inclination to hyperbole and the great incidence of vivid acts of violence, Gogol goes too far. His hero becomes something of a monster in the gratuitous cruelty and wild irresponsibility of his actions. Bulba forces his two sons to leave their mother the very next day after their return from four years away at the seminary; he initiates a senseless, ill-matched engagement between his army and the enemy, murders his son for his treacherous behavior, and attempts to raze the whole of Poland to avenge the execution of his oldest son.

Nevertheless, the tale, carried along by the very ferocity of events and Gogol's uncharacteristically straightforward, dramatic narration of them, conveys a sense of exhiliration and power. The masculine world that Gogol reconstructs out of "the rough cruel times" is uninhibited, uncomplicated, and touched with the breath of epic poetry. The French Romantic critic, Sainte-Beuve, called it "the Iliad of the Dnieper Cossacks," and there is something Homeric in the detailed descriptions of hand-to-hand combat that are veritable orgies of slaughter, in the exultant shouts of warrior to comrade in the thick of battle, in the militant speeches that the leader delivers to his men on the eve of a decisive engagement. The reckless, restless spirit of the lawless Cossacks—owing allegiance only to a leader chosen from among them, living with a superb indifference to death, full of zest for fighting—is admirably portrayed.

For a long time, *Taras Bulba* ranked first in popularity as a historical romance in Russia. In 1842 Gogol made substantial revisions in the text; he sharpened local color patterns, added a number of concrete details to the description of the daily life of the Cossacks, modified the lyrical tone of several passages on nature with the insertion of a keyed-down vocabulary, and intensified its patriotic coloration.

II *Malevolent Magic*

In *Viy*, which is literally witch-haunted, Gogol returns to the combination of fantasy and reality that dominates the *Evenings . . .* cycle. The gist of this swiftly-paced, action-packed tale is the wrestling of a young theology student, Khoma Brut, with a broom-cracking witch who forces him to carry her across the night sky on his back until he overpowers her, jumps on her back in turn, and beats her in a frenzy of wild, sensous delight until she falls to the ground exhausted and is transformed into a beautiful young girl. Khoma, frightened, runs away. He would have forgotten the adventure the next day in the arms of a hospitable and buxom young widow whom he met at the Kiev market, if he had not been dispatched by his university rector to the estate of a wealthy and influential Cossack captain whose dying daughter had requested that the seminarian, Khoma Brut, read the vigils over her coffin for three nights.

The moment he arrives at the house of the grief-stricken father, he recognizes the dead girl as the witch, and for the next three nights he is locked up in the church with the witch's corpse. Khoma fights for his sanity in a bilateral world. The split in his reality is quite primitively conditioned by the change from light to darkness. During the day which he spends with the servants in the captain's yard, he eats and drinks hugely in a futile attempt to forget and even escape his plight. Three times (another insistence on the classic number formula that links the action to a fairy tale) Khoma tries to run away and is brought back. With each hour that brings him nearer to the harrowing nocturnal tryst, Khoma's depression deepens as Gogol masterfully integrates suspense and premonition of disaster into the rustic fun. The intrusion of evil becomes increasingly manifest as the light wanes.

Around the table, with tongues loosened by vodka, the kitchen help vies for attention with hair-raising tales of the master's daughter, known as the witch who had sucked the blood of a neighbor's baby, driven a young lad mad with her guiles, and reduced a huntsman to a heap of ashes. When for the third night, Khoma is taken back to the church, Gogol instills into a few lines a sense of impending doom: "It was a hellish night. Faraway, a pack of wolves was howling and even the barking of the dogs had a frightening sound. 'Something else seems to be howling out there: that's no wolf' said Dorosh. Yavtukh kept silent. The philosopher did not know what to say." [2]

Throughout the nocturnal vigil Khoma is in his other world. Alone, defenseless but for the magic circle that he draws around himself, and the prayers and exorcisms that he repeats at random, Khoma manages to withstand the diabolisms of the witch-corpse and of her cohorts until the third night. Here again, Gogol fills the church with a gradation of horrors that are extraordinarily effective; terrifying movements and sounds are suggested until the apparition of the squat, earth-encrusted monster Viy with a face of iron and eyelids hanging down to the ground that when lifted reveal a look that causes the student to expire.

Written after *Taras Bulba* and the Petersburg stories, *Viy* is the last fantastic tale in the manner of the adventures in *Evenings*. In it Gogol arrives at a more complex treatment of the supernatural as the underlying motive in the conduct of human affairs. A familiar stock character, such as the witch in *Christmas Eve*, who was treated with detached irony and was mischievous but not basically harmful to man, assumes here the dimension of an evil force that forms an alliance with mysterious cosmic powers represented b ythe monster Viy, powers that shaped the tragedy in *St. John's Eve* and *The Terrible Vengeance*.

This fusion of folkloric legend with Romantic literary tradition becomes more dynamic and adds to the tautness of the tale in which Gogol compresses the impact of its imagery into the conscious perceptions of one man. Since his meeting with the witch and her revenge upon him, Khoma Brut starts to exist simultaneously in two conflicting worlds. In his external aspect Khoma appears as an ordinary, unimaginative, easy-going fellow. Caught in a situation about which he can communicate with no one, this haunted and hunted man's vision becomes transformed. In the delineation of it, Gogol shows his own development as a writer. No longer content, as in the earlier tales, to manipulate puppet-like figures within the tested formulas of the fantastic, Gogol suggests another interpretation of the imagery of witchcraft, namely the projection of suppressed desires and anxieties in man.

Khoma becomes a more complex and interesting personality when pressured by the curse that is upon him; he begins to live in an inner world, experiencing new sensations of delight, deep foreboding, awareness of cosmic forces, and paralyzing terror, until finally he is stretched and broken on the rack of fear.

III   *Subjective Realism*

Turning away from the heroic past and the world of the fantastic, Gogol evokes in the *Old-World Landowners* the peaceful existence of the rural gentry in the remoteness of the Ukrainian countryside who live contentedly in the midst of nature's abundance and whose modest needs are satisfied.

The sentimentally rhapsodic tone of the opening lines sets the mood: "I sometimes like to enter for a moment into that extraordinarily secluded life in which not a single desire steps beyond the fence that surrounds the small courtyard, beyond the garden enclosure filled with plum and apple trees, beyond the village huts surrounding it, leaning to one side under the shade of willows, elders, and pear trees." [3] True to habit, Gogol introduces his story with a generalized reminiscence and then settles into the concretization of a particular memory.

The "little house" belongs to Afanasy Ivanovich Tovstogub and his wife Pulkheria Ivanovna, a childless aging couple, unpretentious, hospitable, and kind. In minute and affectionate detail Gogol limns in their mutual solicitude, their gentle appearance ("The slight wrinkles on their faces were drawn so prettily that an artist would surely have stolen them" [4]), the welcome they always extended to the chance visitor, with Afanasy Ivanovich smiling and listening attentively to the traveler's stories and Pulkheria Ivanovna regaling him with her choicest delicacies and pressing him to stay the night, although he may have come only from three or four miles away. A truly delightful pair, and it is with a heavy heart that the author recalls their "humble, bucolic life" now that they are no longer living.

From morning to night—and they rose very early—Afanasy Ivanovich would ask his wife every two hours or so between meals "if it weren't time for a snack of something," and some tempting dish of fruit dumplings or poppy seed pies or salted mushrooms or cabbage and buckwheat cakes would immediately be brought in and consumed. And so the ritual of comestibles filled their days and continued on into the night, when Afanasy Ivanovich would wake up groaning to be relieved only when his wife sent a sleepy maid to the kitchen cupboard to get the master "a snack of something."

The slow and relaxed rhythm of the narration is punctuated by the author's exclamatory praise of his heroes ("good old people!" "dear old woman!"); he likens them to Philemon and Baucis, and the isolated rural setting of the story gives it the air of a sentimental idyll. But as Renato Poggioli points out in a careful comparison between the classical myth and Gogol's tale, the resemblance between the two couples in age, hospitality, and a blameless life is more than offset by the fact that Philemon and his wife spent their days in work and lived by the golden rule of moderation.[5] Gogol's protagonists, on the other hand, are mired in idleness, filling their empty hours with a monstrously excessive consumption of food, and the other inhabitants of the manor follow the example of the masters in gluttony, slothfulness, and waste. The kitchen maids steal into the storeroom after dark, stuff themselves with sweets and complain of stomachaches all the next day. The house-boy is always eating or sleeping. Even the pigs that gorge on plums and apples from the baskets readied for jam-making are unable to devour all the fruit that rains down upon them from trees they shake with their snouts.

Gradually there is a ripening awareness of all not being right in that world. As the narrative unwinds, the idealized version of rural utopia, remote from the sophistication and corruption of cities, is intermittently downgraded and undermined as Gogol vacillates between his attraction and repulsion for a passing social order. By instinct he yearns for it and his nerves clamor for the soothing rhythm of that undemanding routine "in the horn of plenty," and he identifies himself with it through the memories of his childhood. It has been contended that the Tovstogubs were patterned after his own grandparents.[6]

On the other hand, the basic triviality, the inbred apathy to a fuller existence, and the shallowness and mediocrity of that self-contained small world overwhelm Gogol. He brings the force of his irony to bear upon it, exposing its flaws in the damning intensification and rearrangement of realistic elements already noted in *Ivan Shponka*. But these precise descriptions do not reduce his heroes to one-dimensional caricatures. Because he is deeply attached to them, they remain living characters and retain their credibility despite typically Gogolian assaults on their commonplace reality.

Afanasy Ivanovich is portrayed as a flattering and attentive host, who listens to his visitor and with much curiosity questions him about his affairs, but when Gogol adds that "it is like the curiosity of a child who carefully looks over the seal of your watch while talking to you," [7] all that remains of the earlier attractive impression is the old man's lowered consciousness and a basic indifference to anything outside his own palisade. The disarming otherworldliness and charming innocence of the couple take on a different coloration when we learn in rich detail that due to their lack of business acumen and total trust in a steward who knows all the answers when questioned about the management of the estate, they are being systematically robbed of their forest lands and a major part of their annual revenue.

One of Gogol's keenest thrusts against this vegetating existence is in his depiction of the old lady's death, which occurs when her little grey cat runs away to the forest and joins the half-wild cats who terrorize the countryside with their bold raids on farmyards. When the little cat is found three days later, ragged and ravenous, she runs away again to her fierce, free life after having been fed. To her mistress this seemed the sign of her own impending demise. Very soon afterwards, having left minute instructions to the housekeeper about the feeding and care of her husband and requesting that she be buried in her second-best dress, she took to her bed and died.

This death would be inexplicable if Gogol had not used it as a symbol of the old lady's escape from the stagnation she could no longer endure after the sudden impact of a powerful outside force represented by the cat's option for freedom and adventure. Her life collapsed as do the forms of warriors when the archeologist's pickaxe unseals the doorway of a tomb and fresh air rushes in to break the vacuum of a thousand years.

Gogol's last tribute to a way of life that he had cherished and one he was not to evoke again in creative fiction occurs during his visit five years later to the little house "which seemed to me twice as old." It is the most moving part of the narrative, unmistakably sincere, highly charged with feeling, and with no subversive commentary. He finds the widower sadly changed, inconsolable and showing signs of senility. He observes his host's listless stare, his helpless fumbling with food; and is struck by the old man's paroxysm of grief when he is served a dish that his wife used to make, breaking into uncontrollable sobs trying to utter her name. Gogol reflects on the endurance of love and the force of it in a man "who had never once been moved by a powerful feeling" . . . and whose heart "was already turning cold." [8] What was the secret of this deep devotion? How could it be described? No passion had held these two people together, nor could the memory of passion have retained its hold on Afanasy Ivanovich, since in Gogol's eyes passion was a wild, destructive, and fleeting emotion to be feared and avoided. He cautiously diagnoses the feeling as habit. The impression remains that the affection that the old people had shown one another in a hundred minute gestures of solicitude and tenderness, and which Gogol described with infinite care, ironically eluded him when he attempted to give it a final definition. He remains helpless in his amazement and admiration before his hero, who becomes alive only in the violence of his despair when confronted with the slightest reminder of the love that he had lost.

IV *Hilarious Grotesque*

For sheer grotesque comedy, *The Tale of How Ivan Ivanovich Quarrelled with Ivan Nikiforovich* has few equals in humorous fiction. Both the basic plot which concerns a trifling quarrel between two old friends leading to years of litigation, and the title were probably borrowed from Vasily Narezhny's novel, *Dva Ivana, ili strast' k tyazhbam* (*The Two Ivans, or the Passion for Litigation*, 1825). However, the long complicated series of adventures involving scores of characters and the didactic conclusion of Narezhny's novel bear little resemblance to Gogol's tautly constructed and impenitently mocking version. Beginning with a situation no larger than a snowball, Gogol dislodges an avalanche of hilarity. The setting—the small Ukrainian town of Mirgorod; the narrator—a typical, naïve inhabitant of the town; the action— three sharply articulated scenes (the quarrel, the filing of petitions, the attempted reconciliation), are the ingredients of this expertly devised story.

The tale must be read on more than one level to appreciate

Gogol's increasing ability in manipulating comic contrivances into a methodical distortion of reality. The more obvious humor derives in part from caricatured descriptions of people that rely heavily on grotesque distortions of mannerisms or physical traits. A favorite device of Gogol, the utilization of inanimate objects to portray human beings or parts of them, is more abundant and precise here than in the earlier story of Ivan Shponka. The judge is distinguished by his lips that "were very near his nose, and therefore it could meet his upper lip as much as it liked. In this way, the upper lip made a snuffbox, since the snuff aimed at the nose almost always rested upon it." [9] A scribe is depicted as "a darkish little man, no longer young, with spots all over his face, in a dark blue boat patched at the elbows, a real inkwell for hire!" [10] Another person has a waistline "that looked like a tub, and it was no easier to find her waistline than to look at one's nose without a mirror. Her short, small feet resembled two puffed-up pillows." [11] The physical appearance of the heroes of the story is memorable: "Ivan Ivanovich's head is like a radish, tail downward; Ivan Nikiforovich's head is like a radish whose tail is turned upward." [12]

Some scenes are pure farce. For example, rotund Ivan Nikiforovich is stuck in the courtroom doorway, unable to move forward or backward until a broad-shouldered clerk with a drunken look in his squinting eyes folds the poor man's arms together and, with the aid of an invalid who had been standing by the door, pushes in his stomach and finally squeezes him through. Another scene in which Gogol parodies high tragedy is the pantomimic culmination of the dispute between the bosom friends. In this scene, which prefigures the famous *coup de théâtre* at the end of *Inspector General,* Ivan Ivanovich, his arm raised high, confronts a completely naked Ivan Nikiforovich standing in the middle of the room, while a terrified servant woman and a boy in a huge long coat calmly picking his nose look on.

A more mature and subtle Gogol is at work in the development of new comic techniques. An insidious irony bores through the seemingly innocuous utterances of the fatuous narrator, himself a prime target for Gogol's oblique derision. The bleak ordinariness of Mirgorod belies the narrator's enthusiastic description:

What a charming town Mirgorod is! So many different buildings! Some have thatched roofs, some even have wooden ones, others are covered with reeds. There is a street to the right and one to the left, and an excellent fence everywhere; on it hops are entwined, pots and pans hang on it, and from beneath it the sunflower peeps out with its golden head, the poppies are red and one catches sight of plump pumpkins. . . . Marvelous! The fence is always decorated with all kinds of things that make it even more picturesque, such as a checkered petticoat or a shirt or a pair of trousers. . . .[13]

No less stultifying in its banality is the description of the two Ivans, again interspersed with the narrator's ecstatic ejaculations. The story opens with a panegyric:

Ivan Ivanovich has a magnificent hunting coat. What astrakhan! Damn it all, what astrakhan! . . . an excellent man is Ivan Ivanovich! What a magnificent house he has in Mirgorod! There's a porch around it on oak posts and under the porch there are seats everywhere. . . .
Ivan Ivanovich lies clad in a shirt on his porch only after luncheon, toward evening he puts on his hunting coat and goes out, sometimes to the town store which he supplies with flour, sometimes out into the fields where he catches quail. Ivan Nikiforovich lies all day long on the porch; if it is not too hot, with his back to the sun and he won't care to go anywhere. . . . Ivan Ivanovich gets very much upset if a fly drowns in his borshch. He flies into a rage, throws down the plate and gives his host the very devil. Ivan Nikiforovich is very fond of bathing and sitting up to his neck in water, he has the samovar placed in the water also, so as to enjoy his tea in the cool. Ivan Ivanovich shaves twice a week, Ivan Nikiforovich only once. . . . What an excellent man is Ivan Ivanovich! He likes melons, it is his favorite dish. Ivan Niki- forovich is a very good man, also. His garden is right next door to that of Ivan Ivanovich. They are better friends than the world has ever seen before! . . . despite all their dissimilarities, Ivan Ivanovich and Ivan Nikiforovich are splendid people.[14]

In this garrulous account with its profusion of ill-assorted, trivial details, Gogol is mocking the provincial mentality of the narrator whose silly ecstasies over unpraiseworthy matters are made even more ridiculous by their inconsequential, unmotivated presentation. What, for example, has the fondness for melons, or the fact that a man's garden borders a neighbor's, have to do with his excellence?

Gogol contrives another comic finesse in his opening passage.

An apparent break in logic is made more glaringly incongruous by being expressed in a rigidly logical grammatical pattern:

Ivan Ivanovich is very inquisitive. God help you if you start a story and do not finish it! If he is angry about something, he will let you know that he is. Looking at Ivan Nikiforovich, it is not easy to tell whether he is displeased or contented; even if something does please him, he does not show it. Ivan Ivanovich is rather timid. [*and here is the apparent incongruity*] Ivan Nikiforovich, on the other hand, has trousers with such enormous folds that if they were blown out you could put the whole courtyard with the barns and the outhouses in them.[15]

This seemingly illogical statement is based on an inner, personal logic. In Gogol's idiom the wide trousers symbolize Ivan Nikiforovich himself. He is boorish, has an animal indifference to everyone, and cares only for his creature comforts. Why should it matter to him if his wide trousers make him look fatter than he is? On the other hand, the other Ivan has a tightly gathered-up look about him. He is anxious to please, is watchful of his own deportment and that of others, comely in his manners, and extremely well-spoken: "Listening to him can only be likened to the sensation you have when someone is looking through your hair for lice or gently stroking your heel with a finger. One listens and listens and gets drowsy. It is delightful, so delightful." [16] Clearly, it is not the content of Ivan Ivanovich's monologue that brings on the soothing drowsiness, but the manner of his speech. But the narrator is impressed by outward signs only. A man's moral excellence is attested by the magnificence of his house and his hunting coat.

The dominant figure of Ivan Ivanovich comes extraordinarily alive in a masterpiece of indirect, ironic analysis. In creating this citizen of Mirgorod Gogol assembles bits and pieces that later will serve him in the construction of another, much more famous unsavory character, Pavel Chichikov in *Dead Souls*. The outward impression of a paragon of respectability, nimbly avoiding all displeasing social behavior, he is actually riddled with sly, undercutting mockery. Ultimately, Ivan Ivanovich is revealed in all his crass niggardliness.

For example, after Sunday services, being spiritually refreshed, one might say, and propelled by kindliness, Ivan Ivanovich never fails to seek out the most wretched beggar woman on the church steps to talk to her at length, asking her whether she is hungry, what she would like to eat, and when she has last eaten. But finally, he would wave her off as hungry as ever with these words: "Well, go along and God be with you. What are you waiting for? I'm not beating you, am I?" Father Pyotr, the head priest, vouched for this "devout man" with impeccable morals as a good Christian "who knew how to live." This ambiguous commendation is answered forthwith by a sly Gogolian aside. We learn that Ivan Ivanovich is a widower without any children. But Gapka, his fresh-cheeked, unmarried, sturdy-calved house-keeper, has many children who are always running about the yard hoping to receive a slice of melon or a pear from the master.

In the vitalizing incident of the quarrel, this supposedly solid pillar of society is revealed as the vainly pretentious figure that he really is. Gogol handles this quarrel between the two friends with such careful indirection that not only the Mirgorod citizens, but also many critics have dismissed the cause of the dispute as a mere trifle. Actually it is kindled by their inequality in social status. Though Ivan Ivanovich styled himself a gentleman-land-owner of Mirgorod, as the son of a priest, he is not eligible for an officer's commission in the tsar's army. One afternoon, when he is lying on the porch, complacently enumerating to himself his worldly goods, his neighbor's servant brings out a faded officer's uniform to air, a saddlebag with leather pockets for pistols, a cap, and a gun. This evidence of his friend's superior rank dis-tresses Ivan Ivanovich and, perhaps to appease his sense of so-cial inferiority, he crosses over to his friend's house and asks him for the gun. Ivan Nikiforovich snobbishly refuses and becomes incensed when the other offers to trade a grey sow and two sacks of wheat for it. In the heat of the argument Ivan Nikifor-ovich calls his friend a goose. Ivan Ivanovich is reduced to speechless fury, possibly because he had just been reminded of his humiliating lower social class, and possibly because the epi-thet was apt. He was like a gander—pretentious, easily fright-ened, and full of cackle. He vowed never to speak to his old crony again. The feud was on.

The story's pace gains momentum when the two Ivans file their petitions accusing one another of arson, trespassing, and even improper moral conduct and atheism. A trivial incident becomes ludicrously important in this very small, self-centered society. The entire town becomes involved in this private affair.

The two scenes of the deposition at the courthouse are out-rageously funny, almost burlesque. Gogol does not miss the chance to jibe in passing at the indolence of bureaucratic pro-cedure and the unconcern of officials for the business at hand. The secretary's monotonous summing up of a case would have put the judge to sleep had he not been engaged in a lively con-versation with the court assessor about his tame blackbird and the kind of vodka to which he is partial.

The case, duly registered and filed, lies on the shelf long enough for the judge to have lost a molar and two eyeteeth, for many girls to have married, and for two more children to have appeared in Ivan Ivanovich's yard. Only the grey sow that Ivan Ivanovich had offered to trade for the gun reacts with sense and dispatch to the litigation. She runs into the courtroom, paying no attention to the piles of eggs, mushrooms, bread, and other produce that the petitioners had brought for his Honor, snatches the file with Ivan Nikiforovich's deposition and runs away.

The story concludes with the narrator visiting Mirgorod twelve years after these events. He meets the two Ivans both looking shockingly older and learns that they are still absorbed in their lawsuit, each momentarily expecting a favorable judgment. Gogol as narrator becomes depressed. The grey, muddy road, the pene-trating dampness, the monotonous rain, the black, furrowed fields, the drenched crows and jackdaws as he drives away, all accentuate his melancholy: "It is gloomy in this world, gentle-men!" is his final—and now famous—remark.

The somber ending is anticlimactic. It is not justified as it was in *Old-World Landowners,* when the narrator-Gogol, again on a last visit, is oppressed by the old man's senility signifying the passing of a cherished way of life. The tale of the two Ivans functions superbly as a satire exposing the hypocrisy, medioc-rity, self-complacency, and dullness of a limited and self-absorbed provincial milieu. In this stagnant backwater nothing would change. The sterile, senseless squabble of the two aging neighbors was bound to continue. Therefore, artistically, some of the sharp-ness and mordancy of the story is blunted when Gogol shifts his stance from a detached observer to a morally concerned commentator.

CHAPTER 4

The Petersburg Cycle

I Gogol's City

IN a fragment entitled *Year 1834*, written in St. Petersburg, Gogol addressed himself to the new year which he believed would be his most creative one: "Mysterious, ineffable 1834! Where shall I commemorate you with great works? Will it be here, amid piles of houses, thrown one on top of another, thundering streets, buzzing commercialism—in this hideous heap of fashions, parades, government clerks, wild northern nights, glitter, and greyness?" [1]

Let us compare this castigation of Petersburg with the sensations that grip the blacksmith Vakula in *Christmas Eve* when he is suddenly transported on the devil's back from his native village to the capital: "Mercy me! the rumbling, the uproar, the glitter; on both sides, walls rose up, four stories high; horses' hoofs and wheels thundered by echoing and re-echoing from every quarter; houses seemed to lift themselves out of the earth at every step; bridges shook; carriages flew past; cab drivers and postillions shouted; the snow crunched beneath a thousand speeding sleds and pedestrians huddled together, crowding under the buildings that were studded with small lamps and their huge shadows flickered along the walls, with their heads reaching the chimney and the roofs." [2]

Both passages convey a pervading sense of chaos; it is as if the great city belched out meaningless explosions of sound, movement, and lights that acted as an onslaught on the senses, and behind the glittering bureaucratic façade lurked moral and social conflicts and contradictions.

This is the malefic image that Gogol constructs of the Russian capital. It is no less unreal than the Ukrainian tales. But it is even more fantastic, for unhampered by the dictates of folklore tradition, Gogol's exuberant imagination was able to invent freely, allowing for the necessary overlay of facts to substantiate the passionate indictment. The wheels, carriages, and lamps that Vakula stared at are authentic enough, but are houses thrown on top of one another in a city street any more real that Petro's potsherds that turned into gold? As his Cossack chieftain hunted down the sorcerer by the Dnieper, so Gogol stalked the city seeking out its implicit menace and discovered it in the form of the corrupting forces of cupidity, vanity, and social and political ambition that supported the bureaucratic power structure of Petersburg. The Gothic demon reappears again in urban guise. The obsessive conviction that the city is an enemy—a world of impersonality and ruthlessness where it is individual folly to retain the human and personal—is the binding theme of the five Petersburg stories, all set in the capital: *Nevsky Prospect, The Portrait, Diary of a Madman, The Nose,* and *The Overcoat.*

Gogol wrote these stories fitfully, over a ten-year span, working on them most intensely between 1833–1835 and 1841–1842. The first three were published in *Arabesques; The Nose* was accepted by Pushkin for his journal, *The Contemporary,* in 1836. *The Overcoat* composed between 1839 and 1841 appeared in the third volume of Gogol's *Collected Works* in 1842 together with a substantially revised text of *The Portrait.* In an 1831 notebook, the first paragraph of *The Portrait* and a rough draft of *Nevsky Prospect* precede, significantly, the final version of *Christmas Eve.* Gogol was already attracted to the theme of the big city even while he was still at work on *Evenings. . . .*

By the first decade of the nineteenth century, European writers had become fascinated with the concept of Paris or London as a unique, man-made phenomenon with a separate life and unity of its own. Their works on the subject[3] translated into Russian became popular with the Russian public and may have inspired Gogol to draw a profile of Petersburg which in the 1830's was the only modern city in imperial Russia. The more conventional reporting of his Russian literary predecessors,[4] at times no more than tourist descriptions, was at antipodes to Gogol's abstract picture of a megalopolis whose essence for him resided in its intangible elements. The external aspect of Petersburg is mostly eschewed in the stories; only the magnificent main boulevard and a near slum suburb receive specific mention, serving to point up the extremes of squalor and luxury in the city's life.

Pushkin's vision of the capital as administrative center created in his last long poem *The Bronze Horseman* (1833), was, of course, well known. Petersburg stands as a monument to the willpower and ambition of Peter the Great, symbolizing Russia's prestige and enlightenment by the formal beauty of its architecture, the magnificent palaces, and marble-banked canals. But the poem, set during the fearful 1824 inundation of the poorer city sections, centers on the despair and wrath of an insignificant clerk, Evgeny, who shouts his hatred at the Emperor's bronze statue when his sweetheart and her house are swept away. Pushkin's masterpiece has been construed also as a memorial to the hundreds of thousands who died in the construction of the city and to those who continued to live in it in dangerous proximity to the elements. No attempt is made to resolve the moral conflict, although the fact that Evgeny becomes insane from grief and flees across the pavement from the pursuing hoofs of the Bronze Horseman makes clear that public grandeur is bought at the price of private happiness.

In his personal confrontation with the city, Gogol makes this clearer still. In the Petersburg stories he dwells upon the theme, implied by Pushkin, of desperate private rebellions in the climate of huge indifference and impersonality, a theme that was to be developed in all its shattering aspects, after the two World Wars, by American and European writers. The narratives are not subjective in tone, but Gogol's partial identification with his heroes is discernible enough. Like him they are solitary, rootless men with few human attachments. It is as if Gogol were testing himself in their efforts to endure and to succeed despite the ubiquitous malignant pressures of the city. These pressures are not concretized, and no portrait of Petersburg is attempted even in terms of a moral definition. Rather, the effect of a great city on the consciousness of those who live in it is Gogol's preoccupation, and here he breaks new ground. With his enormous imaginative faculty he perceives behind the palpable, organized reality of the city structure its other face of dissonance and friction engendered by its very size, complexity, and diversity. He considers Petersburg a threat to man's self-fulfillment and sanity, anticipating with uncanny prescience the traumatic anxieties and insecurities of modern urban life.

II Nevsky Prospect

Nevsky Prospect, the city's main avenue, "the universal communications line of St. Petersburg" [5] is the hero of the story. The action begins and ends on its wide sidewalks, and the life of the city is telescoped into a description of all manner of people who may be seen there at varying times of the day.

"There is nothing finer than Nevsky Prospect. . . . What doesn't it glitter with, this street, the beauty of our capital!" [6] exclaims the author in a seemingly admiring tone. In the early morning, it is crowded with beggars, peasants, government clerks, old women, errand boys, and other small fry; later these are replaced by tutors and governesses accompanied by their young charges, and during the fashionable afternoon hour—here Gogol's good-natured banter sharpens with irony—the world of privilege makes its appearance, represented by "persons of distinguished occupations and habits." From two to three o'clock daily, "the chief exhibit of all the best productions of man" takes place. Follows a surging catalogue of the "best productions," whereupon a potentially ordinary scene of high-ranking officials strolling with their elegant wives explodes into a splintered distortion of reality:

Here you will meet side whiskers, threaded through the necktie with extraordinary and astonishing art, velvety whiskers, satiny ones, others black as coal or sable, but alas! invariably belonging to the Department of Foreign Affairs. . . . Here you will meet marvelous moustaches, indescribable by pen or brush, moustaches to which the better half of a life has been consecrated, objects of long vigils, by day and by night; moustaches perfumed with the most exquisite scent and anointed with the rarest kind of pomade, moustaches wrapped at night in delicate vellum that are the envy of the passers-by and for which the owner has the most touching affection. . . . Thousands of varieties of hats, dresses, and fragile multi-colored kerchiefs which produce an adoration for them on the part of their owners that lasts two whole days, dazzle everyone on Nevsky Prospect . . . You will meet waists as delicate and slim as you have never seen in your dreams, waists no thicker than the neck of a bottle . . . and the ladies sleeves on Nevsky Prospect! O, what delight! They are two balloons that might lift the lady into the air if she were not held down by her escort; and it would be as easy and enchanting to lift the lady up into the air as one lifts a glass of champagne to one's lips . . . there is a display of all the finest things: one displays a smart overcoat with superior beaver on it; the second, a magnificent Greek nose; a third, sports superb side-whiskers; a fourth, a pair of pretty eyes and a stunning little hat; a fifth, a signet ring adorning the little finger; a sixth, a small foot in a lovely little slipper; the seventh, a cravat that provokes amazement; and the eights— a moustache that reduces one to stupefaction. . . .[7]

This is Gogol at his most exuberant, slyly satirical best, a superb instance of his inventiveness in the extraction of comic effects from prosaic elements by indirect denigration and fragmentation. The breaking up of the external world into single, freely interchangeable animate and inanimate particles is a constant in Gogol's vision of reality. Leaving aside for the moment the subtle ridicule of the effervescent commentary, it may be argued that the scattered, spotty impression of the crowd, in a very literal sense is photographically accurate; an observer, striding quickly in the midst of a moving throng would catch only glimpses of bits and pieces of people and their finery. Nonetheless, the transformation of Nevsky Prospect into a fragmented space peopled with mobile and isolated objects cast into new roles (ladies' sleeves compared to balloons) and new relations (one may lift a lady as easily as a champagne glass) becomes Gogolian fantasy. Since all declared links in Gogol's description of the promenade are fluid and virtual, their only meaning is drawn from the arbitrary persuasions of the author. The comic grotesque produced by the deliberate dismembering of the sumptuously attired crowd suggests Gogol's abhorrence of one aspect of Petersburg which he saw purely as a showcase for the vanity, posturings, and essential triviality of its high-ranking bureaucrats. No faces here, not one real human being, only dressed-up mannequins on show externalizing the emptiness and artifice of that society.

This interpretation is supported by Gogol's concluding remarks evoking the mirage of the city and underlining the perfidious character of the handsome boulevard in yet another way:

O, do not trust that Nevsky Prospect! I always wrap my cloak around myself even more closely when I walk on it and avoid looking at the objects that meet my eye. Everything is deception, everything is a dream, everything is not what it seems! You think this gentleman strolling along in his excellently cut coat is very wealthy? Not at all. All his wealth consists of his coat. . . . You think that the ladies . . ?

but ladies, more than the rest, are not to be trusted . . . and for heaven's sake, get as far as possible from the street lamp! Pass it quickly, as quickly as you can . . . you'll escape with little damage if it only stains your foppish coat with stinking oil. But not only the lamp—everything breathes deception. Nevsky Prospect lies all the time, but most of all when night falls in massed shadows on it, throwing into relief the white and dun colored walls of the buildings, when the entire city is transformed into noise and glitter, thousands of carriages roll over the bridges, postillions shout and the demon himself lights the lamps to illuminate everything in false colors.[8]

Two young friends, the shy idealistic painter Piskarev and the swaggering Lieutenant Pirogov, meet on Nevsky Prospect at this deceiving hour of dusk and the story proper begins. As they walk along, two beautiful women, one after the other, pass them. The officer decides to pursue the blond girl, which gives courage to the artist to follow the other, who seems to him the incarnation of Il Perugino's "Bianca." When she turns out to be an ordinary prostitute, he rushes off in revulsion, but her beauty continues to haunt him in opium-induced dreams in which she appears now a glamorous lady of quality, now as his virtuous and loving wife who shares his modest existence in his studio, keeps it tidy, and encourages him in his work. He experiences such supreme happiness in the second dream that one day, upon awakening from it, he returns to the brothel where the young beauty lives and impetuously offers her himself, respectability, and the rewarding joys of "work shared, side by side." Her coarse and jeering reaction to his proposal leaves Piskarev shattered by the vulgarity of his idol, and he commits suicide.

Pirogov's adventure is no more successful, but it culminates in farce. The blonde whom the officer follows right into her house is the dull, but accessible wife of a German tinsmith named Schiller. In a long vaudevillian aside Schiller is shown as a model of methodical German perseverance who has decided to save 50,000 rubles in ten years and lives accordingly, rising at seven, dining at two, kissing his wife twice every twenty-four hours, and getting drunk only on Sunday. On that day when he is full of beer and catches the enterprising Pirogov covering his spouse with kisses, he gives the officer a sound thrashing and his two assistants enthusiastically join in. Quivering with indignation at the insult to his rank, Pirogov sets off to lodge a complaint with his general, and already sees the trandeseman in chains and on his way to Siberia. But somehow the affair ends quite differently. The lieutenant stops at a pastry shop, consumes two jam puffs, glances at the latest issue of the *Northern Bee,* and walking down Nevsky Prospect in a much calmer frame of mind, drops in at a party where some officers from his regiment and several government officials are gathered. There, he so distinguishes himself in dancing the mazurka "that not only the women, but everyone in the company expressed their admiration." [9]

In the two episodes, one tragic, one comic, each of the young men suffers deception but to a varying degree of intensity. Gogol gives us to understand in two deadpan informative pages that the thick-skinned, pleasure-loving Pirogov is a sciolist, name-dropper, and self-styled amateur of literature and the arts, who dines out nightly and whose only ambition is "to marry a merchant's daughter with 100,000 rubles dowry and a host of wealthy relations, who knows how to play the piano." [10] He is the kind of unimaginative numbskull who would shrug off with self-complacency and aplomb a flirtation that miscarried. We learn that he is a typical product of the middle-echelon military society in Petersburg and an embodiment of self-centeredness and stupidity. His utterly commonplace and crude behavior is intended to bring out the purity and depth of feeling shown in Piskarev. But in this Gogol is only partially successful. Granted the lieutenant's volatile character, he has the winsome and rakish appeal of a man who knows how to enjoy himself and share his fun with others. He remains likable and immensely alive.

Piskarev, on the other hand, is a dreary figure and artistically indecisive. His drama is centered around the theme of the contradictions between illusion and reality beloved by the Romantics that Gogol had explored in his first published effort, *Hanz Küchelgarten.* But he has difficulty fitting the unknown Petersburg artist into the Romantic role. His way of life and his very temperament get in the way. Piskarev is too timid and retiring. Awed by persons placed socially higher than himself, he is content to work away, unrecognized, in his shabby studio hung with his undistinguished canvases and drawings. He has not the stuff of rebellion in him to struggle against materialistic society nor the sense of an esthetic mission that in the "Meditation" of *Hanz Küchelgarten* Gogol deemed essential for the Romantic hero par excellence. In another way, however, the story of the painter is a continuation of the *Hanz* theme.

What Gogol found contemptible in Hanz was his sacrifice of the esthetic ideal for the homespun idyll of Louise and his native village, Lünensdorf. Piskarev does not aim any higher. Seized with a vision of beauty, he does not transform it with its promise of self-realization and a larger freedom into his art; neither does he reject reality to maintain the splendor of his solitary illusion. Instead, Gogol reveals him in his wish-fulfillment dreams as something of a social and moral prig who wants to press his own version of reality upon the unattainable. Both Hanz and Piskarev are fatally flawed by this safe, familiar, and secure attitude toward life, and in Gogol's Romantic terms they must suffer: Hanz is condemned to an "exister's" inglorious lot, and Piskarev, to mental anguish and death.

III The Portrait (Portret)

In important respects, *The Portrait* is unlike Gogol's other works. At the time he wrote it, he was also formulating in articles a system of esthetics on literature, architecture, and the plastic arts, was studying at the Art Academy, and frequenting Bohemian circles where young artists whiled away the hours in interminable discussions on problems in art.

Gogol's esthetic values stemmed in part from the chimerical mysticism and idealism of German Romantic philosophy which sought to reconstruct life as a unified whole impregnated with beauty and virtue. But this yearning to express cloudy, sentimentally colored universals was complicated by another facet of his ideological organization which harbored superstitious, tradition-locked fears of concrete images of absolute evil and which haunted his creative endeavor.

At twenty-five, these problems of creativity absorbed him, and the beliefs that he held concerning the artist in relation to art and to his public blossomed with tropical speed. He used *The Portrait* as a vehicle for these beliefs.

It is perhaps Gogol's least entertaining piece of fiction—serious, philosophical in tone—unique in Gogolian production for its lack of humorous asides and total absence of the grotesque. However, a creator expressing his theories on creativity usually makes for interesting reading. At times such writing is unconsciously self-revealing, and *The Portrait,* coming out of the intellectual forces at work in Gogol, provides more penetratingly than do his critics an understanding of certain basic fluctuations in his approach to his art.

The story is composed of two parts: an introductory parable and a discursive explanation of it. The parable is written in a genre new to Gogol—a psychological novella tightly plotted and melodramatic in style. It centers on the gradual moral disintegration of a poor talented young painter, Chertkov. In the relentless momentum of mental torment endured by one man alone caught in an inner hell of his own making, Chertkov's drama recalls that of Khoma Brut and Piskarev. In Gogol's revised version of the story, we meet Chertkov in a secondhand shop staring at a picture of an old man of distinctly Oriental origin wearing Asiatic dress. He is fascinated by the look of the extraordinarily life-like eyes, becomes frightened, but buys the portrait almost for nothing and hangs it on his studio wall. During the night the old man steps out of the frame and shows the young painter large rolls of gold coins. Chertkov wakes up, realizing that he had been dreaming, but what he thought was reality is also a dream. By accident, a roll of gold coins is discovered hidden in the portrait frame, and with it, Chertkov can now have everything material that he has wanted. He sets himself up as a fashionable portrait-ist, learns to cater deftly and cynically to the public taste: "One word from a sitter was enough to tell him how the portrait was to be painted. If a man insisted on looking like Mars, Mars appeared on the portrait; for those who wanted to look like Byron, he provided a Byronic pose and Byronic gestures. . . ." [11] Once when he is asked to assess a truly great painting that had been sent to the gallery by one of his former friends who had sacrificed everything to his art, he receives a terrible shock, realizing the price that he had paid for wealth and affluence. He locks himself up in his studio in a futile attempt to recover his former techniques. Consumed by envy and despair, he begins to purchase with the banknotes that have accumulated in his coffers all available new paintings showing talent only to slash them. Finally he goes insane and dies.

Money and its vitiating influence on the artist keys this story. In variegated form, the theme runs through Gogol's fiction time and again starting with his first doom-laden Ukrainian tale, *St.*

John's Eve, where the folkloric motif of the corrupting power of
gold acquired through a supernatural agency is treated with
feral directness. Possibly because Gogol was himself rarely free
from financial worries, he came to hate the idea of money and
its hold on men. When he wrote that "the nineteenth century has
long ago acquired the dull physiognomy of a banker, who enjoys
his millions as figures on paper" [12] he voiced an apprehension that
was felt by major literary spokesmen of post-Napoleonic Europe.
In the 1830's, Pushkin printed articles in his journal on the character of English capitalism, the speculative fever that gripped
London businessmen and their absorption in financial operations.
Balzac and Stendhal were announcing the new bourgeois age
represented by the moneyed man to whom the world was but a
buyers' and sellers' market: "I am wealthy enough to buy a
human conscience," declares Gobseck, one of Balzac's heroes.

So was Chertkov bought by moneyed Petersburg society and
transformed into a dehumanized professional hack:

. . . all his feelings and impulses were concerned with gold. Gold became his passion, his ideal, his fear, his delight, his aim. Piles of banknotes thickened in his coffers and like everyone who is privileged in
this fearful way, he began to be boring, inaccessible, and indifferent
to everything. He was about to be transformed into one of those
strange beings whom a man full of vitality and passions regards with
horror, for they appear to him as ambulating stone coffins with a
corpse inside instead of a heart.[13]

The problem posed in the story is that of the artist who
must choose between patronage that offers financial security at
the cost of professional integrity and artistic freedom coupled
with a precarious economic existence. Obviously, Chertkov, at
the moment he finds the gold, penniless and threatened with
imminent eviction from his studio, opts for an immediate solution to his plight. But the miraculous interference of the portrait
in his affairs does not stop at the initial lure of one thousand
gold pieces; the success predicted and realized for Chertkov is
the symbol of the evil that continues to control his life. What is
the source of this arcane power? The second part of the story
furnishes the answer.

The first version of the story had the following plot: Years
after Chertkov's death, the portrait is seen at an auction and the

son of the artist who had painted it reveals its secret. The sitter, an immensely rich ruthless moneylender, named Petromihhali lived in Kolomna, a most unpretentious section of the capital, and it was rumored that the money he loaned at exorbitant rates invariably brought misfortune to the borrower. Here the narrative breaks off to describe the seedy character of the Kolomna neighborhood in a masterpiece of Gogolian Realism that contrasts sharply with the otherwise rhetorical and verbose literary style of the narrative.

The narrator's father, a gifted painter was called when the moneylender lay dying and asked to paint his likeness. When the painter had completed the eyes, they stared back at him from the canvas in such a terrifyingly lifelike way that he became frightened and would not continue. The old man begged him to go on, confessing to him that if something of his life force, even no more than his image on canvas were to remain on earth he would escape hell's torment in the life to come. The painter remained obdurate. When he returned home, the usurer had died and he found the painting on his own wall. Misfortune began to dog his steps; when he gave the picture away it brought trouble and harm to others. He was a pious man and decided to enter a monastery to purge himself of this experience. There he learned that the usurer was really Antichrist who had wanted to visit the earth but could only appear in human form; when the body disintegrated, some part of his demoniacal power would remain if it were preserved—even in a painting. This painting would travel over the world, sowing destruction in men's hearts for fifty years, then its secret would be revealed and its power cease. That time was now at hand. When the speaker had finished his account, the buyers turned to look at the portrait; it had changed into a mediocre landscape.

Never far away, demons stride again across the Gogolian landscape and in the parable of Chertkov's fall, as in *Terrible Vengeance,* the vitality, the life force, the immutability of diabolism receive in space and time supreme emphasis—in this tale, the image of the living eyes on a painted canvas. It was a favorite horror device in Gothic literature and Gogol may have found it in *Melmoth the Wanderer* by Charles Maturin or in Pushkin's *Queen of Spades,* or perhaps in *Der Sandmann* where E. T. A. Hoffman uses the obsession with eyes as a leitmotif.

But as frequently happened with his literary borrowings, the magnetic eyes of the moneylender served Gogol for yet another purpose beyond the Romantic connotation of deathless evil or inscrutable mysteries. In a magnificent passage, Chertkov examines the portrait and reflects upon the limits of successful Realism in art—a problem that preoccupied Gogol throughout his creative life:

This was not art. The eyes, human, alive, as if they had been taken from a live human creature and inserted into the canvas, destroyed the harmony of the portrait. The supreme enjoyment that permeates the spirit at the sight of an artist's work, no matter how terrifying the subject, was lacking; there was a feeling of painful anxiety instead. "What is it?" the painter asked himself. "After all this is taken from nature, why this strangely discomfiting feeling? Or is it the slavish imitation of nature that is a crime and acts upon one as a sharp and discordant cry? Or if one paints unfeelingly and objectively, must the subject emerge in all its fearful reality, unmitigated by the light of some unattainable secret vision? Will it appear with the form of reality when, trying to understand the secret of beauty in man, you reach for a scalpel and dissect his insides to find only the ugliness within? Why is it that simple lowly nature in the work of an artist seems to reflect no degradation? On the contrary, it affords delight and later everything flows more calmly and smoothly around you. And the same subject treated by another painter appears sordid and vile, although he too has been true to nature. No, there was no illumination in it. It's like a landscape; if the sun does not shine on it something is lacking regardless of how magnificent it may be.[14]

Thus, there is no aspect of reality, however unwholesome or repulsive, that may not serve the artist. This central argument is given further coherence and direction in the famous apologia that opens the seventh chapter of *Dead Souls*, when Gogol speaks again of that writer (himself) who is courageous enough to expose to his reader all the fearful shattering morass of details that make up existence. But what is the saving essence of Realistic art, what exactly is the "sun" that illuminates the landscape? Is it ultimately the overworked umbrella concept of "inspiration"? In the description of the canvas that produced the change in Chertkov, Gogol evades the issue by placing the word "inexpressible" on that intangible quality which breathed greatness into the work.

In the second version of *The Portrait* published seven years later (1842), Gogol returns to the definition of true art. It has now taken on a moral and religious coloration. At the end of several austere and contemplative years, the monk-painter expiates his sin of reproducing the exact likeness of the demoniacal usurer by painting a marvelous picture of the Madonna and Child. He is told by his prior that "no artist could have created such a painting with human art alone; Your brush was guided by divine power and God blessed your inspiration."[25] This thought the monk passes on to his son admonishing him to preserve his talent which is God's gift and adding that "the glorious spirit of the Creator permeates it . . . and intimation of God's paradise is found in art and that is why art is higher than all else." [16] Drawing upon the Christian vision to inspire his art, both the artist and his own work are purified, and the reality that he observes through the prism of a religious ideal becomes illuminated in his picture with a higher truth; in this way a masterpiece is produced.

This subservience of art to religion, anticipating Gogol's eventual artistic collapse, was not developed in the revised edition of the story. But the fact that Gogol looked for a supporting moral force in the creative act, opens up the provocative idea that he regarded art as a kind of transgression. In this context the portrait itself symbolizes the sinfulness of all creative expression lacking devout impulse.

In contrast to the much strengthened didactic element, the demonic atmosphere in the 1842 corrected edition has been substantially dispelled. This may in part be attributed to Belinsky's sharp criticism of the "needless fantastic" in his first major essay on Gogol's fiction in "The Russian Story and Mr. Gogol's Stories" (*Telescope*, 1835, XXVI); it also suggests that the Gothic-Romantic hold on Gogol's imagination was weakening. His evils are now more modern; they plague the hero in the shape of his own weaknesses from within. Chertkov's prostitution of his art is explained by his envy of more successful colleagues and his yearning to move in high society. The eerie scene of the old man stepping out of the frame into the moonlit room and offering the roll of gold to the young painter in the first version of the story is now transformed into a nightmare, and the gold simply falls out of the frame when it is pressed hard. No longer is any mystery attached to the appearance of the picture in the studio; Chertkov buys it with his last twenty kopeks and brings it home. It finally disappears in a natural way. When the auction crowd looks for it after the long speech, it is no longer there and the word "stolen" is echoed through the room. Gogol wanted to stress the considerable re-working of the story and may have changed his hero's name from Chertkov to Chartkov for that reason. The later version is by far the less gripping one; what it gains in plausibility, including at least one vividly realistic and ironic scene—the landlord's visit to Chertkov's studio to collect the rent—it loses in the intense and unifying power of the superhuman theme.

IV   Diary of a Madman (Zapiski sumasshedshego)

In style, tone, and subject matter the *Diary of a Madman* is Gogol's most compressed, most driven story.

Its thematic complexity and richness have actuated a diversity of interpretations. The cardinal pattern in the story's design has been variously diagnosed by critics as the eternal divergence between reality and illusion, the tragic fate of the little man crippled by the injustice of the ruling social order, a search for identity, the unfurling of erotic fantasies, the triviality of human life, man's futile quest for a reordered existence, and as a study of insanity as the last resort to a comprehension of reality. That a good case has been made for each of the above themes is a forceful testimonial to the universality of the story that reaches to the core of the slighted human condition.

Gogol wrote *Diary* . . . in 1833–34, just after he had abandoned the dramatic script of *The Order of Vladimir, Third Class* in which he satirized a high-ranking bureaucrat's obsessive desire to receive the distinguished award until the *idée fixe* weakens his contact with reality, and he imagines that he himself has become the coveted decoration. Realizing that the plot as it stood would not pass censorship, Gogol reduced the sacrosanct highly-placed official to an ambitious secondary personage and placed the insignificant clerk, Poprishchin on the lunatic fringe. For greater precaution, the story was given the form of Poprishchin's personal diary composed of twenty entries that record his increasing mental aberration; to the censor the ramblings of a madman seemed harmless enough and few of the diatribes against the aristocracy were deleted.

The setting down of the hero's emotional disturbance in an uninhibited, first person monologue addressed to himself, completely free of authorial interference, is unique in Gogol's fiction and remarkably effective in following the progress of a mind along the knife-edge of encroaching madness. Painful disclosures— of the kind one might overhear in a psychiatrist's office—are made and they provide an intimate revelation of the patient. Even the language is significant: It is a vulgar idiom made up of literary turns of phrase that abound in second-rate novels, crude office slang, and lively journalistic jargon culled by Poprishchin from his favorite newspaper, the sensationalist *Northern Bee*. Poprishchin's mental orientatation is thereby established, demonstrating again Gogol's skill in exposing content through form.

Despite his exterior envelope of a middle-aged, awkward, unattractive, inarticulate copyist assigned to the most menial tasks, orphaned by circumstance and people, Poprishchin is not inert. His is an angry and ambitious ego, seething with pent-up energies, paranoiac, and marked by a pathological gift for collecting injustices. His defense against the careless snubs and humiliations received in his milieu, which apparently ignores the fact that he was born a nobleman, takes the shape of aggressive invective duly noted in his diary. When his section chief jeers at him for trailing after the director's daughter, suggests that the clerk take a good look at himself, and calls him "a zero and not a man," Poprishchin brands him in an early entry as "a damned heron with a face like a druggist's bottle." He gleefully repeats the rumor that the cashier who refused him a salary advance is a "hoary monster," who is known to be beaten at home by his cook. During the tedium of the long office hours filled with suffocatingly inutile, lowly tasks, and in his shabby room Poprishchin engages his discontented thoughts in building up an acceptable image of himself. Humiliations that he has endured, real or fancied, surface to his mind and he asks himself why it has been so arranged that some enjoy prestige and wealth, while others, like himself, submit to daily indignities and do not advance beyond the lowly title of Collegiate Assessor.

The question that thrusts itself constantly into his tormented mind is "Why not I? After all, I am not of classless origin like some tailor or the son of a non-commissioned officer. I am a gentleman and I should receive promotion. I'm 42—an age when a career, properly speaking, gets off to a start. You just wait my good man [implying the section chief], I'll become a colonel yet and perhaps something much better." [17] The verisimilitude of the hero's protest is all the stronger in that Gogol makes it abundantly clear that Poprishchin is not revolting against the bureaucratic system of which he is a product, only against his own inferior position in it. He identifies rank with worth and yearns for recognition within the ruling hierarchy whose principles and attitudes are the same as his. He looks down on the common people, is roused to indignation when he reads in the *Northern Bee* about a current social uprising in France against the established order. He is sharply envious of more fortunately placed personnel in certain government offices where bribe taking is strongly entrenched and where "side benefits" may consist of horses, carriages, and furs.

A self-centered life that feeds on its frustrations and is dominated by a desire to cease being a zero and to become a somebody does not necessarily lead to mental derangement. There is a sign, however, in the very first entry that the clerk is a little "touched," when the section chief berates him for muddled behavior: "Sometimes you dash about like a house on fire and get your work into such a mess that the devil himself couldn't put it straight; you're likely to start a new heading with a small letter and give no date or reference number." [18]

His borderline state becomes more apparent three entries later in a description of the director of the department to whose study Poprishchin is sent to sharpen some quill pens Immeasurable excitement grips him at the thought of His Excellency, and he fixes his attention on his books, porcelain, furniture, and his young daughter with a passion. The director, who is also a general moves in the highest aristocratic circles; he becomes for the clerk the Dostoevskian "Other," a figure of supreme authority and unimpeachable moral and social distinction. He reigns from the unattainable heights of Poprishchin's most daring dreams and his feeling for His Excellency is that mixture of envy and rapturous admiration sometimes seen in the eyes of the very poor when confronted with a magnificent parade of riches. Lying on his bed, Poprishchin gives

himself up to his private ecstasy, oscillating between wonder at the General's erudition (the study is crammed with
French and German books) and erotic fantasies about white-
gowned Sophie, the General's daughter, and the wondrous things
that must exist in her bedroom: "I yearn to look into her bedroom; there must be miracles there . . . a true paradise such as
cannot be found in heaven. To see the little stool that she uses
to put her little foot on when she gets out of bed and the way
she draws a snow-white stocking on that little foot. . . ."[19]

This wish is granted through the letters that Sophie's lap dog,
Madgie, writes to her friend Fidèle whom she meets when taken
out for walks. Poprishchin overhears the conversation between
the dogs on the street, follows Fidèle, manages to grab Madgie's
little notes out of Fidèle's basket, and copies them into his diary.

The canine correspondence (a device previously used by
E. T. A. Hoffman in "The Surly Tom Cat" and "News of the
Latest Adventures of the Dog Berganza" *) that Gogol integrates
into the strictly realistic framework of the story has been explained by some Soviet critics as a phantasmal extension of the
clerk's deranged imagination.[20] This is impossible, however, since
the housepets gossip about events that Poprishchin could not
have known or guessed. It is significant, however, that he credits
Madgie's every word, not only because he is convinced that dogs
are more intelligent than human beings, but also because his
extreme paranoia is receptive ground for disclosures guaranteed
to inflict the deepest wounds upon his psyche.

He learns that the general is no less rank-haunted than himself
and cuts a ridiculous figure in his own household during his
agony of waiting for a medal that may never be accorded him,
striding through the rooms "in a very strange manner" opening
one hand and closing the other, questioning even Madgie about
his chances. His daughter, who can hardly refrain from giggling
at the sight of the quill-sharpening clerk in the study with hair
like hay on his head, is smitten by a dashing court chamberlain
with flashing eyes whom she engages in vapid social nonenities.
Their marriage will soon take place, according to the dog. "Hell,
I cannot go on . . . it hurts . . ." writes Poprishchin after reading

* ("Katir Murr" and "Nachricht von den neuesten Schicksalen des Hundes
Berganza).

Madgie's last letter, and in fury and despair he tears the canine correspondence into shreds.

This is the turning point of his illness. With his idols toppled, his mind gives way. Immediately afterwards, his hatred of the court chamberlain brings on a compensatory vision of himself, as one who might just as easily become transformed into a general with epaulets on his shoulders and blue ribbon across his chest. But the fantasy, as Gogol astutely comprehended, needed *ambiance* and focus in this downward plunge. Poprishchin finds them in the *Northern Bee*'s reports of the death of Ferdinand VII and the disorders surging around the vacant Spanish throne. The news absorbs him entirely; he no longer goes to the office, but remains at home reading newspapers all day. One evening, at dinner he throws two plates on the floor. In triumph he asserts that the Spanish king has been found, shouting, "I am the king!"

He is astonished by his former disguise of collegiate assessor and wonders why he was never discovered and committed to an insane asylum! The new reality throbs with a marvelous sense of order, clarity, and happiness as the delirium gains momentum and previous idealizations are shed. When the director enters the department, the clerk remains seated and given a paper to verify, signs with a flourish in the space left for the director's signature—"Ferdinand VII." Thus the roles become reversed. Accosting Sophie in her boudoir, he hints at their future joys together, but turning on his heel reaches the instantaneous conclusion that the devil is standing behind her and will marry her—a recurring leitmotif in Gogolian fiction. The sexual impulse is blunted by new political responsibilities, although generalized eroticism surfaces from time to time in the form of an anxious query about the moon. The moon is "tender and gentle" (like love), "our noses live on" (an obvious phallic symbol), and "when the heavy earth sits on the moon may it not crush the moon and all our noses with it?" (fear of castration).

The world of officialdom whose haloed image of promotion and rank had motivated his entire previous existence gets the most violent abuse. It is as if a bandage had been removed from his eyes and he suddenly sees with the lucidity of the insane the venality, greed, and egregious egotism of his former superiors: "And all these people, their distinguished fathers who cater to everyone and push their way to court and say they are patriots and all that sort of thing: profit, profit is all these so-called patriots want! They would sell their father and mother and God for money, ambitious creatures that they are, Judases all!" [21]

In a troubled entry the problem of the royal mantle comes up—reminiscent of Gogol's insistence in *Nevsky Prospect* that appearance makes the man—and is resolved when Poprishchin cuts up his almost brand-new overcoat behind a locked door into a suitable garment for a monarch. He is ready for his retinue to escort him to the palace. When he arrives there, he notes that all the people whom he takes for grandees or soldiers have shaven heads.

The madman's final hysterical outburst when his initiated action turns into a reaction to outside stimuli (the beatings he receives from the keepers in the asylum to which he has by now been committed) conveys a sense of dislocation and loss. Beaten and goaded beyond endurance, the clerk calls for fast horses to carry him away from his agony—an escape that Gogol and his heroes resorted to in moments of bewilderment or despair. Poprishchin's feverish appeal to his mother to nurse him in her arms and take him back to childhood foreshadows the author's deathbed delirium fifteen years later.

The story moves on two levels. It is the saga of a man crippled by social alienation, conscious of being *de trop*, needing to be integrated into his society, and spending his abundant energies on the creation of a private world based on his obsessions. But the seemingly straightforward and tragic account of a warped mind's regress into lunacy is distorted with double images which, when placed side by side, become parodies of each other and produce a Gogolian grotesque vision of the world.

Madgie's mundane chitchat, for example, reflects the frivolousness of Sophie, even to the extent of preference in suitors. It is not always clear from Madgie's high-flown prose that mimics Sophie's drawing room accents, whether the backyard dog Trezor or the court chamberlain is being discussed. Nor is it evident whether "the horrible mongrel with stupidity written all over him" whom Madgie despises is the dog next door or the oafish pen-sharpening clerk who is tongue-tied in Sophie's presence.

With carefully placed irony, Gogol has the images flow from one into the other. The disturbances over the Spanish succession, due to the king's untimely death, are juxtaposed with the despair that washes over Poprishchin when his supreme illusion is shattered. Until a figure of authority is reinstated in Spain and in the clerk's consciousness, disorder and bewilderment continue. There is yet another bitterly ironical connotation in the fact that the clerk's surname is derived from the word "poprishche," a lofty term for "career," that, like a broken mirror, projects the hero's shattered ambitions.

The most powerful confrontation of all is between the high-ranking administrator and the lowly copyist in his department. Both are shaped and controlled by the bureaucratic apparatus, and both are entangled in a web of ambition. Is not the director whom Madgie calls "a very strange man" as obsessed as Poprishchin? Where to draw the line between sanity and madness? Insanity (this word is not used once in the story) is projected in one sense at least, as an emancipation from the viciousness and falseness of life. In the asylum Poprishchin understands and rejects the contemptible reality with its conflicts and tensions that had formerly enslaved him, and becomes freer, more sane than his counterpart who will go on grovelling in the real world of "highest lackeydom." And finally, what is reality or madness, for that matter, but mockery and delusion that dissolve into nothingness from which there is no escape other than a headlong rush in a swift troika into another void. The Diary . . . provides no answer. But at the end of the passionate outburst that seems to come right out of Gogol's own spiritual torment, the last wild, superbly incongruous line stabs through the tragic with resurging comic-grotesque: "And do you know that the Dey of Algiers has a boil right under his nose?" [22]

V The Nose (Nos)

The Nose is a gem apart. Pushkin acclaimed it as a merry, fantastic jest, and at first blush it does seem to be a hilarious tour de force, something made out of nothing, with the exact proportion of ingredients needed to produce a completely successful "tall" story: a preposterous event in a realistic framework reinforced with comic but credible incidents, a total lack of compassion for all concerned, and an atmosphere of suspense maintained until the end where it dissolves into bathos, and everything that has been stirred up settles back into its original order.

On March 25th, a Petersburg barber finds in his breakfast roll the nose of Collegiate Assessor Kovalev whom he shaves every Wednesday and Saturday. Did he accidentally cut it off when he had had a few too many? "For like all self-respecting Russian tradesmen, the barber was a fearful drunkard." [23] He wraps the nose up in a piece of rag and tries to get rid of it without being noticed. On the same morning, Kovalev wakes up remembering that a pimple on his nose had broken out the day before, looks into a mirror and sees to his stupefaction that instead of his nose that had resided with dignity and poise between rather full florid cheeks and the magnificently trained whiskers that flew straight up to his nostrils, there was now only a flat empty space, smooth and shining like the outside of an egg. He jumps out of bed, shakes and pinches himself . . . where is his nose? He decides to visit the police commissioner. On his way, he catches a glimpse of a shining gold-braided uniform, tricorn hat, and saber, jumping out of a carriage, running into a building, coming right out again, and riding away. He recognizes the wearer of the uniform as his own nose and from the plumes on his hat realizes that he is a State Councillor, four grades higher in rank than he. He runs after the carriage that soon stops in front of a church, pushes past rows of beggars, and timidly approaches his praying nose to remonstrate with it. The other retorts brusquely that "he is no one but himself" and snubs the "Collegiate Assessor. While Kovalev is momentarily distracted by a pretty woman, the nose disappears. Kovalev rushes off to the police commissioner, but not finding him at home, goes to place an ad in the newspaper for his lost nose. The clerk, after some thought, decides that too many absurdities would get into print if everyone began advertising for vagrant noses. When Kovalev reaches the police superintendent, he finds him reluctant to start an investigation so soon after a meal; the official pointedly adds that noses do not come off decent people's faces. Kovalev now becomes convinced that his misfortune has been brought on by the staff officer's widow, Mrs. Podtochnitsa (Mrs. Undermine) who must have enlisted the aid of a witch to pay him back for courting, but not marrying her dowryless daughter. He writes her a letter full of double meanings and vague threats which she answers immediately and establishes her innocence in the affair. At the nadir of his distraught state, a policeman reports that the nose he is now returning wrapped in a piece of dirty rag had been caught presenting a false passport when boarding an international train in Riga. The Collegiate Assessor is overjoyed and tips the policeman lavishly, but the nose will not stick to his face again. A doctor suggests that its owner let things remain as they are, place the precious object into alcohol, and exhibit it for a fee as a curiosity. On April 7th, Kovalev wakes up to find that the nose is back in its proper place. The epilogue concludes with the regularly scheduled visit from the barber who examines the Collegiate Assessor's face with some concern before starting to shave him, placing his thumb now on Kovalev's cheek, now on his gum, rather than holding him by the nose as used to be his want.

What is the meaning of this jerky, fragmented and improbable tale? Gogol must have felt the need to justify its illogical sequence, for he placed the story originally within the framework of a dream. The first draft concludes with the words: "Everything that has happened here occurred to Major Kovalev in a dream, and when he woke up, he was so overjoyed that he jumped out of bed, ran up to the mirror, and seeing that everything was in its right place, began dancing in his nightshirt a combination of a mazurka and a quadrille around the room." [24] Although this explanation was discarded in the final version, dream-like features continue to dominate the waking fantasy.

At the onset, the awakening of the barber and the official suggests that their sleep may not have been interrupted; the unity of the action is shredded by disconnected episodes that fade away into obscure endings; the dates chosen to begin and end the story—March 25th and April 7th—when reckoned by the Julian and Gregorian calendars, respectively, fall on the same day, an indication that no time at all has elapsed. But it is in the basic structure and pace of the story that the dream framework is most discernible.

When he grafted Kovalev's episodic contacts with routine city life onto the main theme of the traumatic search for the nose, Gogol did not succeed in dovetailing the two disparate elements of the narrative. For all the lively comicality and biting satire that permeate Kovalev's interviews, these vignettes do not fit in with the self-propelled dynamics of the main situation that drive Kovalev on through his nightmarish hunt. Like a train rushing across a dark landscape, stopping briefly at ill-lit stations, ever more than static halts immediately forgotten, so does Kovalev in his restlessness and increasing agitation remain separated from his momentary involvements with reality. Hence, the lack of real communication between him and the forces of law and order to which he appeals. It is significant that faced with a fantastic happening no one registers shock or even amazement. The valet continues to lie on the couch and spit methodically into one spot on the ceiling when his noseless master comes in. The sight of the pale nose within the bread roll that she herself had just baked, incites the barber's shrewish wife to the usual volley of abusive language about her husband's drinking habits; and the policeman remains unperturbed by the transformation of a travelling official into a small whitish object which turns out to be the lost nose. He places it in his pocket and returns it to its owner. This public indifference to Kovalev's catastrophe demonstrates once again, as did the tale of *Shponka* and *The Two Ivans,* the mental torpor of commonplace minds incapable of envisaging anything beyond their limited daily interests. This was Gogol's view of the world, strengthened here by its very consistency and the impression of a superimposed fantasy which is artistically convincing within the dimension of a dream.

Kovalev is a Collegiate Assessor from the Caucasus who calls himself Major Kovalev, a military rank roughly equivalent to his civilian title, and one which he feels gives him more distinction and prestige. He has recently come to the capital to seek promotion and a profitable marriage. Conceited, swaggering Pirogov in *Nevsky Prospect* is a preliminary sketch to this calculated opportunist who is as empty-headed and self-centered as the younger man, but in this new version more intent on furthering his career and more amorously inclined, although careful in avoiding entanglements that would jeopardize his marital plans. It is tempting to speculate on the possibilities that came to Gogol's mind for downgrading his hero whom he had already presented in bits and pieces of moustaches, sideburns, and signet rings promenading along Nevsky Prospect, now put together into a full-blown fop strolling down the fashionable avenue sending meaningful glances to pretty women and bowing obsequiously to acquaintances in uniforms with more gold braid than his own. And why not pillory him with the disappearance of his nose?

With this devastating occurrence the major's ambitions are

felled and his situation reduced to farce. For not only is the happening itself embarrassing and absurd, but the proboscis has something faintly ridiculous about it. The nose, often ungainly and prominent, apart from its olfactory function seems to be an empty, otiose member, extremely masculine, and somewhat uneasily associated with sexual virility. It is a common phallic symbol and it was to be expected that in the psychoanalytical interpretations of the story, the major's nose should represent his sexuality, and the loss of it an impotence or castration dream.[25] In light of this theory much has been made of the Collegiate Assessor's erotic inclinations, his possibly unconscious but consistent concern with sex, his role of a cautious amorist, either because he is uncertain of his sexual prowess or, as Gogol makes it abundantly clear, he is afraid of getting trapped into a nonlucrative permanent relationship. Freudian overtones are attributed to Gogol's feigned amazement at the impropriety of his hero's attempt to publicize his predicament in the press as "awkward, unseemly, indecent."

The obsession with rank, however, is Kovalev's *raison d'être* and it winks from every page. He assiduously cultivates the niceties of external appearance to cut an imposing figure in the only world that matters to him, which itself is composed of appearances and show. It is also a very slippery world where favoritism and bribery grease the wheels of advancement, and although the resourceful and shallow-minded major seems to fit into it perfectly, the fact that he is a parvenu and essentially a fraud stirs in his unconscious and surfaces in a dream.

The flight of the nose symbolizes his fear of failing to achieve the coveted social status, and in this sense the story turns upon a castration fantasy. Noseless, he also becomes faceless, a sort of rudderless non-person, degraded and humiliated, ridiculously inept in trying to remedy his position, and there is comedy enough in his ludicrous attempts to recover his nose—and thereby his former identity.

There is no scene more ironic verging on the burlesque in Gogol than the confrontation in church between the quailing Collegiate Assessor, begging his nose to return to him, and the magnificently garbed impostor insolently rejecting a petitioner, who, judging by his uniform buttons, serves in a different department and at a lower level than himself. Where rank is everything and a human being without it is a nonentity, the nose passing for a State Councillor is bound to win. Here, in a shift of focus, fantasy backs up into reality. The absurd personal situation is toppled by the monstrous absurdity of the bureaucratic hierarchy from which there is no escape, not even in dreams. In the *Diary of a Madman* the pressure of the reigning predatory élite drove Poprishchin to insanity; in *The Nose*, the same concern fantastically deformed, explodes into comic grotesque.

The literary vogue for "nose-ology" themes in the 1820's and 1830's probably inspired Gogol's basic anecdote for the story,[26] and the description of the excitement generated throughout the city when news of Kovalev's accident spread is very much like a similar incident occurring in *Tristram Shandy*. But the treatment of the nose motif is very much Gogol's own. *The Nose* exemplifies his bent for incorporating into one member of the body all the essence or functions of its owner. The nose *is* Kovalev, just as in *Viy* the monster's evil force is in his eyes. In a letter written from Rome in the spring, Gogol reveals again this profoundly physical aspect of his art: "Roses are now strewn all over Rome. But I am even more exhilarated by the smell of the flowers that have just bloomed. Would you believe it that I frequently have an insatiable desire to transform myself into a nose, with no hands, eyes or legs, nothing but one huge nose, with nostrils the size of pails that would draw in all the fragrance of this spring."[27]

VI   The Overcoat (Shinel')

The earlier Petersburg stories are related to *The Overcoat* as certain Stone Age engravings on cave walls are related. Drawn once, the figure of some huge animal is recalled again by being redrawn and cut deeper.

In this last and famous story, Gogol returns to bureaucratic officialdom versus the little man, the theme that dominates *Nevsky Prospect, The Portrait,* and the *Diary,* but with new creative resources in style and ideology. He wrote it between 1839 and 1841, when he was also working on *Dead Souls,* at the zenith of his mature art. It is a literary masterpiece that ranks together with Maupassant's *Necklace,* Flaubert's *A Simple Heart,* and Kafka's *Metamorphosis* among the great short stories of modern European literature.

[88]

The Petersburg Cycle

The seed of the plot was planted in Gogol's mind in 1834 when he heard a story about an indigent civil servant and ardent sportsman who, after several years' privation, was able to buy a good shotgun only to lose it in the thick reeds when he took it out hunting for the first time. Becoming dangerously ill as a result of his loss, he recovered only when his colleagues took up a collection and presented him with a new gun. According to Annenkov, everyone was amused by the anecdote, except Gogol who listened to it thoughtfully, with a lowered head.[28]

The hero of Gogol's story is just such a government underling—an underpaid document copyist whose ragged coat with innumerable patches cannot withstand another Petersburg winter. After long privation and endless economizing, he has a new one made. On the very first day he wears it, it is stolen from his back. His frantic search for it results only in the callous indifference of the high official to whom he appeals for help. He catches cold and dies of pneumonia, but his ghost returns to haunt the city streets, snatching overcoats from terrified pedestrians, until, finding the offensive official, he snatches his and disappears forever.

At first reading, the greater abundance of realistic details distinguishes *The Overcoat* from the other Petersburg stories. We never learned what Chertkov or Piskarev looked like, but the main protagonist here is introduced at once as "nothing much to speak of, a short pock-marked man with reddish hair, balding on top, myopic, with wrinkled cheeks and a complexion that might be called hemorrhoidal." [29] With the same unsavory realism Gogol describes his uniform that had been green," but has now taken on a muddy reddish hue . . . and there was always something stuck to it, bits of hay or thread, and because he had a gift for passing under a window when garbage was being thrown out of it into the street, he would carry a piece of melon rind or similar stuff on his hat." [30] The indiscretion about small intimate matters that reaches its apogee in *Dead Souls* comes through in the clerk's anxious budgeting of his pitiful means and the inventory of his belongings after his death that were not put under seal for they consisted only "of a bunch of goose quill pens, three trouser buttons, a stock of government paper, and the familiar old dressing gown." [31] This concretization of objects brings us into a world that seems palpably near, and the narrator's informal tone strengthens that impression. In the manner of the prefatory comments in *Evenings* and *The Quarrel of the Two Ivans*, *The Overcoat* is given the form of a verbal narrative unprepared and uninhibited, related by a witness to the events, this time a city man, familiar with the bureaucratic milieu, who is not emotionally involved with the hero, but temperamentally unable to maintain the role of an objective observer. He is now ironic, now compassionate, now depressed, now bewildered, and his frequent changes of mood enliven the narrative and tighten its pace.

In the narrator's language, Gogol achieves a perfection of sorts. The occasional colloquialisms, repetition of certain key words for emphasis, avowals of memory lapses ("If I'm not mistaken . . . I cannot say just where the party-giving clerk lives; my memory is beginning to fail me badly . . .") convey the naturalness of unhurried speech near enough to the hero's idiom to be completely authentic; on the other hand, it is a diapason of Gogol's most successful verbal devices tempered by a comic flavor, and in this sense the seemingly effortless and casual flow of expression is studied and contrived. One of these effects, which incidentally constitutes a challenge to the translator, rests on an intricate system of assonance, for the Russian language is rich in words that can be brought together for their auditory appeal and phonal variation. In the description of the hero, the adjectival suffix "-vaty" like the English "-ish" meaning "somewhat," is used to carry along a determined sound sequence ("He was pock-markish, reddish, myopish."). The hero's christening provides Gogol with an exuberant show of minute verbal gestures in the choice of outlandish-sounding names that the godparents read from the saints' calendar to the hero's perplexed mother: Mokky, Sossy, Khozdazat, Trifily, Dula, Varakhisy, until she finally settles on his father's name, "Akaky" ("kaka" is a child's word for feces), branding her son with the unseemly-sounding Christian name and patronymic: Akaky Akakievich.[32] In another comic maneuver, Gogol plays with irreverent meanings, inserted impishly within a strictly logical grammatical sequence, which serve to bring the reader to a hilarious stop: "The hero's name was Bashmachkin. From the name itself, it is obvious that it must have been derived from a shoe (bashmak); but when and where this happened it was impossible to say. Both his father, grandfather and even brother-in-law, and all the Bashmachkins wore boots which they simply resoled two or three times a year." [33] With the tagged-on phrase, the resoling is brought into the main argument with which, logically, it has no connection.

"Petrovich the tailor, in spite of the fact that he was one-eyed and pockmarked all over his face, was quite successful at repairing clerks' and other people's trousers and coats. . . ."[34] Had Petrovich not been pockmarked, would his alterations been more successful?—is the sly question with which Gogol teases his reader. Word puns effervesce in a verbal patina marked by humorous digression, slyly placed incongruities, and anecdotal asides. Akaky Akakievich was so absorbed in his copy work that only when he would be nudged by a horse "and its nostrils would blow a gale upon his face, would he notice that he was not in the middle of a line but in the middle of a street."[35]

In the opening passage, defined by the Russian critic Rozanov as a "flood of mockery," Gogol does not spare the ammunition of his downgrading art to reduce the stature of his elderly hero who seems to be put together of ill-assorted bits and pieces of a human being. Akaky Akakievich seems to have been born to his copyist's job in the civil service as a ninth-grade government clerk. No one noticed him, even the porters "didn't raise their eyes when he walked in, as if only an ordinary fly had passed through the reception room"; papers were shoved at him without any amenities and young clerks treated him as a butt for office jokes. He paid no attention to them and continued to work even when they taunted him with scabrous tales about his old landlady, and it was only when they pushed or poked him and prevented him from writing that he would say quietly:

Leave me alone. Why do you insult me? and there was something touching in the words and in the tone in which they were said. There was something in that utterance that aroused compassion, so that one young clerk who was new to the office, and together with the rest had also jeered at him, suddenly stopped, as though cut to the heart, and from that moment everything seemed changed and appeared in a different light to him. Some unknown force seemed to repel him from his colleagues with whom he had struck up a friendship because he considered them to be well-bred and decent men. And long afterward, during his gayest moments, the figure of the modest little clerk with a bald patch on his head would come before him with his poignant words: "Leave me alone! Why do you insult me?" and within this utterance he heard another: "I am your brother." And the poor young man buried his face in his hands, and numberless times afterwards he would shudder, seeing how much inhumanity there is in man, how much vicious brutality there exists under refined, cultured, politeness, and my God! even in a man whom the world accepts as a gentleman and a man of honor.[36]

The solemn and highly emotional passage coming as it does immediately after the grotesque delineation of the lowly, down-trodden clerk had a tremendous effect on Gogol's public steeped in the "social sympathy" literature of the 1830's and 1840's of which the popular novels of George Sand and Victor Hugo formed the vanguard, and it became a manifesto for a spate of humanitarian fiction that followed. "We all come out of Gogol's *Overcoat*," a statement, apocryphically attributed to Dostoevsky, may have been said by a number of philanthropically-minded nineteenth century Russian writers and the ideational theme of Gogol's renowned story was interpreted as a special plea for the underprivileged.

The fact that Gogol makes it perfectly clear that Akaky Akakievich's own mental limitations stood in the way of promotion (when a more involved piece of work had been offered he broke down over it and begged to "copy something") and that this "human" paragraph is singled out, occurring at the start of a story not yet developed and expressed by a nameless and transient character, escaped the notice of contemporary critics led by Belinsky, who acclaimed the work as an indictment of bureaucracy and charged it with a social message. What was also overlooked until Boris Eikhenbaum, the Formalist critic pointed it out [37] was Gogol's esthetic need at this point for an antithesis to the comedy-laden opening which would bring the grotesque introduction into sharper relief. The pathos-charged musings of the young clerk breaking into the buffoonery of the hero's appearance and origins accomplish exactly that.

But the artistic interpretation, albeit rightly dismissing social import, slights another cardinal function of the melodramatic pause. It presents Bashmachkin as he appears to others—an accidental and paltry vessel upon which a modicum of life has been conferred, and, in the eyes of decent and honorable men, deserving of pity. And since Gogol is about to introduce the leitmotif of the story which is a refutation of obvious psychological probabilities, the dynamism of the narrative requires that a conventional attitude be projected and immediately afterwards undermined in the most forceful and dramatic way. In the very next lines the focus changes: the external world recedes as the private solitary world of the clerk takes shape.

It is a self-sufficient world, made luminous by the contentment that Akaky Akakievich finds in his work, arousing envy rather than compassion. Every morning he wakes up to the lively expectation of getting back to his desk with its inkwell and pens, and at the close of the day he takes papers back home to spend happy hours in the making of capital and lower-case letters. He lives a rapt and poetic life contained in his beautiful calligraphy. He cares nothing about his clothes, is indifferent to food, eating whatever his landlady puts in front of him, and has no distractions. In a sharply satirical page, Gogol compares the compulsive need of his fellow employees to fill up their leisure with some form of amusement, however trivial and empty, with the serenely fulfilling and changeless evenings of the dedicated copyist. His inner life had a "centrum securitatis" or an "immovable anchor" that Gogol, writing to Danilevsky in 1843, insisted everyone needed "since all things are bound to be destroyed and man must have within himself a prop upon which he can lean and by means of which he can overcome all the suffering that comes his way." [38]

The tiny world of the clerk in its established routine and isolation from a larger reality is not unlike that of the characters in *Old-World Landowners*. But the latter are doomed to decay and death while Akaky Akakievich would have lived "the peaceful existence of a man who knew how to be happy on four hundred rubles a year and so perhaps he would have reached extreme old age" [37] if a sartorial crisis had not occurred that changed his entire life.

Here again, Gogol outdistances the expectations of his reader. When Petrovich shakes his head over the ragged old garment and reduces the clerk's pleading for another patching-up job into a frightened silence by naming the inconceivable sum of one hundred and sixty rubles for tailoring a new overcoat, we are prepared to commiserate with the hero in his new predicament. But compassion is out of place. With the prospect of acquiring a new overcoat Akaky Akakievich becomes transformed, and his transformation is the main theme of the story. When the decision is made to order a new overcoat, the hero's static world quickens to new imperatives: he becomes livelier in his speech, more vigorous and self-confident in his manner, his days are filled with purpose and anticipation. By dint of innumerable small sacrifices (walking on tiptoe to avoid frequent resoling, giving up tea and a candle in the evening, getting undressed upon returning home to keep linen fresh as long as possible), he saves every kopeck with the rapture of a bridegroom approaching his wedding. In his keyed-up state, thinking passionately about that object of wool that was soon to be made, "the boldest, wildest notions flashed through his head—perhaps he should even consider having marten put on the collar?"

The carefully placed word "even" that prepares for intensification and produces a risible anti-climax instead, is Gogol's way of projecting the comicality of an absurdly limited world, similar to that of the two Ivans where trifles assume colossal proportions. But contrary to the Mirgorod story where the reversal of dimensions moves the action into farcical gear, the humorous aspect of the clerk's love affair with a fashioned piece of wool, cat fur, and stout cotton interlining is muffled by the drive and precision of his passion. We are reminded of Gogol's bewilderment in *Old-World Landowners* at the tenacity and vigor of the senile landowner's affection for his deceased wife. A like determination directs the behavior of the timid, ineffectual copyist in the acquisition of a new overcoat and, when he is robbed of it, in his consequent efforts to recover it. His despair at the loss galvanizes him into action that may have surprised his creator when his hero proves stronger than the circumstance of his character. The metabolic change of the insignificant clerk into a positive, rebellious, and revengeful figure culminates in a powerful interplay of parallels and contrasts in one of Gogol's finest satirical scenes, when Akaky Akakievich once more wearing his tattered old coat is ushered into the Olympian presence of an Important Personage and begs him for help in recovering the stolen overcoat.

On the face of it this is a demonstration of the normal bureaucratic process at work: a high-ranking official, resplendent and terrifying in his bemedaled uniform shouts down the subordinate for disturbing him about an unimportant private matter, and the berated clerk suffering near collapse from the show of angry authority is thrust out onto the street. In fact, the incident is suffused with Gogolian irony. From an earlier depiction of the Important Personage, "who had become important quite recently . . . and formerly had been quite an unimportant personage" and the narrator's sly asides during the interview, it is clear that the flagellation of the clerk was propelled by a need to show off in front of an old friend who happened to be present. The comicality that clung to the clerk at the start of the story when the narrator stressed the faintly ridiculous external behavior and appearance of the clerk is conferred to the recently promoted general, but on a psychological level. The satirical exposure of the Important Personage who is not named is all the sharper for the careful parallels that Gogol sets up between him and the lowly clerk. It is an astonishing kinship made possible by Gogol's resolute refusal to endorse conventional probabilities (the young man's feeling of pity for the tormented clerk), and the leitmotif of the story emerges as Gogol indirectly but systematically debunks established and obvious attitudes towards power, status, economic security, private happiness.

Words, or lack of them, characterize both the clerk whose flaky stammer of adverbs and prepositions fails to manage a coherent sentence and the general who confines his communication to his staff to three harshly admonishing reprimands. At the party Akaky Akakievich "had no idea how to behave, where to put his hands or feet or for that matter his whole body," while the Important Personage finding himself at a social gathering with lower ranking officials present "is quite pitiable in his inability to join in a lively conversation, stopped by the thought that he would be going too far . . . the high rank had gone to his head, had knocked him off balance, and he simply did not know how to act." [40] This is no longer the one-dimensional bureaucrat of the earlier stories; a discerning and mature Gogol has humanized him into a more complex and interesting figure of a man at odds with himself. Basically kind, not stupid, and a good, obliging friend, he is forced to hide behind an official façade and is far more deserving of pity than the respect and fear that his external image incites. Indeed, it is he who merits compassion in Gogol's insinuation, not the tormented clerk who manages to withdraw from hierarchical tyranny into the comfort of a blissful, inner world.

When Akaky Akakievich, overcome by personal grief, confronts his superior, he rips through the bureaucratic scrim and having nothing else to lose, gains his personal identity and his freedom. What gives *The Overcoat* universality and a touch of greatness is the argument, that a human being, no matter how seemingly inferior, is a man unto himself, unlike any other man, and capable of rising above his predestined condition. The vision of a new overcoat opened for Bashmachkin a larger reality; its loss stirred him to rebellion against the strong articulate forces that had kept him low. When in his final delirium the victimized hero curses "His Excellency" scabrously and abundantly, not unlike Poprishchin at the turning point of his madness, he attains a sudden lucidity about past wrongs inflicted upon him and passively endured.

Critics disturbed by the intrusion, in the concluding episode, of fantasy into the strict realism of the story have been inclined to interpret Akaky's ghost as a symbol of the guilt that nagged the Important Personage after the fatal interview when "in his mind's eye, he saw, almost every day, the bloodless face of the little clerk." But in the Gogolian concept of ultimate reality where evil takes on various irreal forms and fantasy mingles freely with the pragmatic banality of everyday life it is logical that the "little clerk's" revenge upon the society that had trampled him would be possible only in the freedom of the afterlife.

In an exquisitely satirical and insouciant return to the concrete, which serves also to reaffirm his attachment to his hero, Gogol describes the general's state of mind just before the terrifying appearance of the overcoat-snatching ghost of the copyist. Again, beyond the humbug of rank, status, position, the two men are brought together in purely human terms. For what could be more fitting—Gogol seems to imply—than to have the high official attacked by Akaky's ghost and reduced to a paralysis of fear at the very moment when he is in a euphoric mood after a pleasant evening enlivened by good conversation and champagne, just as the copyist had been feeling extremely happy, walking home from a party after having drunk two glasses of champagne in agreeable company before he had been robbed of his new overcoat.

A creative restlessness pervades the Petersburg stories. Working from a full bin of Romantic fictional antecedents and beset by a need to express his own urban experience, Gogol was searching for a new esthetic. He found himself at the crossways of a Romanticism-Realism antinomy. The concrete circumstance of the underprivileged city dweller engaged his imagination, and he brought to it his own kind of Realism, rendered with pragmatic detail, but verging on a parody of reality through deliberate exaggerations and humorously contrived verbal gestures.

But he was still strongly attached to the Romantic canon and the narration is freighted with traditional Romantic themes (illusion versus reality, the sacred mission of the artist), an impassioned play of contrasts, a dependence on the fantastic waiting in the wings to take over from reality when the latter becomes unbearable or mundane.

What ensued was a subjective vision of the world marked by a selectivity of images—more the Surrealist's than the Realist's response to visible shapes and movement—as for example, dogs meeting on street corners to exchange letters, a nose riding off to church in a bemedaled uniform, a moneylender stepping out of his portrait with a bag of gold. It is also a virtuoso balancing act between the intensely emotional and the grotesque. The heroes, to a man, are inept and mentally limited loners who stand in grotesque relationship to their environment, not quite outside but not actively in it, like molecules floating around fields of strength. They are comically awkward in their dealings with others: Akaky Akakievich does not know what to do with his hands and feet at the supper party; Kovalev writes an idiotically inappropriate letter to the widow Podtochina; Piskarev behaves oafishly in the brothel; Chertkov is naïvely taken in by the society woman's vapid and banal comments on art. But these humorous touches that stress the bewilderment of the characters who lack formative contacts in their periodic excursions into daily living are relatively few. The Romantic in Gogol responds melodramatically to his estranged and imbalanced heroes who are unable to get a grip on existence, except in the most indirect and transitory manner. They are victims of the artificiality of the urban mechanism that is all the more terrifying because they are consciously unaware of it. Gogol's irony is pathos momentarily overcome. Too swiftly and too often humor is displaced by emotion-charged passages and intensely dramatic episodes such as the

lurid "crash" endings which are alternated with reflections of a
didactic nature. The overall effect of this narration which proceeds on multiple levels is a certain incoherence and disorder.
Reality is not so much obscured as displaced. Gogol has not yet
learned to control his sensational material—it furthers too actively
the development of his basic theme; realistic specifics—arresting
in themselves—are dispersed, unassimilated, and unable to provide a thoroughly rounded-out depiction of complete human
beings. The ill-starred protagonists, with the exception of the
extraordinarily vivid and realized figure of Akaky Akakievich
Bashmachkin, an immortal in the hall of Russian fiction, do not
come to life. They remain faceless nonentities and of nominal
artistic interest, despite Gogol's careful concretization of their
profession, class, economic rank, and many magnificent realistic
mosaics of the physical squalor that surrounds them. At the center of their inner life is a certain exasperating emptiness; it is as
though the author had created them to give vent to his hatred
for members of the upper bureaucracy who were not prepared
to accept Gogol when he was nineteen and in consequence
treated him badly.

Although the predominance of Romantic influences in the first
four stories offers little clue to Gogol's mature art, which was to
be a satirical exposure of human and social flaws, one powerful aspect of his genius emerges in the character portrayal
of Pirogov in *Nevsky Prospect* and Major Kovalev in *The
Nose*. It is what the Russian emigré critic V. Zenkovsky
has named Gogol's "artistic platonism," [41] that is, the creation of
a personality with distinct individual traits who nevertheless
embodies a universal prototype. Gogol had an uncanny gift for
observing and projecting the archetypical features of his heroes
without impairing or deleting from the rich baggage of personal
idiosyncracies that constitute the total man.

Pirogov and Kovalev are individuals in their own right, with
distinct motivations and behavior patterns, but they are also
similar to one another as typical instances of insensitive, conceited, and shallow-minded braggarts who will go to any length
to be noticed and admired. The need to make an impression is
so deeply incised and is "lived" with such honest rigor that it
passes from being a pose to becoming a total expressive stance.
The outward man becomes the ideogram of a special, initially

private style, and we recognize him not for what he seems to be, but for what he deliberately, scandalously is. The characters of the flirtatious lieutenant in *Nevsky Prospect* and of the self-styled major in *The Nose* are preliminary sketches of this archetypal portrait that Gogol was to bring to ultimate fulfillment in Nozdrev, a major protagonist in *Dead Souls* and one of the most magnificent liars in modern fiction. This type of boastful character seems to have fascinated Gogol, and he casts it again for the principal role in a very short story, *The Carriage*, written in 1835 and published in the first issue of Pushkin's *Contemporary* the following year.

VII   The Carriage (Kolyaska)

In *The Carriage* which records a moment in small-town life, setting it outside the Petersburg cycle, Gogol plunges into the midst of a happening that keys the story into its lock with this opening line: "The small town had grown much livelier since the cavalry regiment had been quartered there. It had been incredibly dull before." [42] In the following half page of masterfully calculated lightening touches the reader is again caught, as in the public scenes of the strolling nose and the overcoat-snatching ghost, by the sudden change of the movement and appearance of the community, jarred out of its lethargy by the unexpected: "Wooden fences between the houses were decorated with soldiers' caps . . . an army coat was carelessly draped over the gate. In the narrow alley-ways one met soldiers strutting about with mustachios as stiff as boot brushes. They were to be seen in all kinds of places. No sooner did a few housewives gather at the market place, than a mustachio was sure to be peeking over their shoulders." [43]

And all the town's produce is requisitioned very soon for the general's gala dinner to which his staff and the neighboring landowners are invited. With this superb indirection Gogol describes the munificence of the feast: "The sturgeon, the whitefish, asparagus, quail, partridges, and mushrooms made it clear that the cook had not consumed any liquor since the night before and that the four soldiers who helped him had worked throughout the night, knives in hand, on the fricassee. . . ." [44]

One of the most elegant guests is the landowner Pythagoras Chertokutsky, formerly a cavalry officer who for some reason had been cashiered from the army, a fact that did not prevent him from attending all the regimental gatherings and parties, making more noise than any of his peers at the nobility's elections, and entertaining the rural gentry at his country house that had been bought with his wife's dowry together with six excellent horses, gilt locks for all the doors, a tame monkey, and a French butler.

It is inevitable in the expansive after-dinner stag atmosphere of coffee, liqueurs, and tobacco when the host leads the admiring company out on the porch to look at his racing mare that Chertokutsky would feel compelled to outboast the boasting. He describes an apparently remarkable carriage of Viennese make that he had won at cards, light as a feather and yet, holding an incredible amount of luggage with room enough in its glove compartment "to stow the whole carcass of an ox," and invites the general and his staff to dine with him and inspect the carriage the very next day. He returns from the party very late and very drunk and is not awakened until the guests were at the door. He panics, gives orders to announce that he had been called away and hides in the carriage. The general, indignant at this reception, decides to examine the famous vehicle anyway. He finds it to be very ordinary and when he unfastens the leather apron to look inside, he sees his host clad in a dressing gown crouching in an unnatural position under it. The general replaces the leather apron and rides away with his officers.

The fable-like ending exposing the basic fraudulence of the hero and reducing him to a humiliating position eloquent of his mediocrity rounds off this tautly controlled tale, not much more than an anecdote, that is a masterpiece of narrative skill. Chekhov, hmself a supreme master in the use of economy and compression, was impressed by the terseness of *The Carriage* and called it a "sheer delight." Urbane in tone, detached and gay, full of movement and dialogue culled from the tools of reality, this miniature literary gem moves in the direction of Gogol's theater indicating the dramatic productions of his mature talent ahead.

CHAPTER 5

A Theater of the Absurd

I *The Play Is the Thing*

SINCE childhood, Gogol had formed a passionate attachment to the theater. The unanimous opinion of contemporaries who had heard his superb readings of his own stories or plays was that Gogol could have become a great comic actor. Like his father and in true Ukrainian tradition, he loved the farcical antics of the Ukrainian puppet show and drew upon them to enliven his first *Dikanka* tales. In the *Mirgorod* stories he continued to project a physical world filled wth plastic, mobile images. Some of the most memorable passages in these stories are the most theatrical ones with Gogol as producer, director, stage designer, and playwright dispensing terror (*Viy*), nostalgia (*Old-World Landowners*), violent action (*Taras Bulba*), and instant farce (*The Tale of How Ivan Ivanovich Quarrelled with Ivan Niki-forovich*) in brief dramatic scenes.

By far the most effective ones were the comedy-charged confrontations that mark the progress of the quarrel between the two Ivans. But in a typical misconception of his own natural bent, which is reminiscent of his first plunge into poetry rather than prose, when Gogol did in fact turn to playwriting it was to compose a hstorical drama focused on the conflicts between King Alfred and his own subjects and the Danish invaders of England in the ninth century. This was during Gogol's university lecture-ship and his fascination with great personalities from the past. He planned a five-act play to dramatize the tragic impasse between an enlightened monarch and a backward, mean-minded people. It did not come to him easily. The extant fragment of a first act and the beginning of a second act are made up of stilted speeches over-rhetorical and patriotic in tone. Gogol must have sensed that *Alfred* was doomed to failure and he quickly abandoned it.

According to Sergey Aksakov, Gogol first expressed interest in Russian comedy when they met in Moscow in 1832 and Gogol criticized the comic playwrght Mikhail Zagoskin for lack of real laughter in his plays. When Aksakov retorted that there was nothing amusing to write about since contemporary life was so dull and empty, Gogol said that "on the contrary, the comic element is lurking everywhere and it is only because we are living in the midst of it that we do not notice it; if the artist transposes it to the stage, we will double up with laughter at seeing ourselves as we are and be astonished that we have not previously recognized it." [1]

In February of the following year, Gogol wrote to Pogodin that he has lost his mind over a comedy that he has not yet written, that he had called it *Order of Vladimir* and "that it was going to be full of malice, laughter, and salt." [2] Only four scenes of it were completed. In the first, "The Morning of a Government Official," Barsukov, the official who covets the Vladimir decoration and is to go mad because of it, meets a colleague who promises to support his promotion, but is actually planning to discredit him. In "The Lawsuit" Barsukov's brother conspires with the perfidious colleague to start a legal action aganst him. The third scene, "In the Servants' Quarters," catches the backstairs gossip that reproduces the snobbism, hypocrisy, and triviality of the masters. The fourth, an unnamed scene, is a dispute between an ambitious, wordly, and stupid matron and her son who is in love with a poor, but charming girl whom one of his mother's hangers-on is about to vilify with a false love letter. This first comedy breaks away from the standard sentimental or melodramatic plot so much in vogue at the time and takes up new themes of preoccupation with rank, moneyed capital, and a profitable marriage, themes that in a later exposition on the theater—*After the Theater* (1842)—Gogol claimed were more interesting and "had more electricity in them" than the theme of courtship and love.

The complexity of a play that promised to bring in several classes of society and to introduce representative Russian types may have discouraged Gogol who had yet to find a central dramatic formula. His purported excuse for abandoning the work was the fear that it would not be passed by the censor, and he began to look for another subject suitable for the stage "to which even the lowliest policeman could not object."

II The Wedding (Zhenitba)

The Wedding, a two-act comedy started in 1833 and completed only after many interruptons—some nine years later—is the result of this search. Gogol could not have hit on a less offensive plot from the censor's point of view nor on a more rewardinng one for comic exploitation. He rewrote it more thoroughly and more frequently than any other of his plays, and the final version is a concentration of comic effects in every line which, when properly staged and acted, keeps the audience in a perpetual state of laughter.

This extravaganza of hilarity is built around a girl's urge to marry and her recruitment of suitable "wooers" with the help of a professional matchmaker. In the early drafts the action takes place at a country estate with landowners bidding for the hand of the wealthy heiress. By transposing it in the final version to the capital's lower middle-class mercantile milieu, Gogol injects the play with the vigor of richly crude dialogue, openly vulgar and bawdy. A rich merchant's daughter, Agafya Tikhonovna, aspiring to gentility, is looking for a husband with a nobleman's status and is about to choose one from the middling officials hungering for her dowry.

The scene in Agafya's parlor with the assembled candidates waiting to "take a look at the bride" is loaded with humor that gains momentum as each suitor becomes a distinct personality in his expressed yearnings for his wifely ideal. Practical Yaichnitsa considers her in terms of the two-storied brick house with waterproof cellar that heads the dowry list; since he has been to Sicily and met young Italian girls "like rosebuds," Zhevakin dreams of a "rosebud" companion in life; and Anuchkin, who is something of a social snob and regrets his own lack of drawing room graces, would like to have a wife who could converse in French.

In the recalcitrant suitor, Podkolesin and his dynamic friend Kochkarev, Gogol introduces traditional comic types played against each other in deliberately overdrawn behavior patterns. Podkolesin is a direct predecessor of Goncharov's famous hero, Oblomov. Indolent, indecisive, fearful of any action that would take him away from his couch where he reclines all day in his dressing gown smoking a pipe, he resists his friend's attempts to marry him to Agafya. Kochkarev has no particular reason for urging the match, but he is a compulsive busybody, driven by a restless energy to attach himself to some action for action's sake. His character recalls the clever intriguer whom Molière immortalized in Scapin and other less clever and more good-natured meddlers that figured frequently in the Russian vaudeville of the 1820's and 1830's. Although Podkolesin is swayed toward matrimony by the matchmaker's description of Agafya's opulent charms and is finally pressured by Kochkarev to visit her, he is fearful of marriage that is "somehow strange to him because he has not been married before." When he has already proposed, been accepted, and for a few moments left alone in Agafya's parlor, he is overcome by panic and makes his escape by jumping out the window.

The strength of the play and its originality rest on Gogol's skillful interlocking of the comedy of character with the comedy of situation. The passivity of Podkolesin (the name means "under the wheels" in Russian) and the unbridled vitality of his friend are brought into heightened comic relief by the absurd contest they engage in. Besides this, leaping out the window which is farcical in itself is sound psychologically, being the desperate break for freedom by the timid and vacillating bachelor. This, however, was not understood by the theater-goers of Gogol's day who considered Podkolesin's final action ridiculous and unseemly behavior for a gentleman.

Some fifty years later, Alexander N. Ostrovsky [3] recreated for a more appreciative public the private world of the Russian merchant and stressed the ambitions and vitality that Gogol had intuited in *Marriage*. The two women in the comedy that were to serve as models for a dozen Ostrovsky plays are particularly fine; the shrewd, supple, bargain-minded matchmaker who speaks almost exclusively in the indirect speech of the Russian proverb exudes the tough competitive climate of the market place. Agafya Tikhonovna is Gogol's most successful young female character, and in two short scenes she becomes fully alive as the typical dowried girl who earns both pity and derision. Gogol treats her fumbling attempts to rise above her station and become "a lady" with unprecedented sympathy, all the while exposing her devouring triviality and her shopkeeper's respect for cash that is typical of her upbringing and class.

III   The Gamblers (Igroki)

A cardsharp meets three professional gamblers who win his confidence by promising to cut him in on a lucrative deal, but instead swindle him out of 80,000 rubles that he has just won with a skillfully marked pack of cards. This is the anecdote that Gogol heard from Shchepkin and expanded into a tautly constructed one-act play. *The Gamblers*, first produced in 1843, was poorly received and rarely staged since.

The theme was very much in the air. In Russian society, card playing was an endemic pastime, and stories of predatory swindlers who fleeced honest men in gaming houses and roadside taverns abound in Russian fiction. Gogol's innovation was to eschew the moral bias. He eavesdrops on the gamblers when they are boasting to each other about their successful coups, and it becomes clear from their conversation that these arch rascals, gentlemanly and decorous in appearance and social manner, are difficult to distinguish from men who live within the law. Gogol does not fail to point out in a sly aside that their ambitions are identical to those of any government official who yearns to squander his salary as they do their illicit gains on frequenting the theater, dining in elegant restaurants, and dressing in the latest fashion.

The interest of the play which has only male roles is not in the characters, however, but in the action. Gogol works a conscious mystification with the old device of substitute personages, and does it swiftly and deftly, so that the climax boomerangs unexpectedly both for the hero and the audience. As an exercise in dramatic construction it is the most polished of the plays. But there is hardly a laugh in it. In his concentration on successfully bringing off this trick of the theater, Gogol seems to have laid aside his extraordinary power to make the stage live with the exuberance, spontaneity, and sparkle of his comic art. In his most famous play, *The Inspector General*, this talent is brought to full maturity and fruition.

IV   The Inspector General (Revizor)

Many years after he had written it, Gogol told in his *Author's Confession* how Pushkin had supplied him with the plot for *The Inspector General*. In October 1835 he wrote to the poet

about his lack of funds and begged him to suggest "some anecdote, humorous or not, but purely Russian. My hand trembles
from eagerness to write a comedy. Do me a favor, give me a
subject; I will instantly make a five-act comedy of it and it will
be funnier than hell."[4] Whereupon Pushkin told him that once
when he had been travelling through Nizhny Novgorod, he had
been mistaken for a government inspector and had had some
fun with the worthy burghers maintaining the pretense while he
was there. But the anecdote of a false inspector's appearance in
a provincial town was a currently popular one and had been
used more than once by Russian writers as a variation on the
comedy of errors theme. The first critics were quick to notice
the resemblance between *The Inspector General* and Gregory
Kvitka's play, *The Newcomer from the Capital,* written in 1827,
from which Gogol did borrow some details and which was based
on a similar theme. Having latched on to a plot, however, Gogol
began to reshuffle its elements and so radically transformed
Kvitka's straightforward story of a pseudo-government official
who enriches himself at the town's expense until he is caught
and punished that the only features shared by the two plays
are the basic cast of municipal officials and the small-town
setting.

   The Inspector General is Gogol's most ambitious dramatic work
and far superior to the other two completed comedies. At the
lowest estimate, it is a great play. It is also Gogol's nearest approach to Realistic art. The profusion of comic material is developed within the discipline of credibility and does not erupt into
the customary Gogolian extravaganza of verbal and physical
grotesque. The action is tight and circular. Nothing is wasted.
Unexpected happenings that create havoc are made plausible by
hints carefully planted in advance. The fact that the postmaster
had dared to unseal the inspector's damning letter, for example,
and read its shattering contents at the end of the play does not
startle the audience who remembers the mayor's precautionary
measure in the first act that provides for the interception of all
the inspector's mail. The piece is crowded with characters: all
the public life of a small town is represented with the exception
of the church and the military. The single day in which the
action takes place is crammed with incidents, and the atmosphere
is tense and confused. Yet, a kind of inner organic order directs

the movement of the play promulgated by the unity of the plot and the dazzling economy of its structure. Every one of the five acts announces and leads inevitably into the next, while at the same time maintaining its own center of gravity with one major happening that gives it autonomous strength. The total effect is one of tremendous dramatic power.

The opening lines of the first act strike at the very heart of the action: "I have called you, gentlemen, to tell you a most unpleasant piece of news," announces the mayor of a small town to his municipal officials. "An inspector general is coming to visit us . . . from Petersburg, incognito, and with secret orders." [5] From this moment to the final curtain, everything that occurs will be totally involved with the inspector.

In this introductory scene, Gogol is at his satirical best as he exposes the disorder of town affairs. The worried mayor advises each of his subordinates to clean up his own department. We learn that the porter breeds geese in the vestibule of the town court; that mental patients wander about the wards unattended, looking like chimney sweeps and smelling of vodka; that charity cases at the city hospital are left to die because "those who are meant to get better will survive by themselves"; that the policeman is constantly drunk and terrifies the population; and that the streets are made impassable by the accumulation of garbage. The history teacher breaks up classroom chairs to illustrate more realistically the victories of Alexander the Great; the postmaster habitually unseals letters for diversion's sake (keeping the ones that please him best); the mayor allows the merchants to sell rotten produce in return for exorbitant bribes and has embezzled funds granted for the building of a hospital chapel that he has reported as having burned down although its construction had not even been started.

The apprehension gripping the company changes to downright fear when two town gossips burst in with the news that a young government official from Petersburg, Ivan Khlestakov, has been staying at the local inn for two weeks, seems inordinately inquisitive, and "looks into everything." Everyone becomes convinced that this must be the dreaded *revizor*, and the mayor decides to confront him head on and placate him with money and hospitality.

In the second act the previous confusion and dismay coalesce into a preposterous misunderstanding that veers the plot toward the absurd. What gives it particular zest is that Gogol takes the audience into his confidence by disclosing before the mayor's arrival that the "inspector" is in actual fact a menial copy clerk from the capital, very small fry indeed, who has lost all his money at cards on his way to visit his father, and is now stranded, penniless and hungry, and about to be evicted from the hotel. High and low comedy are superbly conjoined in the meeting between the mayor and Khlestakov. There is something farcical in the confrontation of the portly mayor staring with a frightened expression, about to present his unctuous respects, and the agitated and scrawny young clerk fearfully goggling back, certain that this official in full uniform has come to take him to prison. Their dialogue crackling at cross-purposes is not unlike a vaudevillian interlude, but the psychological motivation is knife-edged—both men are riddled with fear. When the mayor ingratiatingly offers the town's hospitality "to the passing visitor" suggesting a move to other quarters but not quite daring to specify them as "his own," Khlestakov panics and attempts to bluff his way out by shouting that he is an official from Petersburg, knows the minister, and will not go to prison. The other takes the words to mean that Khlestakov will not go to prison for him, and his wrath conveys to the older man that the "revizor" has already found out everything. Standing at attention, quaking with fright, he begs the august personage to spare him, consider his long years of service, ignore the slander of his enemies and the complaint of the sergeant's wife who had been flogged at the police station by mistake the previous week. From among these bewildering allusions, Khlestakov only catches the word "flogging," sees himself whipped in prison and decides to make a clean breast of it, confessing that "I am staying here because I do not have a kopek to my name."

And suddenly the whole tone of the interview changes. To the wily old bureaucrat the mention of money from a high official means that he is now ready to be bribed and the tall story he tells is his way of preserving his incognito. When Khlestakov accepts two hundred rubles, and the mayor slips him two hundred more, he is confident that the young man has come to investigate his municipality. For otherwise why should he accept a bribe? In the mayor's world of officialdom, bribery was a commonplace exchange for favors expected or rendered, and it was impossible for him to imagine that anyone would take a large sum of money, offhandedly, for no reason other than needing it. But that is exactly what Khlestakov does. It is completely in character, and his character is one of Gogol's unforgettable portraits and a key to the play.

In a directive to actors who play the part, Gogol sums up his hero as "a mediocrity, rather stupid, without a thought in his head . . . and who speaks and acts without any reflection. . . . He is so much of a nothing that the most stupid people consider him trivial. He would never do anything to deserve the slightest attention. But the power of overall fear has made him a remarkable comic figure." [6] The feckless and irresponsible Khlestakov has inherited Lieutenant Pirogov's meaningless agitation and Kovalev's empty-headedness, but he is made more negative by his lack of impact on his environment. With Khlestakov, who has no center of gravity and who floats into the principal role on a current of events instigated by others, Gogol achieves a master stroke of dramatic invention. The very passivity of his hero makes credible the absurd development of the plot and moves it into a more complicated and subtle comic dimension.

It is exquisitely ironical that during two whole acts of being feasted, flattered, and lavishly bribed, Khlestakov remains unaware of the reason for his good fortune; being himself he accepts it unquestioningly with the spontaneous pleasure of a child. If he had been less simple-minded and incurious he might have given himself away. Instead, the copy clerk allows himself to be lionized by the alarmed officials and, molded by their fawning attention, begins to throw his weight about and act like he is expected to. Scenes move exuberantly through thickets of comedy as Gogol negotiates the transformation of the featherbrained scamp into a worldly Petersburg nobleman. The process of the pseudo-inspector becoming a convincing public figure begins when Khlestakov, in his cups, mesmerizes the gullible town fathers with an account of his life at the capital:

O, Petersburg! What a life it is, truly! . . . I can't begin going out anywhere without people saying, "There goes Ivan Alexandrovich!" . . . I know all the pretty actresses . . . And literary chaps. Pushkin and I are buddies. I often say to him, "Well, how goes it, Push, old boy?" And he answers, "Oh, just about as usual." Great character . . . I con-

tribute to all the journals, Besides, I've written many works: *The Marriage of Figaro, Robert the Devil, Norma*. . . . I also give balls. . . .
Beyond description. A watermelon, for example, a seven-hundred-
ruble watermelon. Soup delivered by boat right out of Paris; you lift
the tureen cover and such steam comes out as you can't find anywhere
else. . . . The Minister of Foreign Affairs, the French Ambassador, the
German Ambassador and I—we've formed a whist group. . . . The director disappeared . . . So there was nothing to do, they came to me.
And along the street dashed messengers . . . They sent me messengers
and messengers; imagine 35,000 of them! . . . The Council of State itself is afraid of me. . . . I drive to the Palace every day. Why, tomorrow
I shall be made field-marsh . . . (He slides to the floor, sprawling, but
respectful officials hold him up.)[7]

"Khlestat'" means to lash with a whip and conveys to the
Russian a sound that is brittle and without substance. In this
monologue that has made its fortune in the Russian theater,
Khlestakov lives up to his name as one of the most spontaneous
and unconscious liars of all time. Gogol once wrote that there
was something of a Khlestakov in him,[8] and indeed his hero does
display Gogol's self-intoxicating gift for outrageous fabrication.
Khlestakov's super-swindle of the imagination is composed with
meticulous care. The copy clerk, not much nearer to the elite of
the world than those listening to him with rapt attention, presents
to the provincials a scattered and limited vision of high society
overcharged with "quantity" effects precisely expressive of their
own vulgar dreams. Little wonder that they are taken in.

The fourth act opens on the offering of bribes—an essential
aspect of an official investigation—in which Gogol conjoins the
comedies of character and situation. The defilade of nervous
bureaucrats in full-dress uniform, formally introducing themselves to the unsuspecting Khlestakov who has just had a refresh-
ing nap and is now ready for new diversions, is replete with
humor. Individual officials stand revealed in a sly cartoon-like
sketch in their various approaches to the "revizor." The welfare
commissioner hopes to win favor by disclosing the judge's illicit
love affair; one landowner begs Khlestakov to arrange for the
legitimacy of a bastard son; another named Bobchinsky, "humbly requests" that upon his return to the capital, "your Excellency
will tell all those great gentlemen that in such and such a town
lives a man called Pyotr Ivanovich Bobchinsky." Not the least

hilarious element in this hugely funny scene is Khlestakov's behavior which grows progressively more inspector-like with each successive bribe as he catches on to the rules of the game. The judge enters first with banknotes in his fist and Khlestakov, mesmerized by the sight of them, asks him what he has in his hand. The judge, taken aback, drops the money and Khlestakov cannot resist picking it up and asking for it as a loan. The request is so eagerly and quickly granted that with each successive official the copy clerk becomes more brazen and brief in his interview, and when the last one comes up to him he abruptly asks him for a thousand rubles.

The arrival of the merchants and peasant women who now crowd at the windows and doors waving petitions against the mayor's misdeeds and offering money, wine, and bread on a silver platter to the "benefactor" is a raucous, brutish, Kafkaesque scene that serves as a splendid contrast to the decorous overtures of the authorities. Nineteenth-century radical and later Soviet critics have singled it out as proof of the social significance of the play. Gogol shows scant sympathy for the "persecuted" group of the town population, however; the sergeant's wife who has been beaten by the police is truculent and stupid, and the thievish merchants only complain about the mayor because he demands bribes larger than those customarily offered to someone of his rank.

Having flushed out the last local ruble, even Khlestakov begins to sense that he must be mistaken for some other—important— person and is advised by his shrewd servant that the time has come for them to depart. But germane to Gogol's habit of inoculating a story with a virus that will lead to ultimate chaos and disorder is the letter that Khlestakov writes before leaving, to one of his Petersburg cronies, a small-time gossip columnist, relating what has happened to him and suggesting to him that he make a skit of it. While the horses are being harnessed, Gogol obtains yet another volley of sparks from his hero's irrepressibly frivolous behavior by having him flirt indiscriminately with the mayor's wife and daughter, and finally proposing to the daughter when the mother catches him in front of the young girl on his knees. A few moments later he leaves his fiancée forever because the carriage is ready. The extraordinary fecklessness with which Khlestakov pursues his courtship, studded with sentimental clichés, transforms the only romantic moment in the play into a hilarious parody of one and serves as a build-up for the excitement of the last act.

Although total involvement with the inspector continues, the figure of the mayor dominates the fifth act. As the future father-in-law of the all powerful "revizor" he is basking in a vision of himself as a decorated general with a sumptuous residence in Petersburg that cedes nothing in glitter and grandeur to Khlestakov's fabrications. While his wife is picturing herself at her first brilliant reception among the grandees of the capital and is condescendingly accepting the congratulations of the townspeople who have just heard news of the engagement, the postmaster rushes in with Khlestakov's letter that he has intercepted and unsealed. It is passed around the officials who now realize that a young fool has made even greater fools of them all.

The reaction of the mayor is terrible; it constitutes the most memorable scene of a comedy which now discloses something of its serious nature. To the sudden humiliating miscarriage of all his plans and the mortification of having been outwitted by a mere "inkslinger," he responds with a diatribe against himself of such excoriating candor that he ceases to be ridiculous. From behind the mask of a corrupt provincial administrator, we catch in this moment of self-revelation, a glimpse of an emotional but able man—like Poprishchin a product of the regime, but more ambitious, flexible, and intelligent—who has risen from the lowest ranks to his present status, playing lucidly and shrewdly the competive and tricky bureaucratic game. This lucidity and surging anger detach the mayor from the other complacent officials with whom he has been locked in a ridiculous situation. Through this experience that has unsettled him and with which he still does not know how to cope, he emerges as that rare phenomenon in Gogolian fiction—a total and vulnerable human being. In a final passionate utterance the mayor charges everyone, including himself, with being guilty of what has happened and turns to the audience whom the author had already taken into his confidence: "What are you laughing at?" he asks the spectators, most of them—like himself—civil servants of the tsarist regime. "You are laughing at yourselves." This might have been a thunderingly effective curtain line to the play. But Gogol has yet one more *coup de théâtre* in store for his comedy that has been moving at such a precipitate pace that there has been no time to stop for the question: "What happens next?" Suddenly, a gendarme enters with the announcement that the "revizor" from Petersburg has just arrived and is summoning the town officers into his presence. These words fall like a thunderbolt on all. During the mute scene before the curtain falls, the officials are seen in the same position they occupied at the opening of the play.

This final scene neatly closes the cyclical action as is befitting a satirical exposure that leaves the people and state of affairs basically unchanged. But Gogol's insistence on a four-minute lapse between the gendarme's entrance and the curtain suggests that the unexpected appearance had a function beyond that of dramatic surprise. It is not likely that the *deus ex machina* was meant to symbolize the just and benevolent state that would make everything right, as in the comedies of Molière and those of Gogol's immediate Russian predecessors, Fonvizin and Kapnist. There is no hint given anywhere in the play that the municipal officers would have reacted to the visit of an officially sanctioned inspector's visit in a different way.

In his first assessment of the comedy, Belinsky defined Khlestakov as "the creation of the mayor's frightened imagination, a phantom, a shadow upon his conscience"[9] and Gogol concurred with this interpretation when he wrote in 1842 that Khlestakov is "a phantasmagoric figure which like a mendacious embodiment of deception has been carried away on a troika, God knows where."[10] In this light, the summons from the inspector general is a call for the real play to begin and all that has happened before has only been imagined by a frightened community. The fifth act is a return to reality centered upon the mayor's awakening from a dream. The dream was a collective one—this is Gogol's dazzling innovation—and everyone believed in it, including the audience, for it exuded the fears and unconscious desires of all concerned. If it is indeed a fantasy-charged experience that the play is all about then the driving tension of it registers precisely the obsessive dream sequence in pursuit of an image. The image that the officials create of Khlestakov is both a menace and a lure. That is why he must be portrayed as vacant and pliable, easily fitting the role that their fantasies dictate.

But as the play proceeds from Khlestakov's monologue to the

marriage proposal, the fascination he exerts as a representative of the arcane, glittering world of Petersburg grips the provincial minds. Out of his vulgar posturings and senseless talk, the burghers fashion an image of power and prestige inspired by their own yearnings, and the vapid, incredibly trivial Khlestakov becomes the incarnation of their dreams.

The comedy succeeds on two levels and in the spirit of contradiction that informs Gogol's art. It is, on the one hand, a hilariously funny play clicking zestfully to a variety of comic effects that turn on a simple incorrect assumption. The fact that in this exuberant showdown of small town corruption no positive characters appear, and Gogol has no pity for any of his heroes—first-class swindlers that they are—provides for the release of liberating laughter when they are caught in humiliating situations. On the other hand, it is a savage metamorphosis that Gogol inflicts on that visible provincial world which seems harmless enough until he exposes its inner visions and aspirations in the form of the inconsequent copy clerk. Again, in his horror and scorn at the mediocrity and stultifying ordinariness of that world, he reduces the heroes to derisive grotesque as he did the vanity-swollen bureaucrats in *Nevsky Prospect*, the meanly caviling two Ivans, the Important Personage in *The Overcoat*. In a final impression *The Inspector General* presents a gloomy picture of vulgar, complacent life in all its galling emptiness and meaninglessness that to the present-day reader recalls the Existentialist definition of the life-vacuum confronting contemporary man.

V   *First Critical Reactions*

The Inspector General was first performed at the Alexandrinsky Theater in Petersburg on April 19, 1836. Its presentation to the Russian public was stormy and marked, like the climate of the play itself, with unexpected developments, improbably and slightly absurd. To the author's astonishment and delight, the imperial censor's veto to produce or publish this picture of civic waywardness was overriden by the emperor himself who had the comedy read to him and was delighted with it. At the première, the sovereign laughed heartily, was quoted as saying that "everyone got his due, and I most of all" and ordered all his ministers to see the play. It is doubtful that Nicholas, who had advised Pushkin to try his hand at fiction in the Walter Scott manner and whose taste ran to vaudeville skits, had savored in *The Inspector General* anything more than a quick-moving gamey farce. The rest of the audience, however, composed for the most part of the bureaucratic élite, appeared to be more discerning and consequently apprehensive and hostile. Pavel Annenkov, the critic, who attended the opening night noted the changing mood of the spectators in his reminiscences:

Even after the first act everyone looked bewildered as if they could not decide what to make of it. And yet certain features and scenes in this "farce" were so realistic that once or twice, especially where the conventional idea of comedy was not contradicted, there were gusts of laughter. In the fourth act the reaction was quite different: there was still laughter rippling occasionally across the theater, but it was rather timid and stopped as soon as it began; there was barely any applause; but the concentration of the audience on the development of the action and the dead silence in the hall manifested the deep impression that the play was making on the spectators. At the end of it, bewilderment gave way to general indignation that was loudly expressed in the fifth act. Some called for the author because they thought he had written a comic masterpiece, others thought some of the scenes showed talent, most applauded because it had made them laugh. The unanimous opinion of the select public, however, was that "this is impossible, this is libel, this is farce." [11]

Gogol sat in his loge in agony, one kind of despair hammering at another. The signs of consternation and disapproval among the spectators shook him badly, all the more so because the actors who were trained in the style of Neoclassical comedy or outright farce did not know how to interpret this new kind of comic realism and gave an appallingly bad performance. Gogol understood how difficult it was for the actors of his day to lay aside their stock-in-trade of individually showy stunts of heightened gesture, tone, and carriage of the traditional farce-hyperbole and submit themselves to the discipline of realistic portrayal within the subtly built-in comic situation of his play. At the first rehearsals he urged the cast to underplay their parts and aim for naturalness and veracity in the construction of their roles. This advice, largely unheeded, was set down by Gogol in a prefatory note to the play entitled "Characters and Costumes—Remarks to the Actors" in the 1842 edition. In it he insists on the actor's need to think through the universal significance of his part, its ideological meaning, and its projection in terms of a total personality; he urges the actor to be less concerned with the invention and variety of external and isolated laughter-producing tricks than with the continuous creation of life-like and natural behavior. In these admonitions he anticipated the stage-directing innovations of Konstantin Stanislavsky, co-founder and world-famous director of the Moscow Art Theater. Stanislavsky demanded that each actor learn to fuse all his dramatic resources with the action of others so as to produce a deliberately collective mood of fear, anticipation, eagerness, exultation, or frustration that would shape and color the scenes. Above all, there was to be no caricaturing or exaggerating of the written lines, even in the secondary parts: "The less the actor thinks of being funny, the funnier he will appear. The comic comes through the seriousness with which each person in the play goes about his affairs . . . the more modest the actor, the more successful he will be in the execution of his role."

After the first-night performance Gogol went to Prokopovich's apartment where his host presented him with a copy of *The Inspector General* that had just come off the press. Gogol threw it on the floor and then leaning against the table said sadly: "If only one or two people had sworn at it, I would not have minded, but everyone, everyone did. . . ." [12]

This was not strictly true. But from the outset Gogol nurtured an extraordinary sensitivity to reactions to his play and seemed to seek out adverse opinion with a kind of paranoid passion. "Everyone is against me," he wrote to Shchepkin at the end of April 1836.[13] "The older and honorable officials shout that I hold nothing sacred since I dared to write about public officials; policemen and merchants and men of letters shout the same thing," complains Gogol. "I see now what it is to be a writer of comedies. You tell the smallest bit of truth and they are all up in arms against you. . . ." A month later he was even more bitter in a note to M. P. Pogodin, the journalist. "Scoundrels are presented on the stage and everyone attacks me for having them there. Let the scoundrels be angry; but even those whom I do not consider scoundrels are also angry. I am dismayed by this sign of a deep, stubborn ignorance which is spread throughout our society. . . ." [14]

The first critical reaction to *The Inspector General* was mixed.

Unfortunately the favorable reviews did not appear immediately. Prince Peter A. Vyazemsky's article in *The Contemporary* of June 1836 acclaimed the play as an outstanding literary event comparable to Griboedov's masterpiece, *Woe from Wit* (1825) and Fonvizin's *The Minor* (1782), considering it stronger than the latter because of the absence of positive heroes. The comment of V. P. Androsov, literary critic and editor of the *Moscow Observer*, following the première in that city classified it as a new type of social comedy that was justified in shunning the traditional love interest and complicated plot in its concentration on the exposure of currently significant social vices. At the same time Belinsky devoted a long review to the originality of Gogol's play, its inexhaustible humor, the author's uncanny skill in projecting individual traits within typification of character, and predicted its pioneering role in the creation of a national theater.

The conservative literary camp represented by Faddey Bulgarin and Joseph-Julian Senkowski lost no time in castigating the comedy. Both journalists were already provoked by Gogol's scathing essay on the Russian press that had just appeared in the liberally slanted *Contemporary*.[15] In the May 1836 issues of the *Northern Bee* (Nos. 97–98) Bulgarin denounced both the play as a libel against Russia and her government and its author as a counterfeit writer who had been overpraised by the literary circle to which he belonged. The play itself, he insisted, was unreadable, the characters exaggerated to the point of caricature, and the general impression was a most unpleasant one with "not a single noble feature seen of the human heart." In a more restrained tone, in *The Library for Reading*, 1836 (Vol. 16), Osíp I. Senkovsky agreed with Bulgarin that the piece was vulgar and tasteless, and that Gogol had erred in adopting a flimsy anecdote for the stage and turning it into a plotless and indecent farce.

VI *Gogol's Defense of His Play*

These attacks from reactionary critics, hurriedly composed and clearly of a partisan nature, nevertheless, stung Gogol to the quick. He felt the need to defend his play. In April–May 1836 he jotted down all the unfavorable comments that had been printed about it within a framework not unlike Molière's *Critique de L'Ecole des femmes,* where Bulgarin's most disparaging remarks are quoted verbatim, and in a sly and protean manner refuted by the author. It is cleverly done. Entitled *After the Theater* the author conceals himself in the theater lobby to listen to the comments of spectators who have just seen *The Inspector General* and are now leaving. Gogol obviously enjoyed making up snatches of talk that reveal less about the play than the obtuseness and general dimwittedness of the Petersburg élite. One well-dressed gentleman liked the farce, although there was absolutely no meaning in it; his companion would not venture an opinion until he had read some notices about it; and a highly placed official admitted to laughing a great deal during the performance, but he did not know why and did not care.

But a more serious analysis that gives credence to the work and points up its originality follows. One theater lover complains about the lack of love interest; another retorts that the day for all this has passed, now people are more interested in money, rank, a profitable marriage—themes that have "electricity" in them—and a playwright should exploit these subjects. A third is caught by the novelty of a plot lacking a happy ending and pulling all the characters together into one large tight knot. "Everyone is a hero; the movement of the play sets all the pieces of the machinery in motion and no part of it becomes rusty, so to speak, or remains inactive." [16]

To the objection voiced by many that all the characters are odious, someone replies that one positive hero would have drawn all the sympathy of the audience and weakened the impact of the others. "But why bring out the vicious and not the virtuous," indignantly asks one spectator to which he receives the answer that to ignore social vices is like stitching up an untreated wound that is bound to infect the entire body.

Here Gogol takes up the cause of the writer's moral obligation to his public. A young lady admits having found the play amusing because the baseness and corruption in it are typical not only of that particular small town, but exist everywhere. And a very modestly dressed man, one of Gogol's first positive characters, an official from the provinces who refuses an important post at the capital, because he fears that a corrupt civil servant might replace him in his own town, admits that he laughed to see the villains in the play stripped of their hypocrisy and their corruption revealed. This projection of Russian officialdom impressed a number of spectators. To one man who is discomfited by it, another replies that "since we all belong to the government and many of us serve it, it is only natural to have it represented on the stage. . . . Besides, a sort of unswerving faith in our government is rooted in our hearts." [17] The same virtuous official is used by Gogol to laud the common people's belief in the beneficent monarchy when he overhears one peasant saying to another in the lobby: "I daresay our governors were sprightly enough in the old days, but they all got scared when the Tsar's justice caught up with them." [18] The lobby empties and the author steps out with a long reflection about the role of laughter in his great play:

No one has seen the honest character in my play. It is laughter. It is noble because it has appeared in spite of the low esteem in which it is held. . . . Laughter is more meaningful than people think. Not the laughter that is evoked by a passing irritation and a morbid, jaundiced disposition, nor that trivial laughter that is meant to amuse and entertain, but the laughter which comes from man's serene nature . . . that deepens everything, points to what might have passed unnoticed and without whose penetrating force man would have been disheartened by life's frivolity and emptiness. . . . [19]

After the Theater was published in an expanded and greatly revised final version only in 1842. Of little artistic merit, it is nevertheless a valuable record of Gogol's increasing insistence on the didactic role of literature and his need to explain his art in terms of moral and social philosophy. This is not the creative Gogol, when he is most abundantly himself, standing in front of his small high desk, testing aloud his own solecisms, acting out dramatic effects, and constructing hyperbolic silhouettes out of the damning physical quirks of speech, appearance, and gesture caught in his distorting vision of the world. Whatever social meaning could be derived from the final result of that exhilirating creative process came through the wider lens of his satirical genius and became part of the irreducible whole that is the mark of great art.

VII *"The Petersburg Theater, 1835–1836"*

During the winter season of 1835–36, Gogol lived, breathed and thought theater. He wrote *The Inspector General* in two feverish months from October to December, supervised its production, came into personal contact with many actors, saw a number of new plays presented on the Petersburg stage, constantly bemoaned the woeful state of the Russian theater, and formulated ideas for its reform. His notes, emotionally phrased and subjective in tone, were published posthumously as "The Petersburg Theater, 1835–36"; the main ideas in this article found their way into a longer essay, "Petersburg Notes for 1836," printed in *The Contemporary* the following year.

Deploring the preponderance of luridly sensational French melodrama and monotonous vaudeville routines that had been cluttering the Russian stage for the last five years, Gogol called for Russian comedies: "For God's sake, give us some Russian characters; let us look at ourselves, our own scoundrels, our own eccentrics! Onto the stage with them and let's have a laugh at them! Laughter is a mighty thing; it steals neither name nor property, but to be laughed at is to feel as helpless as a trussed up hare." [20]

He is struck by the enormous potential of acted out drama as a medium for propagating useful art, where at one performance a great moral lesson may be persuasively communicated to five or six hundred people through the immediacies of dialogue and graphic intensity of human gesture. In this context Gogol gratefully examines the earlier Russian playwrights Fonvizin and Griboedov, who still form part of the current repertory. But he concedes that the present-day public is justly disaffected by these Neoclassical comedies that treat ethical and social problems that are "no longer ours." Even classical Molière is considered "long-winded and dull on the stage. His plays are cleverly constructed, but according to old dramatic rules and in an unvarying pattern. . . ." [21] Modern plays must deal with contemporary concerns in a contemporary manner.

These disparaging comments indirectly point up the innovations brought about by Gogol's dramaturgy: on the one hand is the rejection of traditional devices such as love interest, the conventional happy ending, the "raisonnneur" who is the author's mouthpiece and the commedia dell'arte type of role development. For this last device he created more complex, live characters that combine both typical and individual traits. On the other hand, Gogol infuses his comedies with a hitherto unknown mobility and versatility of action tautly and rapidly integrated.

The need for greater realism in the theater is one of Gogol's most pressing concerns and, characteristically, he introduces it in the most roundabout way with the rhetorical question—what is Romanticism? His answer seems to reflect his own dramatic aims and the problems assailing him when he was composing his comedies. He speaks of Romantics as "daring and desperate men who organize rebellion in society," who hack their way out of the stability and tradition inspired by the ancients into a modern world, and who by writing plays attempt to grapple with modern questions. But they are demolition experts who produce chaos. Does Gogol identify himself with them or with the "great talent" who, he argues, will build a new edifice out of chaos by means of the inspired calm and the precision of his art, to whom the laws of society are accessible, and who sees and understands "the supreme ordinary" while the exceptional is visible to everyone else?

The "supreme ordinary" as a function of Gogol's dramatic art, for example, in the Petersburg and Mirgorod stories, becomes "extraordinary" in an erosive interplay of reality and imagination. The comedies appear to be realistic in the authentic ring of their dialogue and the exactness and reliability of physical detail. But the ludicrous situations that emerge from prosaic settings, motivating characters who resemble ordinary people to behave in irrational, highly risible ways, produce an impression of a world permanently out of tilt. It has been averred that Gogol was greatly indebted to August Schlegel's definition of the Romantic grotesque in creating a supremely comical world.[22] The German critic and poet stated that the comic is less concerned with mundane reality than with arbitrary and witty inventions that are not subject to the laws of reality. The content of the play must underline the comicality of lifelike situations and characters.

Whether or not Gogol was influenced by Schlegel's theory, his own vision of life, centered on discord, was sympathetic to it. But he went further. He did not skirt reality in the development of his comic confrontations; rather he took it head on and discovered that its dynamics consisted of a clash between appearance and substance, the real and the unreal, life as it is and as it should be. This disharmony that seemed to him the very essence of reality he reduced to comic grotesque through the abrasive chemistry of laughter. In this, Gogol anticipated by a little more than a century the Western European theater of the absurd. Absurdity that is pivotal to all human relations is the master served by Ionesco, Beckett, and Gogol. Theirs is the theater of destruction, distortion and hyperbole, and it is also a moral and angry theater in that it teaches, through tragi-comic slapstick, a lesson in shattered complacencies.

The same urge to escape from a hostile public took hold of Gogol after the première of *The Inspector General* as it had after the *Hanz Küchelgarten* debacle. He made hurried preparations for going abroad. Despite earlier promises, he did not visit Moscow where Pogodin and the Aksakovs, sponsors of the production of his comedy at the Maly Theatre, expected his assistance, while Shchepkin who was playing the mayor's role wanted him to be present at rehearsals. He did not even inform Pushkin and Zhukovsky of his impending departure, although he wrote to the latter from Hamburg that "I didn't say goodbye to Pushkin and I couldn't; however, he himself is to blame for it." [23] On June 18, 1836, he sailed for Lübeck in the company of his old chum Alexander Danilevsky and a mutual friend, Ivan Zolotarev, thus beginning twelve years of self-imposed exile, returning to Russia only twice during that time, in 1839–40 and in 1841–42, each time for an eight-month stay.

CHAPTER 6

Years Abroad

I *New Places . . . New Contacts*

N sooner had Gogol left Russia than the glamour of the open road began to work its magic on him and his depression disappeared. He wrote to Zhukovsky from Hamburg: "I feel the strength of a lion stirring in me. I swear to you that I am capable of great things that are inaccessible to ordinary men . . . this is going to be a real breakthrough. I know that there is much unpleasantness ahead, that I will endure privation and poverty, but I will not return soon for anything in the world." [1]

Indeed, as he had predicted, Gogol suffered loneliness; recurring illness dogged his lengthy sojourn in the West and he was often dependent on financial aid from friends for physical survival. The escape from what seemed to him at the time an unbearable situation at home eventually brought on a still more tragic moral and intellectual transformation within him. And yet, the first six years abroad that produced *Dead Souls* and marked the apogee of his art, also brought Gogol rich new sensations and some of the happiest moments of his life.

One such happiness was travel. He would speak of "the open road ahead of me" as the one certain cure for all his ills and jokingly added that no job appealed to him more than that of a courier who spent his time galloping across the length and breadth of Russia. In the summer of 1836 Gogol visited Lübeck, Hamburg, Bremen, Düsseldorf, Aachen, sailed down the Rhine to Baden-Baden, then went to several Swiss cities and stayed for two months in the magnificent autumnal setting of Vevey. When it became colder he joined Danilevsky in Paris. In the early spring he travelled on to Genoa and Florence and finally settled in Rome. For the next several summers he escaped the heat of the Italian capital by making the rounds of various German spas. It is evident from his letters that when he was not seeking relief from his various stomach ailments by taking the waters or simply following the good weather, he confined sight-seeing to esthetically impressive places, particularly to memorials of a romantically flavored past. Like other major Russian writers, such as Turgenev and Dostoevsky, he sought to make, during his travels, a romantic exploration of Western Europe, expecting to find a way of life that had been idealized in the German and French novels of his youth. Of course he was disappointed.

The German natives and English visitors are described with condescension, even with a certain contempt. Besides, like any average Russian tourist and most Russian intellectuals residing abroad, Gogol frequented exclusively Russian circles. In Baden-Baden he met a former pupil, Maria Balabin, her family and their friends, Prince and Princess Repnin. Flattered by their attention, Gogol became his most entertaining self and prolonged his stay to three enjoyable weeks. In Paris, with his constant companion, Danilevsky, he was invited to the house of a famous court beauty, Alexandra Rosset-Smirnova, to whom Pushkin had introduced him in Pavlovsk, and he became acquainted with the Polish poet Adam Mickiewicz and his entourage. Although Gogol liked Italians and learned to express himself volubly if not always correctly in their language, he spent most of his time in Rome with Russian painters, travellers from Russia, and expatriates like himself.

His remarks about Paris where he lived from October 1836 to February 1837 are more interesting in what they omit than in what they contain. The most superficial and colorless descriptions of large window displays, busy streets "splendidly lighted by gas," and banal reporting of visits to the Louvre, the Jardin des Plantes and the theater of Molière fill the letters to his mother. Only the excellent dinners served with ceremony in marvelous restaurants receive his unstinted praise. "Paris is not as bad as I expected it to be," [2] but its brilliant and animated life leaves him unmoved. He is put out by the profusion of newspaper stands and Parisians reading their newspaper in every café: "Everyone is absorbed in politics and people care more about what happens in Spain than about their private affairs." [3] In fact, Gogol remained oblivious to the exciting political and social events that were agitating the France of Louis-Philippe, perhaps willfully so. The ability to remain aloof from the mainstream of foreign living that surrounded him and to keep secret and inviolate the creative processes that were working within him made it possible for Gogol to continue writing his novel about Russia whether facing the lake-encircling panorama of the Swiss Alps or sitting in a Parisian apartment above the traffic din of the Place de la Bastille. Once in a sordid Italian tavern to the noise of clicking billiard balls, the rushing of pot boys and orders for drinks shouted in several dialects, Gogol ordered a small table to be brought and wrote without stirring from it one entire chapter of *Dead Souls*.

In the early spring of 1837 when Gogol was planning to visit Italy, the land of his youthful dreams, he learned that Pushkin had just died. The news shattered him; he could no longer work. Everything in Paris became repugnant to him and he hastened his departure writing to Pogodin that "my loss is even more terrible than yours. You mourn him as a Russian and a writer . . . while I cannot express even a hundredth part of my grief. The most luminous moments of my life occurred when I was writing. And when I wrote, it was always Pushkin whom I saw in front of me. . . ." [4] Given to emotional excess, Gogol was undoubtedly sincere in the violence of the feelings that came over him at the loss of the only man he really admired, who was for him The Poet as Raphael was for him The Painter. He had not written Pushkin all the time he had been abroad—Zhukovsky was much closer to him; it is noteworthy that he mourned him not as a friend but as a sure and attentive critic and guide. Gogol knew that for him no one could take the poet's place; to him only he had been able to confide his writing plans with no fear of mockery or rejection and then be urged to persevere in the realization of his talent. But this is not to say that Gogol, as he so heatedly claimed, could not continue to create with the poet gone. He had long been confident of his own writing powers and by 1837 was constructing a novel out of his own creative resources following a bent that was alien to Pushkin. This death was not a catastrophe for the author of *Dead Souls*, but it orphaned Gogol in another deeply personal way. If Pushkin had lived longer, his balanced and lucid intelligence, his unshakeable artist's conscience toward art might have saved Gogol from castigating his own genius and retarding his plunge into a religious aberration that finally destroyed him.

II *The Spell of Rome*

The shock of the bereavement wore off sooner than even Gogol, who boasted of his powers of resilience, had anticipated. Less than a month later he came under the spell of a new enchantment. He fell in love with Rome. "When I first rode into the city of Rome I did not know what to think of it. It seemed small to me; but the longer I live here, the bigger it appears to me, the buildings are larger, the views more beautiful, the sky lovelier, and there are enough paintings, ruins, and ancient monuments to last one a lifetime. You fall in love with Rome slowly, gradually but then for as long as you live. In short, Europe is to look at, but Italy is to live in!" [5] Life seemed all the brighter since he was solvent again. At his request, Zhukovsky had appealed to the tsar for a small pension and 5,000 rubles had been granted—enough to live on for at least a year and a half. There were days when he stayed writing in his sunlit apartment, others that he spent walking around the city discovering new churches and new squares, stopping to have gargantuan Italian dinners at the Café Greco in the company of Russian painters who found the writer loquacious and amusing. He also became a frequent guest at the villa of the Princess Zinaida Volkonskaya who had caused a scandal at the Russian court by adopting the Catholic faith and had surrounded herself with Polish priests who would have been happy to convert the well-known Russian author. His mother sent him several frantic letters, friends in Moscow became alarmed. If the princess had attempted to weaken Gogol's Orthodox attachments he, on the other hand, may have only appeared to play into the hands of a wealthy and generous hostess. When she left Rome, Gogol rejected all further advances from her Catholic entourage. For this, or for some other unknown reason, the princess later refused to see Gogol again and did not like to have his name mentioned in her presence.

Nevertheless the ubiquitous climate of religiosity in his beloved city seemed to have made an impact on Gogol's sensibilities. Ivan Zolotarev who had shared an apartment with Gogol for a time noticed that the latter had become extremely religious, often went to church, and liked to see manifestations of religiosity in other people. Zolotarev noted that a kind of stupor often came upon him in the midst of a lively conversation, and Annenkov, who spent much time with Gogol in Rome, also commented on the writer's strange behavior "as he would lie motionless for hours on the terrace of the Volkonskaya villa propped against the ancient wall staring at the sky and the marvelous Roman campagna." [6] It was a withdrawal for Gogol into the kind of bliss that Rome now personified for him as years ago did the vision of his native Ukraine that he was creating in the *Evenings.* "I feel as if I had dropped by to see some of the old world Ukrainian landowners. . . . Everywhere else I've been, things are changing; here everything has stopped and will go no further." [7] The child's need for a static world in Gogol was fulfilled by the Eternal City. He admitted calmly to its political stagnation, was indifferent to the Vatican's stranglehold on progressive ideas and to the poverty that stalked its dank, refuse-laden streets. The vivaciousness, spontaneity, and good humor of the Roman populace appealed to him much as the vigor and simplicity of the Ukrainian peasant did, and he had impressed his readers with these qualities until they forgot that these peasants were also serfs. That cherished Ukraine was now replaced by Rome, "his true native land." He felt irresponsible and free in it—free to drink in the clear and vivid landscape, to lose himself in the centuries-old reminders of a heroic past, free from family ties and troubles, and free to indulge in reveries of a vaguely mystical and Messianic nature brought on by the grandeur and immutability of Rome.

These reveries form the core of a lyrical monologue, *Rim* (*Rome*), that Gogol wrote during his first three years abroad and had planned as an introduction to a novel, entitled *Annunziata*. Much against his will this fragment was published in Pogodin's *The Muscovite* in 1842. The hero, easily identified with Gogol himself, is a young Italian prince who, studying in Paris, is at first fascinated by the variety and mobility of the Parisian scene, but is finally disenchanted by the "fearful kingdom of words rather than deeds." Back in Rome he becomes immersed in the deep, eternal calm of "the ancient world, stirring from behind the dark archetype of the formidable Middle Ages that is to be found everywhere in the work of the great artists and enduring through the generosity of the popes and the greatness of its artisans." [8] The images of the city that Gogol scattered in his letters are gathered into a poetic contemplation of nature, art, and antiquity. The prince finds it necessary to justify his backward native city historically as well. Reading deeply into the past he finds that Rome has become the esthetic conscience of bustling, industrial Europe, a warning against the materialism that is permeating the other nations of the West. The lofty tone of these reflections and exhaustive overcharged descriptions of nature make for heavy reading. But the genre scenes of Romans taking part in the carnival, gossiping in the streets, shouting at each other across clotheslines are delightful. The mobile, animated crowd, reminiscent of a Brueghel canvas is realistically caught in its movement with characteristic gestures defining individuals as in the Ukrainian tales. Peppe, the handy man, with his huge nose upon which the rest of the face hangs as upon a hatchet and his boundless trust in lottery luck is drawn with swift and deft mastery. How much less lifelike is the portrait of the heroine, Annunziata, whose flawless beauty is powerful enough to enhance nature itself with her presence.

III   The Failure with Women

The rapturous account of Annunziata's physical perfections— thick, lustrous hair, full dark eyes, alabaster shoulders—that transfix the prince when he catches a glimpse of the young girl at the carnival, differs little from the description of the Polish princess in *Taras Bulba,* the prostitute in *Nevsky Prospect,* and other young and sexually desirable girls in the Ukrainian stories. The endowment of his heroines with the same kind of conventional attractions has something of the same mechanical formula-like quality that the effect of this beauty produces on Gogol's male characters. The women are invariably either idealized like Annunziata or the lovely Alcinoë in the essay *Woman* (1833) who is "poetry, thought", a spiritual inspiration that is inviolate, distant and humanly unbelievable, or they represent a threatening, destructive force. For having known the witch in *Viy,* Khoma pays with his reason and his life; the governor's daughter causes the collapse of Chichikov's carefully laid plans; if it had not been for Agafia's malicious meddling, the two Ivans would have patched up their quarrel; Shponka is haunted by wives with frightening goose faces. Only vulgar women like the matchmaker in *Marriage* and old crones are successfully depicted in Gogol's fiction.

His inability to break away from a literary stereotype inspired

by German idealistic philosophy and its lurid Gothic counterpart
while creating a whole gallery of young women totally lacking
any single credible and full-dimensioned figure, has puzzled
critics and inevitably has aroused speculation about his intimate
life. It has been said that like his hero Ivan Shponka, whom he
treats with sympathy, Gogol was sexually impotent, had a fear
and revulsion of any serious emotional involvement with the
opposite sex, and was incapable of imagining normal intimacy
between men and women.[9] Certainly no such relationships appear in his work. He had apparently never been in love with a
woman, and Sergey Aksakov, who knew him well and revered
him as a great artist, made the chilling statement that there was
something in Gogol's personality that kept people away from him
and he did not believe it was possible to care for Gogol as a
human being.[10] This incapacity to arouse love in others immured
him in a solitude made even more impregnable by his instinctive
distrust of people and natural reserve. The effusiveness in many
of his letters filled with exaggerated terms of affection may have
been Gogol's way of trying to relate more closely to his family
and friends although some critics have interpreted this ingratiating epistolary manner as yet another sign of his effeminacy
extending it to his taste for sewing, cooking, and the excessive
adornment of his person. Only one further step was needed for
the psycho-critique to claim that Gogol's sexual tendencies were
strongly homosexual in nature.

Very little is known of this side of the writer's life—a life shown
by a voluminous correspondence to have been conducted almost
entirely in public. There are two impressive exceptions. In what
one biographer describes as "one of the most violent crises of
his life," [11] Gogol formed a sudden and overwhelming attachment to Alexander Danilevsky during a week's stay with him in
Paris in September 1838, and upon his return to Rome sent several undeniably ardent and pining letters to his old school friend.
Another poignant relationship seemed to have unsettled Gogol
emotionally; he broke out of his usual solipsism to the extent of
considering the life of another more precious than his own. In
December 1838 he met the twenty-three-year-old consumptive
Joseph Vielgorsky, son of Count Vielgorsky who was attached to
the retinue of the tsarevich then visiting Italy. The young man
was working on a history of Russian literature. Gogol and he

became inseparable friends. By May, when it was evident that Joseph was dying, Gogol spent many sleepless nights watching over him at his father's villa and later in a diary fragment, "Nochi na ville" ("Nights at a Villa"), expressed in feverish lines his despair at the cruel and untimely loss: "It was so sweet for me to sit by him and look at him. We had already for the last two nights used 'thou' to each other. How very much closer he was to me since then! . . . What happiness, what utter joy it would have been for me if I could have taken on his illness and if my death would have restored him to health; how ready I would have been to die in his stead!" [12]

The clinical analysis of Gogol's complex emotional relations, or the lack of them, remains the domain of the psychiatrist. The presentation of the author and his character mutations as tempered by his kind of emotional fulfillment, not as a problem but as an experience, rests on the critic's ability to accept and share in his sensibilities. These sensibilities were heightened and nurtured by an extraordinary receptivity to external stimuli which were transformed by his ardent imagination into sensuous images. He had the gift of surrender to sensuality. The ecstasy of the nerves after which he constantly hungered was brought on by an extreme delectation for colors, textures, tastes, smells. A Ukrainian landscape shimmering in the noonday sun stabbed at Gogol with the impact of a physical blow (*Sorochinsky Fair*). He had a highly developed olfactory sense, and for the first time in Russian literature fragrances, odors pleasant and unpleasant, are used to distinguish people (Petrushka in *Dead Souls*), food (*Old-World Landowners*), and even city districts (*Rome*). Alone among major Russian writers who are notoriously reticent in matters of sex, Gogol creates a highly amatory mood in describing the voluptuous movements of a young woman's body. Nowhere is the vibrantly sensuous pursued more ardently than when he builds up the sensuality of desire kindled by fabric touching soft flesh or stirred by an erotic dream or fixed in a lover's look: "The young beauty tossed about in enchanting nakedness that the night's darkness hid even from her and could not sleep" (*Christmas Eve*); "He saw how the taut young breasts were raised, their voluptuous, enlarged cupola-shaped nipples quivering all the while under the linen shift" (*Taras Bulba*); "Her foot, brilliantly bared, bound at the ankle with scarlet ribbons, stepped forward and did not seem to touch contemptible earth" ("Woman").

IV *Physical and Spiritual Peregrinations*

Disturbing news from his mother about a possible foreclosure of the estate and the fact that his two sisters who were graduating from the Patriotic Institute in Petersburg would have to be provided for obliged Gogol to return to Russia in the early fall of 1839. He travelled by easy stages, stopping in Marienbad where he came to know the poet Nikolay Yazykov. Gogol was extremely depressed. He had very little money left, the prospect of going home was distasteful, and a play about the Ukraine, *The Shaved-off Moustache*, that he had been turning over in his mind since he landed in Germany refused to be written.

What is of primary interest in the eight-month stay in Moscow and Petersburg is that surrounded by welcoming friends, besieged with invitations from the Aksakov coterie, and obliged at the same time to arrange for the future of his sisters, Gogol seemed spurred to greater productivity by external pressures. We have a rare photographic glimpse of him actually writing, recorded by Sergey Aksakov: "Gogol stood before me in a bizarre costume, in long Russian woolen stockings that stretched above the knee and instead of a jacket—a velvet vest over a long flannel shirt, his neck wrapped in a vivid scarf and on his head a plum-colored velvet "kokoshnik" embroidered in gold, not unlike the headdress of Finnish tribeswomen. He was busy writing; we had obviously disturbed him, and he looked at us for a long time unseeingly, quite oblivious of his get-up. . . ." [13]

At last, one sister, Elizaveta, was placed as a companion in a wealthy Moscow household, and Annette returned to Vasilevka with her mother who had come to Moscow to see her son. Pogodin defrayed the girls' expenses, and with a 4,000 ruble loan from Zhukovsky in his pocket, Gogol felt that Rome was his again. He left Russia on May 18th, but remained in Vienna the entire summer. It was a period of intense creative activity. The variety and sum total of his production are impressive: a major revision of *Taras Bulba* and the servants' scene from the *Order of Vladimir, The Overcoat*, another chapter of *Dead Souls*, and further attempts to construct scenes from Cossack life for the *Shaved-off Moustache*. Was it the failure to complete this historical play or overexhaustion from the tremendous creative tension that caused Gogol's serious physical collapse at the end of that summer? Some of the symptoms such as pressure on the chest, severe gastric disorder, shortness of breath, blank despondency and fearful unrest recalled to him Vielgorsky's last moments; he began to fear for his life and even composed a will.

A Russian financier, Nikolay Botkin, who took care of him in August was certain that Gogol would not leave Vienna alive. Fearing "to die among the Germans," Gogol ordered a post coach to drive him in the direction of Italy. By the time he reached Venice he felt much better. Nevertheless, that illness was a turning point in Gogol's spiritual life. He confided to Botkin that he had a vision and knew that he had been spared by God so that henceforth he could dedicate his art to the revelation of the eternal truth. This vision he felt was to illuminate all his future work. Despite the difficulty, the frequent frustrations, and the debilitating strain of writing, despite the fact that artistry stood in the way of the pleasures of life, the creative act was now to be infused with a moral purpose. The author was to become a spiritual guide and prophet to other men. Gogol's adolescent ambition of doing great things for mankind was to be realized. "My miraculous recovery fills my heart with inexpressible happiness; it seems that my life is still a useful one . . . only God's wondrous will was able to save me," [14] he wrote to the older Aksakov in March 1841 from Rome while he was finishing his novel. With his bent for impassioned rationalization, Gogol needed little more to convince himself that his "deed of valor" in bringing salvation to others was not to be limited only to literary action. He was chosen, he felt, to use his moral suasion in the ordinary things of life, in simple daily words, as a teacher would. An admonitory, didactic tone gains ascendance in his letters to friends. Writing to Danilevsky whose mother had just died and who was drifting along in restless idleness, Gogol urged him to pull himself together and take over the supervision of his estate. In biblical turns of phrase he begs Yazykov to heed his advice and severely reprimands practical-minded Pogodin, to whom he is in debt, for pressing him to write a piece for his weekly paper.

It is a rare experience to enter Gogol's life and come across a pellucid moment in it when the writer was not self-conscious and was happily himself. We owe the recounting of such a period to the indefatigable and sensitive memorialist, Pavel Annenkov, who was living in a room next to Gogol's apartment in the summer of 1841 when *Dead Souls* was completed. Gogol needed to have a clean copy made of his manuscript and for an hour each day Annenkov volunteered to take dictation; Gogol would read each sentence to him, slowly and expressively, remaining serious even during the most hilarious passages when Annenkov would throw down his pen and roar with laughter. A dramatic moment was reached when Gogol was dictating the famous chapter of the visit to Plyushkin's house. The writer stood up and "raising his hand accompanied his reading with a proud, imperious gesture. At the end of this entire extraordinary sixth chapter, I was very excited, laid down my pen and said in all sincerity: 'Nikolay Vasilievich, I consider this chapter the writing of a genius.' " [15]

Anticipating possible objections from the censors, Gogol decided to submit his novel in person and by mid-October 1841 he was back in Russia confronting the Moscow Censorship Committee. Although his nerves became shattered from worry and frustration in battling the literary watchdogs of the empire, he could not help savoring the grotesqueness of the censors' reactions which together with the absurd point and counterpoint of their dialogue seemed to have been lifted from the most satirical pages of the novel itself. The title caused great consternation; it struck everyone as a heresy against the Orthodox dogma of the immortality of the soul. When it was explained that the "souls" in question were only serfs, the chairman voted against the novel on the grounds that it was an attack against the sacred institution of serfdom. Chichikov's buying operation was considered dangerous material that might provoke readers into following his example, although, as it was pointed out, the author had exposed the swindle from the start.

Some members were apprehensive about the low price that was offered for each dead soul that in reality was nothing more than a signed slip of paper. "No matter. What would the French and English think of us for selling a man for only 2 rubles and a half? They would never come to Russia!" Permission to publish the work was refused. But Gogol did not lose hope. He met Belinsky at the capital and appealed to his highly placed friends— Prince Odoevsky, Alexandra Rosset-Smirnova, Count Vielgorsky—

who were at last successful in persuading the Petersburg censor, Nikitenko, to give a favorable report on the novel. He did so on condition that the Captain Kopeykin incident be omitted, but with substantial revisions it, too, was finally accepted for publication.

Other matters riled Gogol as well. His host, Pogodin, was still demanding the contribution which irked Gogol all the more because he was in deep financial debt to the publisher. Still, he was reluctant to part with *Rim* (*Rome*) or with *The Overcoat* that he planned to bring out for the first time in a new edition of his collected works.

In the Slavophile Aksakov milieu Gogol fared no better. Sergey Aksakov found the writer greatly changed and his bewilderment at Gogol's evasiveness, bouts of bad manners, and irritability colors his detailed account of that second homecoming.[16] There was misunderstanding on both sides. The father and particularly his son, Konstantin Aksakov, looked upon their cherished guest as the literary spokesman par excellence for the nationalist Orthodox ideology they held dear, and they attempted to draw Gogol into passionate political discussions. Gogol was also conservative in his views, but knew little and cared even less about politics to be drawn into a factional struggle. His personal kind of mysticism was beginning to absorb him, and he behaved badly because he felt uneasy among his generous admiring friends whom he did not want to offend and whose hospitality he was too weak-willed to resist. He had tried, for example, to keep secret his meeting with Belinsky, the arch-enemy from the opposite political camp. When the Aksakovs learned about it, they were deeply hurt. When *Dead Souls* was finally published in May 1842, Gogol commissioned Prokopovich to bring out an edition of all his collected works in Petersburg and immediately left for Italy.

CHAPTER 7

Dead Souls

I *Genesis*

A GAIN from Pushkin, Gogol had received the impetus to compose his masterpiece *Dead Souls*. The poet had advised him in 1835 to concentrate on a longer piece of work where he could exercise his uncanny gift of satirizing banality in all its many forms. Pressed by Gogol for a subject, he suggested to him one that he had thought of using himself for a picaresque novel in which the hero would traffic in dead souls and travel all over Russia meeting all kinds of people. The idea was based on the fact that the Russian population was counted only once in a decade, and landlords were required to pay poll taxes for any male "souls," as serfs were then called, who might have died between visits from the census taker. A clever swindler could easily purchase such "dead souls" for a nominal price, ostensibly settle them on a piece of land, and obtain a big mortgage on them at the State Landlords' bank. "I began to write with no definite plan in mind, without knowing exactly what my hero was to represent. I only thought that this odd project . . . would lead to the creation of diverse personalities and my own inclination toward the comic would bring on amusing situations that I could alternate with pathos." [1]

Then a year later when he was abroad, Gogol envisaged the work on a more ambitious scale. Images of Russian life crowded upon his imagination, representative types from provincial officialdom and the landowning class began to take shape; he aspired to recreate in depth multiple aspects of contemporary Russian society and make a psychological assessment of his countrymen—according to the protocol of Gogolian perception—in an exposure of prevailing vices and weaknesses. Caught up by the magnitude of his enterprise which now unfolded its epic proportions for him, he discarded the original idea of using the light picaresque or adventure novel pattern popular at the time. "The work I am now writing, that I have been thinking about for a long time, and that will continue to absorb my thoughts, is neither a long short story nor a novel. It will be very long, running to several volumes, entitled *Dead Souls*. If God allows me to compose my poem it will be my first decent piece of writing. All Russia will be in it." [2]

On the frontispiece of the first edition, designed by Gogol himself, the word "poema" was placed in the center of the page, in larger print than either the title or the author's name. In the text, however, Gogol speaks of his work sometimes as a novel, sometimes as a poem; and his own indecision regarding genre started a lively polemic among Russian critics when *Dead Souls* was first published. Four years later, Gogol answered them with a definition of the epic that bears a strong resemblance to that of Fielding, whom in the earliest drafts he mentioned together with Pushkin, Shakespeare, Tasso, and Cervantes as his literary teachers who were always with him when he wrote.

Modern times have given rise to a literature placed somewhere between a novel and an epic whose hero may be a private and unimportant person, but significant in many ways for an observer of the human personality. The author leads him through many changes and adventures for the purpose of presenting all the most significant habits and traits of the period and giving an almost statistically drawn picture of abuses and vices that he has noted, for the benefit of his contemporaries who seek a solution to the present in the lessons of the past. Such writings have appeared from time to time in many countries. Although many of them were written in prose, they may be considered epic poetry. [3]

Among authors of such minor epics, Gogol mentions Ariosto and Cervantes, and undoubtedly he considered himself one of their company. Although the action in *Dead Souls* takes place in contemporary Russia, the disclosure of moral and social flaws is the mainspring of the work and its motivating force is a "private, unimportant person, Pavel Ivanovich Chichikov."

II *The Opening Scene*

Gogol's major work, one of the world's greatest comic epics, starts with a leisurely description of Chichikov's arrival in a provincial town:

Through the gates of the hotel in the provincial town of N. rolled in a rather handsome traveling *brichka* * on springs, of the sort used by bachelors, retired colonels, staff captains, landowners with about a hundred serfs or so—in a word, all those who are known as the fair-to-middling kind. In the brichka sat a gentleman who was neither good-looking nor ugly, not too stout nor too thin; you could not call him old, but he was not too young, either. His arrival did not produce any stir in the town and was not accompanied by anything unusual.[4]

While we watch the traveller settling in his room, eating, dressing, talking to the waiter, Gogol details with relish the dingy discomforts of the inn, which he takes pains to persuade us are common to all provincial inns everywhere, such as the room "with cockroaches peeping out of every corner like so many prunes," [5] and the cushions in the common room downstairs seemed to be filled with "pieces of brick and cobblestones instead of elastic wool." [6] A walk through the town reveals that it is no different from other provincial towns: "on the buildings the paint was the usual yellow color and just as hard to look at . . . the signs that were all but washed away by the rain showed pretzels and boots . . . along the streets were stalls with nuts, soap, and cookies that looked like soap . . . and the pavement everywhere was in need of repair." [7]

The following day is spent in visits to members of the municipal hierarchy. As Pavel Ivanovich Chichikov, Collegiate Councillor, pays his respects to the governor, he says in passing that coming to his province could be likened to entering paradise—so velvet-smooth were its roads; to the chief of police he makes several flattering remarks about the local guardians of the law; and twice he addresses the vice-governor and the chairman of the administrative officers—as though inadvertently—as "Your Excellency." These compliments, uttered with a dignified and yet modest air, earn him numerous invitations to teas, dinners, and supper parties. Among these bureaucrats who seem utterly commonplace—although Gogol makes the governor memorable in a glinting aside as "a good-hearted fellow who even occasionally embroidered fancywork on tulle with his own hands" [8]—Chichikov makes impressive headway. The patience and diligence with which he charms his social entourage are common to his other

* brichka—a light carriage.

activities. One, unforgettably, is the fastidiousness with which he takes care of his own person. Another, his inquisitiveness regarding the number and wealth of neighboring landowners and recent local diseases and epidemics, surpasses ordinary tourist curiosity. The incidents filling the visitor's social calendar are imperturbably prosaic, yet Gogol manages to convey an air of mystery to that pleasantly rotund and affable gentleman whose obliging ordinariness makes him agreeable to everyone while all the time remaining totally evasive about himself and his past. Nothing about the reason for his trip is disclosed by the end of the first chapter, which closes with the tantalizing hint that Chichikov's enterprise would upset the entire town.

III *Gallery of Portraits*

Chichikov now sets out to visit members of the neighboring gentry, and we learn the nature of his delicate and gruesome mission. The account of his four days of travel about the country-side comprise chapters two through six—each one given over to an interview with one landowner—and is structurally similar to the picaresque novel technique. While discarding the traditional dynamic flow of complicated adventures in favor of one central action instigated by the hero, Gogol retains the threading process of self-sustaining episodes that are static. There ensues a defilade of character portraits that make up the gallery of the most famous grotesque comic types in Russian literature.

Gogol created his eccentric country squires with infinite care. In the unruffled calm of a social visit unhampered by the histrionic urgencies of *The Inspector General* or by the need to develop a story as in *The Quarrel of the Two Ivans,* he chooses deliberately and with precision familiar elements in an intimate setting that provide the widest latitude for his distorting satirical gift. The narrative is relaxed, the sting kept hidden under a congenial surface. We witness Chichikov's various approaches to the serf-owners with whom he strikes deals for dead souls, and the constants observed during each conversation are the same: the host's physical appearance and manner, his speech, the furnishings of the house, a description of his estate, and his reaction to the hero's fraudulent proposal. These seemingly harmless ingredients sifted through the Gogolian alchemy of awareness furnish a profusion of caricatural effects that gradually shape a hyperbolic image of a certain kind of man.

Here is Manilov, blue-eyed and blond, with vacuous looks and a sweet smile who at first glance appears extremely attractive. But a few minutes' talk with him brings on mortal ennui; there is no life in it and Gogol complains that he does not know what to make of this person who unlike others seems to lack any handle to grab him by. Whereupon he proceeds to delineate the most masterful portrayal of cloying and sentimental insipidity in all his fiction.

To his slatternly, drunken servants and his thieving steward, Manilov appears as the paragon of the incompetent landlord, so inert that he lets the estate run itself and does not even know the approximate number of his serfs, living or dead. But he is far from inactive. Although he has not read beyond page fourteen of a book lying in his study for more than two years, he fills his head with euphoric reveries that break into indefinite fragments as easily as do the clouds over his summer house, which he named the Temple for Solitary Meditation and where his days are spent. When there is nothing else to do, he knocks small mounds of tobacco from his pipe onto the window sills and arranges them in neat little rows or settles on the sofa with his wife where "they would exchange such a long and languishing kiss that it was possible to smoke a small straw-stemmed cigar to the very end while it lasted." [9] And neither would notice that two dining room chairs are still covered in rough matting, for there had not been enough of the rich silk upholstery to go around, or that a cheap copper candle holder, twisted and covered with tallow is brought to the evening meal together with a magnificent candlestick of patinated bronze with the three Graces and a mother-of-pearl escutcheon. Although he had met him only once at the governor's reception, Manilov greets Chichikov as his most cherished friend. He cannot thank him effusively enough for honoring his house and is so bewitched by Chichikov's fawning courtesy that he immediately begins to imagine their future life together bound by ties of eternal friendship. But, of all the squires whom Chichikov asks to sign over their deceased serfs, it is Manilov alone who questions the legality of the transaction. As the extraordinary notion sinks into his muddled and sluggish mind, his strangled cluckings of bewilderment grow steadily funnier and end in farce. The visitor's reassurance that Russia and the state treasury could only benefit from their private deal quiets him at once and he gives over a list of dead serfs without compensation.

In a late revision Gogol added a final magnificent touch: upon meeting Chichikov on the promised date at the administrative offices, Manilov presents him a paper decoratively bordered, rolled up in a tube, and fastened with a pink ribbon. When Chichikov asks him what it is, the landowner coyly answers: "The little muzhiks."

Upon leaving Manilov's village, exultant about obtaining the defunct serfs without payment, Chichikov plunges into a maze of agreeable speculations and does not notice that his coachman Selifan is now trying to cross a freshly furrowed field in the pelting rain. The carriage turns over, spilling its owner into mud up to his knees. Finally, driving on they reach a dimly lit manor house and are given shelter for the night. Everything in that dwelling—the fluffed-up feather bed in a room with striped, papered walls cluttered with a miscellany of letters, packs of cards, and stockings stuck into the corners of fancy antique mirror frames, and a hissing grandfather clock with a painted face—breathes the parochial past. The owner was "one of those petty, elderly ladies, with a motherly air, who complain about crops and losses, holding their heads a little to the side, and at the same time tuck away in various bureau drawers tidy sums of money in small striped money bags." [10] When Chichikov looks out the window the next morning and sees a well-kept and well-stocked barnyard with a large vegetable garden stretching beyond it, bordered with solidly built peasant huts, he decides to turn his accidental stop into profit. In no time at all he learns from his hostess that eighteen of her peasants had recently died and he offers her fifteen rubles for the lot.

In the ensuing dialogue, which for side-splitting comedy rivals the choicest scenes in *The Inspector General*, the landed proprietress, Korobochka (her name means "little box" and neatly labels her hoarding instinct), is profiled with extraordinary vividness. Intensely superstitious, ignorant of all matters not bearing directly upon the operation of her farm, she seems simple-minded and is at first frightened by the outlandishness of the offer. Her stolid answer is that the serfs cannot be sold because they are now dead, but since the gentleman comes with money in hand she will sell him feathers or honey or lard that passing merchants like to buy. His exclusive interest in the deceased serfs rouses her suspicions, she begins to reflect on the possibility of some special value attached to them, and "that they might even come to be useful around the farm, somehow." [11] Her woodenheadedness reduces Chichikov to a profusely perspiring fury.

Gogol does not fail to point out the change in tone and manner of the generally obsequious Collegiate Councillor as he addresses the owner of a mere eighty serfs. But his shouts and chair-banging impress her less than his gratuitous lie of having access to government contracts. She sees a way of unloading her flour and some of her cattle at run-away prices through Chichikov, so she immediately agrees to sign away the defunct serfs and has lunch prepared for the visitor. The meal of mushrooms, patties, and baked onions, poppyseed, and clotted cream and curd is bountiful enough, but Korobochka's calculated hospitality is demonstrated by having the pancakes made from left-over dough. Upon completion of his business, Chichikov has the brichka harnessed and within a few miles of Korobachka's manor stops at an inn to fortify himself with suckling pig garnished with horseradish and sour cream, evoking from the author a page of mock envy on the Pantagruelian capacity for food that distinguishes the fair-to-middling Russian gentleman.

A ruddy-faced young man with flashing white teeth and jet black sideburns, whom Chichikov recognizes as another landowner he had met in town, bursts into the tavern, clasps our hero into an enthusiastic embrace, launches into a voluble account of his carousing spree at a fair where he has lost everything at cards including his carriage and horses, and bending Chichikov's head so that it just escapes hitting the window frame, shows him the tattered and ill-harnessed team outside he had been forced to hire. Nozdrev, whose name comes from "nozdrya," nostril—i.e., the impudently open, heavily breathing part of the face—is seen in a flash as an irresponsible braggart, reveller, and gambler powered by a natural dynamic of undisciplined energies expressed in rough gestures and raucous laughter. Unerringly, Gogol stages this encounter at an inn, for Nozdrev exudes the atmosphere of a public place where diversion is found in food, drink, and cards. Widowed early with two children "whom he absolutely did not need," [12] he rarely stayed more than a day on his estate whose dwindling income was spent at fairs that he frequented with the compulsion of a hound on the scent. Here his passion for a deal took the form of swapping the most sundry objects bought as bargains at stalls for a gun, a horse, a set of pipes, only to lose them at the gaming table or in an unlucky bet. His language characterized him admirably: it rushed forward in a torrent of disorganized chatter, punctuated by exclamatory jerks, and seasoned with barroom profanity and the card gambler's jargon.

There are literary kinships to Nozdrev in Gogol's own earlier work when he was assembling him in the thick-skinned, pleasure-loving Pirogov (*Nevsky Prospect*), the bustling Kochkarev (*The Wedding*), and the mendacious hero of *The Inspector General*. But the composite image is the more powerful for it projects the dominant features of those earlier characters in the extreme situation. The lieutenant's friendliness and social charm become in Nozdrev an addiction to indiscriminate and fulgurating friendships that do not last longer than the first drinking bout and end in a fight. The vision of Petersburg with which Khlestakov, the copy clerk, dazzles himself and his audience seems like a harmless fib compared to the outrageous fabrication woven into Nozdrev's stories. He swears that he drank seventeen bottles of champagne at one sitting, claims that two of his men managed to pull a huge fish out of his obviously empty pond. In another vein he unfolds with eloquent ease a well-rehearsed anecdote featuring a calumnious tale about a dear friend—and the closer the friend the more damning the story—that he had made up entirely, complete with graphic and gratuitous detail. He comes nearest to Kochkarev in his ability to live in high gear and a perpetual state of agitation with action for action's sake as the terminal goal. Nozdrev is always ready for anything; his arrival at a social gathering holds the promise of an assault on the sensibilities of all those present.

This kind of assault is made on Chichikov in order to talk him into dining at Nozdrev's house. In a barrage of speech that lasts over thirty pages, Nozdrev stupefies his guest with a detailed and effusive inventory of everything contained in his run-down estate, presses upon him a mixture of suspect vintage wines, tries to force prudent Pavel Ivanovich to try his luck at cards, insults him, and finally submits him to bodily attack. By this time, the chameleon-like Chichikov has adapted himself to his host's direct and explosive utterances, and so he asks him abruptly, on his word of honor, to grant him a certain request. Gogol uses the dispute that follows to spotlight Nozdrev's extraordinary frivolity. He plays with the offer as with a new toy asking impudent questions about his visitor's business, but cannot keep his mind on it. He starts his own kind of swapping game and whips himself into a fever of haggling when Chichikov grimly refuses to buy his light chestnut mare or two hunting dogs for an extravagant sum, or his hurdy-gurdy or yet other bargains with the dead souls thrown in. The situation resolves into burlesque when Nozdrev steps up his bids with increasing truculence, calls his guest a scoundrel to be hung on the nearest tree, and finally orders his two brawny servants to beat him up. By pure chance, the humiliated and frightened Chichikov escapes unhurt and, ordering his coachman to take him to Sobakevich's estate, drives away with a feeling that he has just been through a terrible illness.

The property Chichikov now approaches boasts soundly constructed barns, stables, and sheds of heavy timber; the peasants' log cabins lack all adornment, but appear solid and weatherproof. The landlord who greets Chichikov gives the effect of rough-hewn massiveness described by Gogol with pungent overemphasis:

"When Chichikov glanced sideways at Sobakevich he appeared to him very much like a medium-sized bear, and this resemblance was completed by his frock coat that was the color of a bear's pelt; the sleeves and his trousers were long and he put down his feet in a lumbering fashion, constantly stepping on other people's feet." [13] The disquieting quality of the animal-like Sobakevich is underscored by objects in his house that reflect the look of his person. Full-length pictures of Greek military leaders are striking for their display of imposingly thick arms and huge moustachios; the thigh of the Greek heroine Bobelina is larger than the torso of an ordinary man. The pot-bellied bureau with its "preposterous legs" is bear-like, and the stoutly built armchairs also have an ursine appearance.

During dinner, the taciturn host becomes almost loquacious, contemptuously berating French and German delicacies while engorging with systematic greed immense portions of a side of mutton with buckwheat groats, a stuffed turkey the size of a calf, and curds each larger than a dinner plate. When the talk turns to their common acquaintances, Sobakevich, in contrast to Manilov who found all the town officials equally delightful, brands them with laconic rudeness as swindlers and Judases. He is not taken in by their conviviality any more than he is impressed at that particular moment by the cautiously circumlocutory, flowery language with which Chichikov introduces the shady business that he wants to discuss with him. But the demonstration of the visitor's ability to woo a prospect by means of digressive tactics, testing the terrain for the chance of success is humorous since it is in this case absolutely unwarranted. At the end of a long tirade, Sobakevich simply asks whether he needs some dead souls and Chichikov realizes that he has met his match. Disgruntled by the fact that he is forced to part with three times the money that he had expected to pay under the seller's threat of exposing the nature of the merchandise, Chichikov hastens to leave his host. He is buoyed up, however, by the landlord's vituperative comment about his neighbor Plyushkin, who starves his peasants and lets them die like flies.

To introduce us to the last landowner on Chichikov's shopping list, Gogol transports us into the luxuriant disorder of his vast overgrown garden:

Against the skyline, tree summits that had reached their full growth lay joined together in green clouds and irregular cupolas of trembling foliage. The white colossal trunk of a birch whose crest had broken off in a tempest or thunderstorm thrust itself upward through the dense green tangle like a round regular column of gleaming marble and the jagged break at the top showed darkly against its snowy whiteness like a cap or a black-feathered bird. The hop vines that stifled the elder, rowan, and hazel bushes underneath and ran over all the tops of the paling, finally jutted up entwining the broken birch. Halfway up the middle the vine hung, now catching at other branches, now trembling loose in the light breeze. In places, the thick sunlit verdure parted and disclosed in its midst a hollow that yawned sunless and gaping like a maw; it was all in shadow and in its dark depths could just barely be seen a narrow path across it, shattered railings, a broken down summer house, a decaying willow trunk, a hoary Siberian pea tree that pushed from behind the willow—a mass of twigs and leaves, dried out by the fearful underwood—and at last, a young maple branch stretching sideways its green paws of leaves. Under one of them, the sun got in, God know how, and suddenly transformed it into a firelit wonder, burning in this dense darkness.[14]

Nature's wanton extravagance and profusion furnish a dramatic contrast to the sterile and sordid avarice that reigns in Plyushkin's house. When Chichikov first catches sight of the long house with all but two of the windows boarded up looking like a "decrepit invalid" and next sees on its porch a figure in tattered clothing resembling a woman's dress and crowned by a greasy servant's night cap, he cannot make out the person's sex. Only when the figure barked at him hoarsely that he was the master and waited for him to state his business, all the while staring at him with suspicious little eyes which "darted under his high bushy eyebrows as mice do when thrusting out of their dark holes their sharp little snouts, their ears perked and their whiskers twitching"[15] did Chichikov realize that this is the owner of over one thousand serfs and formerly one of the most distinguished members of the local gentry. How can a man change to such an extent is Gogol's agonizing question prefacing Plyushkin's former life.

He had been a hospitable, happily married country gentleman, who had brought up his children with care and affection and whose efficient and wise husbandry was the envy of his neighbors. With his wife's death and the departure of his grown sons and daughters, Plyushkin began to withdraw into himself, and his tendency to thrift gradually accelerated into avarice. What he previously husbanded, he now hoarded; all his vitality fed a single vice. His literary antecedents such as Molière's Harpagon, Dickens's Scrooge, Balzac's Gobseck are cheerful and sociable fellows compared to the tatter of humanity that Plyushkin has become. He is the complete miser-prototype in his dread of all expense, in his ragged attire, in the fear of being robbed, in his hostility to his own undernourished and over-exploited peasants, and in his gradual recession from the world. There is no humor in Chichikov's encounter with this neurotic acquirer who grabs avidly the pennies that he is given for his deceased serfs and who rounds out the sale with the even more illegal offer of making out a deed of sale for his runaway peasants of whom, not surprisingly, there are many.

Of all the characters in the novel Plyushkin comes nearest to tragedy. Harrowingly, seeming to dread what he has to tell, Gogol picks out the absolutely right specific to record the landlord's dehumanization and physical decay. Plyushkin's gradual disassociation from reality is illustrated with windows which were boarded up one after the other to guard against thieves and so "with each year, the important aspects of his property disappeared more and more from his view, and his interest centered on the scraps of paper and stray feathers that he had accumulated in his room." [16] That he exists in a kind of death in life is stressed by the word "cellar" (in Russian, "pogreb") that is close to "grob," meaning grave. As Chichikov entered Plyushkin's house "he stepped into a dark, wide vestibule, out of which cold air came as out of a cellar . . ." while in the landlord's room, "from the center of the ceiling hung a chandelier in a canvas bag so dusty that it had taken on the appearance of a cocoon with the silk worm still inside. . . . There was an indescribable heap of things in a corner, and the dust upon it was so thick that any hands touching it would take on the look of gloves." [17] To this heap Plyushkin would add any bit of metal or wood or other rubbish that he would find on his daily rounds of testing the locks of the storerooms to which most of the serfs' produce— wheat grain, flour, vegetables, salted meat and fish, linens, clothing, sheepskins—was brought. The commission merchants had stopped buying from the owner who haggled over every half-kopek, and he was content to keep everything, including the rotting hay and wheat, hay ricks that had become manure, flour so stone-hard that only an axe could split it, and clothing that crumbled into dust.

The buyer of the dead souls pilots the novel. In relation to him all the other characters are portrayed, and, inversely, in his contacts with them during his visits, his own image is defined and takes shape. Against the background of feudal nobility and its attendant civil servants, Chichikov emerges as a new social type. He is the harbinger of the moneyed urban class generating a more complicated economy no longer depending on rural production for revenue and—with the middleman—dealing in services rather than goods. He is peculiarly modern. Today he is the broker, the advertising executive, the insurance agent, the public relations man. With something of the prophecy of genius Gogol created him out of the serf-bound Russia of the nineteenth century and gave him the externals that distinguish the business entrepeneur of our time.

We know him by the kit he carries when he visits a prospective client. Like a workman spreading out his tools before starting a job, he produces from that kit a stock of assets that include a self-confident manner, inexhaustible good humor, an air of relaxed vitality, and the ability to get along with all kinds of people. Also, since much of his business relies on the number of contacts made, he gives the feeling of being in perpetual transit. Good looks are an important factor, and we perceive a Chichikov who is particular about his physical appearance, a point to which Gogol returns repeatedly, underscoring his roundness and smoothness. Andrey Bely thinks of Chichikov as a wheel that is not only smooth and round, but one that will also roll sideways, for he is frequently shown bowing a little to the side, coming through a door sideways, mincing as he walks, and turning his body with each step to the right and left. Another distinguishing sign is Chichikov's extreme physical cleanliness. Clearly, Gogol uses this imagery for his hero to restate and develop again the theme of what life appears to be and what it really is, a theme that has haunted all his previous works. That Chichikov's seemliness, his decorous exterior and fastidiousness mask moral squalor is suggested early in the extreme obsequiousness with which the genteel conniver charms the burghers and predisposes the rural gentry toward his mission. His servant Petrushka, who is always in his proximity, resembles his master in his compulsive and undiscriminating reading habits, but always emits a strong unpleasant odor. Gogol ties it in neatly with a bit of brilliant word play. When the officials try to find out from Petrushka something about his master's former life and activities, they only catch the scent of "domestic tranquility" and the real Chichikov eludes them and the reader until we learn about his past in the very last chapter.

"Humble and obscure were the origins of our hero. . . . Life, from the start, looked at him dourly, as if through a murky little window drifted over with snow." [18] From his childhood that knew neither a mother's care nor a single playmate and was spent over lessons in a tiny room with a harsh, ailing father, the boy carried away his parent's last admonition to please his superiors, trust no one, and consider the kopeck one's best friend. In school he was known only for neatness, diligence, and a fawning attentiveness to his teachers. He had already developed a tremendous respect for the ruble and denied himself everything in order to add to his little hoard. The bleakness and drudgery that he endured as a fledgling government clerk were equalled only by the tenacity and will with which he tried to advance in the service by any available means. When he finally became promoted by courting the daughter of his section chief, jilting her immediately afterwards, he set up a carefully planned system of bribe-taking and relaxed his Spartan regime. Named member of a government commission for construction projects, he expanded his venal operation and was at last able to hire a French chef and sport a carriage and pair. But he was caught red-handed, lost his post, and endured privations again while learning to divert the largest possible personal profit from the customs department into which he managed to worm his way.

A foolproof smuggling operation was the result of a long and patient study, and he began to live on a large scale. Because of a quarrel with his partner who subsequently denounced him, he barely escaped prison, was again dishonorably dismissed, and crawled back into his hole to eke out a living as a legal agent. During an investigation he came across the lucrative possibility of the sale of defunct serfs, and with the few thousands that he had cached away when the smuggling scandal broke, he started anew. At the end of this mean, stifling saga that reads like the reverse of a success story, fortitude and endurance being used to shabby ends, Gogol asks himself whether Chichikov is really a scoundrel or whether the modern name for him can be expressed by the word "acquirer." [19]

But Chichikov is not a Plyushkin; he does not crave possessions for their own sake, nor is he riddled with anxiety to achieve status like Major Kovalev in *The Nose*. His is the more Philistine yearning to enjoy the pleasures that a small fortune brings: ease, material creature comforts, a buxom wife, and a host of descendants. With ruthless single-mindedness he places his not inconsiderable resources of patience, cunning, and flexibility at the service of these petty ambitions.

In contrast to the humdrum manor life that he enters, Chichikov appears as a dynamic figure. He is shown as a man set apart from the static mores of the country squires by his mobility, his apparent rootlessness, and his operative environment consisting of one brichka, two servants, and three pieces of luggage. Again Gogol holds us with an illusion of reality based on pragmatic effects. This is the realistic texture of the hero and he seems to bring a fresh current of life. When everything about Chichikov is revealed, we realize that he is not less fixed in his world than his partners in chicanery are in theirs. The sordid adventures that earmark his career do not move outwardly, but circle spirally around his single obsession to which he remains as fettered as Plyushkin to avarice, Nozdrev to fertile lies, Manilov to sentimental reverie. Like them he is indifferent to the larger world, but as a creature dedicated to the fulfillment of a devouring ambition, he excels in ruthlessness, cynicism, cunning, and greed. Manilov's qualms about the transaction are easily dismissed; the indignation expressed by Sobakevich concerning Plyushkin's starving of his peasants has no effect on Chichikov other than spurring him on to visit an estate where there are so many casualties. To Korobochka's objection to the fearful nature of the merchandise, he answers crudely that she need not worry about graveyard bones.

A ripening awareness that Gogol has conceived his hero, despite a contradictory show of appearances, as a reflection of the moral and spiritual bankruptcy of the milieu that he visits is strengthened by his very behavior, recalling the mannerisms of his hosts. There is a touch of "Manilovism" in the over-refined way in which Chichikov holds a violet to his nose each time his unwashed servant approaches him; he shares with Sobakevich the predatory skill of the money grabber; and the constant preoccupation of looking for the most lucrative bargain, shared by Chichikov, is one that consumes Nozdrev's time. But ironically enough, it is the landed proprietess who seems to have stepped out of an earlier century whom this representative of the new mercantilism resembles most. They are both full of bustling energy and thrive in the intensely practical, limited world of moneyed detail that clicks contentedly to the cash register of petty calculation; and although shrewd, neither is endowed with strong mental equipment. Korobochka is monumentally stupid. Possibly, an intelligent man might not realize what a dangerous fool she is, much in the same manner as the perceptive mayor of *The Inspector General* is duped by Khlestakov's simple-mindedness and unbelievable frivolity. And Chichikov himself is not overly bright; it is downright silly of him, for example, to disclose any part of his swindle to the obviously unreliable and mercurial Nozdrev.

The casket that Chichikov always carries with him and which symbolizes him contains a tiny secret drawer—his heart—so quickly pulled in and out by its owner that one never knows how much money it holds. Overladen with all kinds of trashy souvenirs, the box reminds one of Korobochka's money bags hidden among layers of petticoats and shawls. Gogol draws another comparison when he invites the reader to wonder with him at the widow's immunity to a new idea "that bounces off [her] the way a rubber ball bounces off a wall." [20] Chichikov is round and bouncy like a ball, and his name—one that the author had once read on a store sign—when voiced, gives off precisely the sound of a ball being hit against the wall twice.

In the Gogolian reconstruction of the world, untoward happenings cut through the fiber of logic and the normal sequence of events, leaving everything in disarray. Chichikov plunges headlong into disaster at the very moment when he seems to be most successful and secure. The alerted reader is ready for the unexpected climaxes, usually planned with studied care. When Khlestakov is writing his damning letter, for instance, we know in advance from the order given to the postmaster in the first act that the mayor's humiliation must inevitably follow. In the same way, at the ball given in Chichikov's honor, Nozdrev's tipsy appearance and what has been told of his flair for scandal, leads naturally enough to the consternation of all present when he jovially and loudly acclaims the most important guest as the famous buyer of dead souls.

During the night of the ball a curious-looking conveyance rumbles through the outlying streets of the town "that was not a tarantas, nor a carriage, nor a chaise, but rather a full-cheeked melon on wheels" filled to bursting "with cushions shaped like tobacco pouches, rolling pins, pillows stuffed with bread rusks, biscuits, doughnuts, pretzels, a chicken pie, and even one of salted beef that peeped coyly over the top." [21] Its owner was Korobochka, and with her arrival, Chichikov was doomed. For she has hurried to town—and this is Gogol's supreme hyperbolic flourishing of her cupidity and dimwittedness—to find out what price dead souls were now bringing, as she quaked with apprehension that she might have been cheated.

IV   *The Dynamics of Rumor*

With Chichikov's return to the town where he registers the deeds of sale, the texture and rhythm of the narrative change as radically and abruptly as does the atmosphere of a quiet room when its doors are suddenly opened onto the noonday traffic of a busy street. In the following four chapters the intensified portraits of the rural eccentrics cede place to the collective image of a provincial capital. In a preliminary outline to this second part, Gogol jotted down his ideas of the town: "Extreme vacuousness, empty chatter. Uncontrolled gossip stemming from lack of anything to do that becomes highly comical." [22] These jottings take on body as he describes the excitement generated among the urban elite when it becomes known that Chichikov has bought four hundred serfs—the standard price for each male serf was 200 rubles—that he is going to settle them in an outlying province, and that he must therefore be a millionnaire. Such is the latent power of the word that he becomes a hero even to those who have nothing to gain from him, but simply wish to be admitted into his moneyed presence. This camera obscura view, in antithesis to the slow-moving pace of the visits where the characters were solidified cumulatively, is dynamic with abundant incidents, fragmentarily and impressionistically drawn. Clearly, Gogol is enjoying himself. His pen, vibrating with malice, blocks out representative groups from among the bureaucrats who remain nameless, and as in the Mirgorod stories, he flashes exposés of the least attractive aspects of the provincial milieu.

The pretentiousness and hypocrisy of the town ladies receive special attention. In the minutiae of etiquette, rivalling their Moscow and Petersburg sisters, they are careful to drive about in open carriages, as fashion decrees, with a footman in gilded livery swaying behind. Their sartorial elegance and refined speech shun such crudities as "I blew my nose" or "I sweated" or "I spat" replacing them with "I relieved my nose," "I had to resort to my handkerchief."

As for their husbands, Gogol assures us mischievously—catching them at orgies of eating and drinking, followed by the serious business of sitting down to cards—that these officials were exceedingly enlightened men: "This one would read Karamzin, that one the *Moscow News*, and another perhaps would read nothing whatever." [23]

Marginally, Gogol jabs again as in his great comedy at the flagrant venality prevailing among high and low ranking civil servants. The head clerk of the purchasing division, for example, has so developed the art of demanding a bribe without seeming to, that even the experienced Chichikov is taken aback. But it is for the visitor's sudden aura of wealth and the heady chemistry it works on his entourage that the author reserves his most savage satirical thrust. Gogol had been repelled and fascinated by gold early in his life; that a yearning for it may destroy a man is the theme of his first Dikanka tale, and it drenches in Gothic horror certain scenes in *The Portrait*. Here he grapples with it on a mean human level, reducing its odium by a denigrating mockery of those who are affected by it. All the local dignitaries become effusively friendly to Chichikov after the recording of his purchase deeds. The ladies who on first meeting had barely noticed him, now grow ecstatic over his charm and good looks, each feels secretly in love with him, and he receives an anonymous letter whose writer begs him to escape with her from the suffocating city to an unspoiled country retreat.

The conversation which takes place the morning after the ball, resulting from Korobochka's trip to town, is possibly the best known in Russian fiction. It is a masterpiece of excited feminine chatter. A "simply agreeable" lady hurries to the house of her friend, a "lady agreeable in all respects," to impart the thrilling news. Gogol apologizes, as he has done many times before, for not revealing the ladies' names for—who knows—there may very well be persons with similar names who could be offended. Therefore he keeps to soubriquets by which the ladies are known in the town and which now have become immortalized. The affectedly effusive dialogue punctuated with emotional exclamations and sprayed with French words—which Gogol unfailingly makes fun of—is of stupefying triteness. Only momentarily diverted by a discussion of the latest fashion in scalloped bodices, which nearly ends in a quarrel over a dress pattern, the "agreeable" visitor plunges into the excitement of Korobochka's alleged encounter with Chichikov who, armed to the teeth had awakened her in the dead of night and at gunpoint had demanded all her dead souls for a fifteen ruble note. Both ladies are still puzzled by the reference to "dead souls," and the "simply agreeable" lady who is not mentally overactive could do no more than remain agitated. Her hostess of a more inventive turn of mind, still smarting from Chichikov's preference at the ball for the governor's sixteen-year-old daughter, immediately surmises that the nature of these purchases is only a smoke screen for the far more complicated plan of the abduction of the governor's daughter.

In yet another pseudo-genial aside Gogol—happy to ruffle academic feathers—begs the reader's indulgence toward this feminine way of establishing evidence not much different from the zealous university scholar fitting an appealing conjecture into a pattern that he projects as fact. The two ladies set out in different directions and within half an hour the entire town, galvanized by the news of Chichikov's perfidy, gives itself up to a frenzy of speculation, suspicions, and slander.

Gogol seems happiest in creating chaos that stems from irreversible, snowballing rumor. His talent for distortion and hyperbole is peculiarly suited to exploit the comic possibilities of a situation wherein shallow and simple minds are swayed by piquant hearsay. The depiction of an agitated crowd shaken by a fantastic rumor, which Gogol also employs to animate the last pages of *The Nose* and *The Overcoat,* is exuberantly funny. It is but a trial balloon, a prelude to a new high in comedy reached in the wild conjectures about Chichikov which run their course through Chapters Nine and Ten.

All the townspeople are stirred up; even those who have not left their houses for years, preferring to vegetate on a sofa in a dressing gown, now appear in drawing rooms to join the gossip. The female contingent organizes a highly efficient defamation campaign which centers upon the abduction, to which a hastily-summoned Nozdrev adds specific and colorful details. When asked whether Chichikov intends to elope with the girl, Nozdrev answers unhesitatingly that the affair has been long planned, identifies the priest who is to marry them, states precisely the cost of the wedding and the names of the coachmen who are to have relays of fresh horses at every post station, and garnishes the account with so many spectacular irrelevancies that in their perplexity and bewilderment the officials refuse to believe him.

Besides, the visitor's amorous adventure worries them less than the ambiguous and menacing angle of the dead souls. It touches off suspicions among some of them that these "dead bodies" are related to recent mismanagements of the law in hushing up two gruesome incidents of manslaughter and a mass murder. Others are certain that Chichikov's appearance is tied in with a letter from the Governor General warning of a band of counterfeiters operating in their district. Could it be that Chichikov had been sent to investigate the matter or is he himself a forger hiding among them? Who *is* Chichikov? Invention upon invention spirals uncontrollably among the bureaucrats. Some say he may be Napoleon in flight from St. Helena and bent upon ruining Russia once more. The chief of police, veteran of 1812 who had once seen the French emperor, concedes that Napoleon and Chichikov have a certain resemblance in height and profile.

The postmaster suddenly believes that Chichikov is no other than Captain Kopeykin who had lost an arm and a leg in the service, was refused a pension by the war minister despite vigorous personal petitioning, and in revenge has organized bands of run-away peasants to steal money from state banks and give it away—Robin Hood style—to the poor. The long story, strung along with the most hackneyed clichés of provincial officialese, is listened to carefully, but reluctantly rejected on the grounds that Kopeykin after all was armless and legless.

Gogol set great store by the Kopeykin story but not, as some Soviet critics would have it,[24] because it offered him a way of casting his satirical net ever wider to draw in examples of callousness and indifference to the public welfare even among the highest government echelons. He readily modified the tale to avoid the censor's objections by transforming Kopeykin into the author of his own misfortunes. Nor would it seem that the Kopeykin episode serves only as a set-in piece to break and vary the narrative in a novel already richly embroidered with entertaining digressions. More likely, since the dynamics of rumor were used to hold up a mirror to the backwardness and stupidity of the provincial mentality nourished on dime novel fiction, the essential absurdity was deepened and enhanced by the transformation of the portly, dignified Chichikov into a bandit, a romantic abductor, Napoleon travelling incognito, and finally into an armless and legless war veteran. While gossip rolls and surges around him, Chichikov, confined to bed with a cold, knows nothing about it until he emerges again for a round of social calls and finds all doors closed to him. After Nozdrev's impromptu visit initiates him into all the refinements of his bankrupt romance with the sixteen-year-old beauty, the dazed and frightened councillor gives hasty orders for his departure. His *brichka* is held up for a few minutes by the funeral procession of the prosecutor who had brooded so long over the town's disturbance that one morning he simply dies. Afraid of being seen, Chichikov settles deeply into a corner and is unaware that the ladies in mourning caps, gesturing animatedly as they pass him in a closed carriage, are now completely absorbed in discussing the arrival of the new Governor General and the gowns they plan to wear to his first ball. For them Chichikov has become a non-presence. As the procession moves on and Chichikov's light carriage turns off into a side street, Gogol has his hero exit in a superbly designed finale. It is as if two halves of a stage-set were being rolled off into opposing wings, the actors no longer speaking, but maintaining their stance until the fall of the curtain. Created by rumor and destroyed by rumor, his departure as little noticed as his arrival, Chichikov drives out of town, passing rapidly mile after mile of "water wells, dreary villages, sooty samovars, peasant women . . . wretched little towns and their counter shops with floor barrels, bast sandals, loaves of bread" [25] and vanishes into the distance.

V *Critics' Interpretation of the Novel*

What is the meaning of this work that does not conform to the standard definition of a novel? The middle-aged hero lacks all heroic quality; he is as dull as his "adventures" which are practical to the extreme, and although everyone is concerned with them, they do not affect any of the characters, and the situations throughout remain basically unchanged. Chichikov's activities in dealing with things that do not exist take place in a kind of vacuum. Nothing really happens, the swindle does not materialize, and the plot that never gets off the ground is arrested as the hero disappears in a whirl of dust, forgetting everything he just left behind.

In *Dead Souls* Gogol aspired to recreate all of Russia. He had to devise a structure that allowed him to introduce representative Russian types from the landed gentry, government officials, and the peasant class and he solved the problem with the use of the main episode—Chichikov's travels across provincial Russia in search of dead souls. Beyond the estates he visits and the friends he makes in the town of N, there is implied in the nature of his undertaking an endless vista of similar visits and similar contacts made in other similar towns. The synecdoche principle is at work giving us an open-ended view of the entire country as it is represented by a typical part of it where the hero under observation is making one of his many business stops.

This impression is strengthened by consistent generalizations. The brichka symbolizing Chichikov's income and status is of the kind used by middling bachelors; the features of the inn are those of any other inn; and the town is like all other towns. Nozdrev, Gogol assures us, exists everywhere among us; Mme. Manilov's education which consisted of speaking French, playing the pianoforte, and knitting small gifts summed up the offering of any school attended by girls of her class; and her husband's steward behaved like any other in a job catering to prosperous villagers and creating hardships for the poorer ones. Against the background of provincial officialdom only the chief of police is singled out, probably because this smooth and skillful bribetaker, also a genial and garrulous imbiber and a good hand at whist, reflects the way of life of his milieu. Through this correlation of the particular and the general, Gogol attempts to assemble and project the main elements of contemporary Russian life. Did he succeed in realizing this first objective? Or was it replaced, as he wrote and labored over his writing, by other illuminations that gave another significance to his masterpiece?

The liberal-minded critics of Gogol's day viewed *Dead Souls* as a superbly realistic re-creation of modern Russia. For them Gogol's debasing portraits of the landed gentry were a direct and valid criticism of the decaying landowners' class, and his revelation of the venality and pettiness of small town life was a castigation of the tsarist bureaucracy. To the most gifted and most important avant-garde critic of the age, Vissarion Belinsky, Gogol's images appeared as real reflections of life because they epitomized the malignant tumor of Russian society. Gogol's concern for preserving the national flavor and the concreteness of his characters was for Belinsky a guarantee of their authenticity. Belinsky brought to his critiques a high sense of personal com-

[156]

mitment and an incorruptible judgment. But as a member of the radical intelligentsia he was pledged to show abuses of the autocracy, and since strict censorship stifled the expression of all but official opinion, he saw in literature the only effective weapon for combatting the intolerable conditions of poverty, inequality, bureaucratic corruption, and serfdom. He bestowed on artistic endeavor the burden of moral and social reform and decreed that it was to deal with the contemporary, the typical, and the national. Above all literature had to be truthful. These qualities he believed were to be found in Gogol.

As early as 1835, he had singled out the almost unknown author of the Mirgorod stories as the leader of Russian literature that was moving away from the poetry of the ideal to prose fiction— that is, the poetry of reality. For Belinsky, Gogol was the supreme realist, and he praised in his work the simplicity of plot, a faithful representation of actuality, emphasis on the national character and humor that he explained as a mercilessly accurate exposure of the negative aspects of Russian society. When Gogol's novel was published, Belinsky had already consolidated his position as an embattled propagandist for social reform.[26] Consequently he interpreted *Dead Souls* as a call to arms for Russian writers to fight for civilization, culture, and humanity in their struggle against official Russia. It is difficult to overestimate the prodigious influence that this critic exerted on the Russian intelligentsia with the peculiar vibrancy and drive of his polemical articles and from the vantage point of his passionately held ideological certitudes. Almost singlehandedly he engaged the more progressive-minded men of letters to discard the still very popular but outworn literary forms derived from German and French models which came under his special attack and to create works out of the native reality that "Gogol had been the first to look at clearly and boldly." [27]

This became the slogan of a new literary movement organized by Belinsky in the early 1840's. While contemptuously tagged the "Natural School" by Faddey Bulgarin for its predilection for the unseemly side of life,[28] Belinsky eagerly picked up the epithet to convey the authentic and the natural as opposed to the artificial and tendentious literary fiction favored by the reactionary press. Realism based on the contemporary understanding of Gogol shaped the program of the school which encoded social awareness, democratization, naturalness of approach, and observation as method. Typicality that in a prescriptive control over subject-matter selects the particular to imply the general was brought out time and again in the "physiological" sketch that became the hallmark of the school. This sketch profiled in densely descriptive, near-photographic detail, with frequent recourse to the Gogolian taboo-lifting technique, representative figures preferably from among the by-passed portion of the population where poverty and social injustice remained unresolved.

These sketches appear in *Otechestvennye zapiski* (*Notes of the Fatherland*) which Belinsky, the chief editor, made into the most prestigious progressive journal of the day. When in 1846 he was invited by Nikolay Nekrasov, a spokesman for revolutionary youth and prominent radical publisher, to join his staff on the *The Contemporary*, it became the rallying ideological guide and forum for members of the Natural School.

The school's earliest adherents included Vladimir Dahl (1801–1872) who wrote short stories and novelettes about the common people, but is better known for his valuable *Dictionary of the Great Russian Language;* Vladimir Sollogub (1814–1882), author of *The Coach*, a miscellany of loosely linked candid camera shots lined with a satirical inflection of merchants, landowners, clerks, and peasants met on a journey; and Yakov Butkov (1815–1856) whose *Summits of St. Petersburg* evoke the tenement atmosphere of *The Overcoat*, reaching in its sympathetic treatment of the garret dwellers to the philanthropic sentimentalism of *Poor Folk*, Dostoevsky's first published work. The latter increased the prestige of the school when it was enthusiastically greeted by Belinsky as a true successor to Gogol's fiction not only in its stylistic manner,[29] but in its humanitarian approach to the downtrodden copy clerk. Other vigorous and important works identified as belonging to the Natural School included Turgenev's *A Sportsman's Sketches* first published in *The Contemporary*, and the publication of *A Common Story* by Ivan Goncharov in which a strong plea for pragmatic reality is made as the hero gradually sheds his generous but impractical ideals, acclaimed by Belinsky as a masterpiece of Natural literature.

This literature, produced in the climate of moral and social protest against existing political conditions, held uppermost the need for educating the reading public in the hope it would lead to its own betterment but the school did not last much longer than the life of its founder and most passionate advocate. Writers who had been discovered and encouraged by Belinsky gradually freed themselves from the demands of a one-sided and partisan civic emphasis and began to enlarge their perception of life. The treatment of people became many-sided and objective. The type of Realism that was to dominate Russian letters for the next fifty years was far removed from Gogol, its putative master. As the critic D. S. Mirsky phrased it, little was inherited from Gogol but a keen observation of external detail, the device—particularly favored by Leo Tolstoy—of catching the essence of character through a physical trait or gesture.[30] During the decade of the 1840's the Natural School provided budding Realists with a common workshop for experimentation and realization of these writing techniques, but with respect to Gogol, the school and its presiding spirit caused wide and enduring harm.

By the power of his fiery polemic, personal persuasion, and intransigent dogmatically expressed convictions, Belinsky was able to impose his own belief in the social significance of Gogol's art on all his contemporaries of the liberal camp. No attack, however virulent, could have rendered a greater disservice to the writer than the density of adulatory barrage through which, improbably, Gogol appeared as a social and political reformer. Belligerent criticism of the world around him and a plea for moral and social betterment seemed to Belinsky, clearly and compellingly, the pillars that supported the edifice of Gogol's works. Because fact and contemporary circumstance interested him most, he saw in the writer's fiction—the abundance of concrete detail which had the look of actual life—the only reality. The inner reality that Gogol intuited—that of man's precarious balancing act between the norms and anti-norms of existence, and the ensuing ambiguities and absurdity of human behavior with its forays into the subconscious, the irrational, and the fantastic upon which Gogol brought to bear the great imaginative resources of his grotesque art—Belinsky either overlooked or was unable to recognize. His immense reputation insured his opinions as literary canon for the remainder of the century, thus, several successive generations of Russian readers taking their cue from Belinsky were to read Gogol narrowly, with only a dim awareness of the mainsprings of his dynamic and intractable genius.

After Belinsky's death in 1848, in the tense climate of brewing political reform, the progressive critics took their lead from him and recruited artistic literature into their opposition to the tsarist regime. Thus N. G. Chernyshevsky praised *Dead Souls* for its sociological relevance; N. A. Dobrolyubov detected a deep love for the common people in its author, and for the active social reformer, Alexander Herzen, Gogol was an ideological ally. This interpretation of Gogol's art, understandably enough, was taken up by Soviet critics who do not conceive a serious literary work without underlying political import. As early as 1912, Lenin defined Gogol as a political forebear, pointing to the enormous social significance of the portrait gallery in *Dead Souls,* and giving credit to Belinsky for recognizing the writer as the initiator of an attitude toward the landowning class that was to culminate in the revolution of 1917.[31] These statements have been variously echoed by Soviet scholars for the last five decades until they have crystallized into permanent articles of faith.

The close of the nineteenth century marked a temporary slackening in the revolutionary movement. Among writers and critics forging new, purely esthetic literary forms, a reaction set in against the myth-makers of the "sociological" Gogol. A reassessment of the writer was inevitable. Leaders of the Russian Symbolist movement took up the cudgels for him as an imaginative artist of the highest order unfettered by the demands of history, tradition, or class. The worlds he created, to their way of thinking, were imaginary worlds where actuality serving as a point of departure diffused into the private reality of the poet's vision. What Gogol once wrote about his heroes being the embodiment of his own vices and weaknesses [32] now gained legitimate status among the Symbolists. The poet Andrey Bely described Gogol's novel as an intricate geometrical design which shaped the ideal world of his creations.[33] To Vasily V. Rozanov, his characters were grotesque masks—tragic, comic, all caricatures—and *Dead Souls* itself, a huge edifice of waxworks.[34] Valery Bryusov held the sum of the novel to be one enormous inflated grotesque, a bizarre distortion of the real world beyond the range of normal experience,[35] while Dmitry Merezhkovsky was fascinated by what he sensed to be the universality of the devil permeating the Gogolian gallery of portraits.[36] Vladimir Nabokov continued the anti-sociological tradition in his brilliant and witty monograph on

Gogol by stressing the elements of the absurd and irrationally poetic in Gogol's stories and by pointing out the inconsequentiality of landscape: "Gogol's heroes happen to be Russian squires and officials; their imagined surroundings and social conditions are perfectly unimportant factors. . . ." [37]

Literary criticism, like trees, bends with the prevailing wind. The interpretations of Gogol's novel just summarized reflect the climate of particular current urgencies and seem to be mutually exclusive. And yet, upon impartial examination of the author's relation to his work and to his society, a middle position may be reached to accommodate Gogol as a social critic and as an introspective artist. There is little evidence to support the Soviet claim that Gogol felt a deep compassion for the peasants and underscored the cruelty of their masters.

When common people are introduced they are treated coldly and with brevity. This attitude is reflected in several passages. For example, during Chichikov's ride through a village, as part of the passing panorama "several muzhiks in sheepskin jackets, squatting on benches in front of the gates, were yawning as usual; fat-faced women, their breasts bound in shawls, leaned out of upper windows; out of the lower ones, a calf would be staring or a sow would be poking out its short-sighted snout." [38] A meaningless four-line dialogue on the sturdiness of the brichka's wheels that might or might not get as far as Kazan takes place between two countrymen lounging in front of a tavern. Servants appear throughout as a slatternly, irresponsible lot. Only two are named: the hero's valet Petrushka, distinguished by a special and disagreeable body odor and the dull-witted coachman Selifan, who is inclined to the bottle. In a prefatory comment to the description of the pair, the author apologizes to the reader—a man of his own class—for taking up his time with the lower orders. This attitude is natural to Gogol, himself a member of the nobility and a serf-owner. He takes serfdom for granted, as most American plantation owners at the same moment in history took slavery for granted, considering it an established institution in which certain human beings were regarded as chattel goods.

In the delineation of the main personages, however, there is a clearly discernible social indictment. Gogol himself may have been only dimly aware of it. Inherent in his power for distortion was the power to give form to a character by singling out one dominant trait, or "quirk" as he called it, and blowing it up to grotesque proportions with a mass of studiedly assembled detail. It was natural for him to choose those traits that made the most effective targets for his hyperbolic satire; moreover, since Gogol had given himself the mandate to present typical Russian phenomena "if only from one side," it was imperative that these traits be prevalent in the milieu of the Russian rural gentry. What gives commanding focus to this portraiture and makes it immortal is the universality of its types that have the finality of Molière's characters or of Jonson's humors and transcend local markings.

Bustling, stingy, silly widow Korobochka seems to have stepped out of a commedia dell' arte, while the hoarding Plyushkin is close kin to Harpagon, to Pushkin's *Avaricious Knight,* and other famous prototypes of the miser in Western literature. "Sobakevichism," "Manilovism," Nozdrevism" are expressions that have become part of Russian everyday speech and convey meanings which radiate beyond the country of their origin. Nonetheless, as Gogol's avant-garde contemporaries were quick to point out, the eccentricities of these three landowners have a native flavor. The parasitic mode of life of the Russian landowner, supported by plentiful, unpaid labor did tend to breed mental indolence, sloth, self-indulgence, and arbitrary and ruthless exploitation of human beings. Exposure of these conditions throughout the novel remains derivitive and unstressed. The scenes full of externality tell us only what serfbound Russia looked like, not what was really happening in it.

But Gogol shows a sensitivity to the social and economic realities of his society in yet another way. Drawing upon the sources of national and historical life, he points out the signs of degeneration among his peers with thematic explicitness. Vestiges of the eighteenth-century aristocrat remain in Nozdrev's dissipations and reckless impudent behavior. Manilov, stripped of all literary pretensions, appears as a blurred and drivelling remnant of the effete sentimentality that permeated Russian fiction in the wake of the pre-Romantic movement that swept over early nineteenth-century Russia. In a typical flash of Gogol's genius for the unexpected, from unimaginative Sobakevich who seems impervious and immune to change we hear the sentiment, regretfully expressed, that the vital forces of the nation are ebbing away, that people among the living "are so many flies, not people," and the implication that he, too, compared with his father, is inferior in toughness, vitality, and strength.

There is support for the argument of the Symbolists that the Gogolian world for all its apparent attachments to nineteenth-century Russia, was the creation of Gogol's imagination and was inhabited by unreal and hollow men. A unique feature of Gogol's art was the reconstruction of life in terms of a reality packed and stuffed with "things." These things, chosen ingeniously and described with satirical care, are made to represent the nature, attitude, and state of mind of their owners. Inanimate objects that in the usual way of storytelling are subordinate to people become living symbols of them and take on a life of their own. Imposing the inanimate upon the animate, the narrative slants into comic distortion. Ivan Shponka, for example, sees his future wife as a piece of woolen yardage (*Ivan Fyodorovich Shponka and His Aunt*), a handsome Greek nose strolls down the avenue (*Nevsky Prospect*), virile military whiskers peep into the bodices of young countrywomen (*The Carriage*), Akaky Akakyvich yearns for a new overcoat as he would for a bride-to-be (*The Overcoat*).

In *Dead Souls* this reversal of images dominates character delineation. So persuasive is this rearrangement of reality that we are not sure whether we remember Sobakevich, a heavy bear of a man, or his pot-bellied walnut bureau on four huge legs—a "perfect bear of a bureau"—which implies that it is like its owner. Not Manilov, but his chairs, one upholstered in expensive silk and the others waiting eternally to be recovered, seem to be real. Nozdrev, with his incessant scatter-brained chatter, is a personification of his own hurdy-gurdy; as though something had gone wrong inside, it plays a mixture of mazurkas, marches and waltzes long after it has run down. The process is transposed when Gogol speaks of a young woman who, wearing a patterned shawl, takes her place self-effacingly at mealtimes: "There are faces that are there not as primary objects but just to be foreign spots or dots upon objects. They always sit in the same way and on the same seat and you might consider them as furniture. . . ." [39] A world where things are in the saddle, driving people on, and where objects are summoned to identify a man in the same manner that a mask tags the puppets of a marionette theater, appeared to the Symbolists as an irreal world. They described

Dead Souls as a huge fantasy made up of a hyperbolic profusion and variety of externals that Gogol's vision distorted into magnificent grotesque and that was completely detached from the actual and the human.

VI *Who Are the Dead Souls?*

Who are the dead souls? Not the deceased peasants certainly, whose very names read off the bill of sale evoke for Gogol the strength and endurance of the Russian people. Sobakevich extols the soundness and dexterity of the late shoemaker Maxim and the carpenter Probka. The possible fate of Plyushkin's runaway serfs who face flogging, imprisonment, and death by the roadside in their bid for freedom draw poetry even from stolid Chichikov as he checks off the list. The intense life of these invisible and non-existent serfs is pitted against the weak will and moral decay of the landowners who stagnate in an immeasurable spiritual wasteland and are indeed vacuous, inert, dead souls. The impression of immobility is deepened by Gogol's presentation of them as fully fashioned at the moment when they first appear. Only Plyushkin, the "corpse's corpse," [40] is granted a flashback into his past intended to humanize him just as Chichikov's antecedents in the last chapter serve to explain his absurd and ghoulish undertaking. Nevertheless, in human terms, Chichikov does not seem to exist. He arrives out of nowhere, bringing with him like an agent of the devil a greedy and gleeful interest in the appurtenances of death—epidemics and famine—and a devil's concentration on the success of his enterprise. There is something mechanical in the nimbleness and affability of his behavior, and significantly when he leaves the town to disappear into the void from which he came, the havoc he has caused is already forgotten.

The reader is caught and held by the bleakness and stagnation of the world Gogol pictures. The author seems to make an unflinchingly personal appeal to our understanding of the pessimistic drive of his art. That he was haunted by the fear of being vilified and misinterpreted comes through very early in the strain and exultation of the lines written to Zhukovsky when he was first settling down to "this, my first decent thing: Vastly great is my creation and not soon will it be finished. Still new classes and many kinds of people will rise up against me, but what can I do? It is my fate to be at war with my countrymen." [41]

Dead Souls

Using pages of the novel itself as a forum, Gogol presents an apologia in the much quoted opening of the seventh chapter for the unsung writer who, in contrast to the fortunate author of lofty subjects and virtuous heroes, "dares to expose everything that is always present but remains unobserved; all that fearful, overwhelming, slimy mire of trivialities that entraps our lives; all that is deeply hidden within everyday, cold, broken characters with which our life path, at times sad and dreary, swarms." [42] He forestalls the "judgment of the epoch" (a phrase solemnly invoked four times) that considers lowly and unimportant Gogol's own heroes and does not recognize "that much spiritual depth is needed to illuminate a picture drawn from the despised layer of life." [43] In ruminating upon Chichikov's unsavory character and the ruthless exposure of his skullduggery, and anticipating the popular demand for some redeeming trait to make the hero more palatable, Gogol chastises the reader who refuses to look "at mankind's poverty laid bare," preferring to lull his mind with only that which is "splendidly beautiful" and enticing.

The teaching role of the artist who takes upon himself to bring out the contemptible, the trivial, and the unworthy becomes clear and confirms Gogol's moral purpose already implicit in *After the Theater*, his answer to the critics who had been indignant at the absence of virtue and perfection in *The Inspector General*. But the sensitive expatriate writer felt that he still had to confront the "so-called patriots," those to whom he scathingly refers as "accumulating neat little bank rolls, living at the expense of others . . . who will come running out of their cozy little nooks if they get wind of . . . some bitter truth that in their opinion insults the fatherland," [44] and who will hasten to defame the one who pronounces it. With uncanny precision, Gogol had predicted in these last passages of the novel the objections that would be raised by the literary censor. One way of battening down the hatches against the storm of protest from chauvinistic censors who would consider *Dead Souls* a slanderous view of Russia, was to argue and plead personally with the authorities for permission to publish his work.

There was yet another subtle, writer's way: While he was completing *Dead Souls*, Gogol also took on the rewriting of *Taras Bulba*, the new version differing from the original in its stronger emphasis on national unity, the beneficent power of the mon-

[165]

archy, and the author's own evident love for his country. It appeared shortly after the publication of *Dead Souls,* and it seems more likely that he hoped to weaken the charges of anti-patriotism his work would incite by having an antithesis to it.[45] The national coloration of the Cossack epic is painted more vividly: everywhere the word "Ukrainian" is replaced by the word "Russian." The Cossacks now display the Great Russian character and a tremendous show of Russian strength pours into battle. Fervent speeches about Holy Russia are uttered by the leaders, and even Andrey who had been portrayed previously as somewhat cowardly, now becomes a daring Russian warrior who rushes into the fray with reckless courage, eager to be worthy of the love he had won.

The internal and external defense that Gogol had constructed in an effort to win the approbation of patriotically inclined or morally timorous readers collapsed, or so it seemed to him, and for a reason that he did not foresee. In a post-mortem reflection on *Dead Souls,* Gogol wrote that it was not the disclosure of Russia's social evils that had disturbed the public, but the ubiquitous presence of *poshlost'* in the novel. This *poshlost'* had tainted all the characters and situations, and what had frightened everyone was the fact that his "heroes follow one after the other exuding more and more *poshlost'.* I would sooner have been forgiven the invention of outright monsters, but *poshlost'* I was not forgiven." [46]

What is "*poshlost'* "? It is not easy to find an English equivalent. In several pages of bravura Vladimir Nabokov pronounces it untranslatable.[47] The Russian meaning compresses protean forms of mediocrity and banality, self-complacency, vulgarity, total absence of longings or aspiration, and a self-centered existence unruffled by any but the most trivial things. It is best conveyed by the impression its ordinariness and triteness makes upon a sensitive and vigorous mind, and this was strikingly imaged by Gogol when referring to his frightened reader as one "to whom it seemed after having read the whole book, exactly as though he were emerging from some stifling cellar into God's world." [48] And Gogol himself was frightened by it. The Romantic in him was appalled by the stagnant human morass that the satirist had created. Oppressed and revolted by what he was doing, he would at times turn away from the object of his satirical observation toward "God's world" in an outburst of personal emotion that yearned for the spontaneous, the generous, the beautiful. These lyrical thrusts into the impassively good-humored and yet maliciously woven texture of the narrative give it yet another dimension in which the author communicates his underground protest against his own compulsively grotesque vision of the world and the limitations of that vision.

How else can one interpret the indubitably sincere and poignant writer's soul-searching of his art in the following well-known passage: "But for a very long time I am still destined by some magic power to wander together with my strange heroes, to gaze at the whole, huge, rushing movement of life, through laughter heard by the world and through tears that are unperceived and unknown to it." [49] Clearly, the artist laments his inability to widen his creative horizons; he can do no more than reflect as in a crooked mirror a distorted and truncated world; but even as he expresses his anguish, he senses in the succeeding lines that new sources of artistic power will be revealed to him and he will be stirred by images and shapes as yet barely understood. "And still far away is that time when awesome inspiration will break forth like a storm and well up like a fountain in another head that is clothed in sacred terror and radiance and when men will hear, in fearful trepidation, the majestic thunder of other eloquent words. . . ." [50] The geared movement of this uterance that shifts abruptly from present near despair into a rhapsodic prose aria of a vision into the future beats more forcibly and with a swelling undertow of self-liberating lyricism in Gogol's two great appeals to Russia.

In picturesque, monument-studded Italy, the exile recalls the flat monotony and desolation of the Russian plains and wonders at the mysterious pull that his own land exerts upon him despite its bleakness and sadness. Just as the artist perceives new vistas for his art, moving him to abandon his grotesquely shaped world, so the expatriate, losing sight of the spiritual and moral void of the Russian provinces that he had been laying bare, is struck by the potential greatness of the vast, unexplored land. "Is it not here, within thee and of thee, that there is to be born a limitless idea, when thou art thyself endless and boundless?" [51] Again, reality is loser to the dream. Russia's underdevelopment, regarded by the Slavophils as a sign of her spiritual purity and moral endurance and becoming for Dostoevsky the guarantee of her Messianic role in Western Europe, caused Gogol to make a similar prophecy in the panegyric that concludes *Dead Souls*. As Chichikov is driven away in his brichka, the author also rushes ahead with winged words, carried away by his own emotionally charged rhetoric:

And art thou not flying onward, my Russia, like a fiery, never to be outdistanced troika? . . . The horses—what horses! Your manes are whirlwinds! . . . You hear from above the familiar song and at once, in unison, your bronze chests swelling and your hoofs barely touching the earth, transformed into straight lines, cleaving the air you gallop ahead, God-inspired. . . . Where art thou going, Russia? Give me thy answer! But Russia gives none. Wondrously does the jingle bell thrill; the air torn to shreds becomes wind; everything that is on the earth and in the fields flies past, and all the other peoples and nations stand aside and give thee right of way.[52]

Other emotionally-charged pauses had afforded Gogol respite from the stultifying *poshlost'* of his universe: he romanticizes about the spellbinding lure of the fast troika "along a long, long road," or just before moving into the description of Plyushkin's avarice-wrinkled senility, weaves a reverie of his own youth always avid for the excitement of new places and new impressions.

Time and again Gogol deliberately retards the flow of his story in the manner of Sterne or Pushkin in *Eugene Onegin* by ambushing the reader into spirited digressions on such diverse and incongruous subjects as the vigor of the Russian language, habits of country bachelors, or the quality of a meal at a roadside tavern. In a show of exuberant irrelevance that curves the narrative into yet another direction, he treats us to a plethora of "never again" people who burst into the novel with an irrepressible life of their own. The camera-shot of a nameless lieutenant whom we catch only once in his hotel room after midnight, sunk into an admiration of his new boots which he tries on over and over again, is pure virtuosity in writing. It defies analysis. Quite independent of Chichikov's adventures, such people who have no relation to the story live for an instant in a bright, marginal reality. Similar parenthetical characters appear in *The Inspector General*, as well. There, for example, we learn from a letter about sister Anne's brother "who has grown very fat, but still plays the violin." Or, while the police sergeant explains why the main street is not patrolled, we hear fortuitously that the policeman Prokhorov, just brought in from the suburbs where he was sent out to break up a brawl, himself got drunk, was doused with two pails of water, but has not yet come to.

In *Dead Souls* these digressive "never again" personalities are not so simply introduced. For the most part, they appear under the guise of similes taking on momentary life as subjects of subordinate clauses.[53] Here are two superb instances of this literary tour de force. A description of Plyushkin's smile:

All at once, something like a ray of warmth glided over those wooden features; an expression of—no, not feeling, but of a reflection of a feeling; a phenomenon like that of the unexpected surfacing again of a drowning man that brings a joyous shout from the crowd gathered on the bank; but it is in vain that his rejoicing brothers and sisters cast a rope from the bank and wait for another glimpse of the back or the arms wearied from the struggle—he had come up for the last time. All is over and the stilled surface of the implacable element becomes even more fearful and desolate. So did Plyushkin's face, after the feeling that had momentarily glided over it, look even meaner and more callous.[54]

A first glimpse of Sobakevich's face peering through the window: ". . . full and round as a Moldavian calabash, called 'gorlyanka,' out of which in Russia balalaikas are made, light two-stringed balalaikas, the adornment and delight of a smart, twenty-year-old peasant lad, a saucy dandy who not only winks at but whistles after the snowy-breasted and snowy-necked young girls who gather round to listen to his soft-stringed strumming." [55]

VII *Gogol's Language and Style*

Not until 1902, when the Symbolists discovered the originality of the Gogolian method and mode of composition, was any serious appraisal made of Gogol's verbal art. The critic V. Vinogradov first noted the "impudent" intrusion of "low" vocabulary dealing with such hitherto taboo functions as snorting, snoring, belching, spitting, and nose-blowing that Gogol had appropriated, bringing thereby a new plebeian flavor into polite Russian literature.[56] In *How Gogol's "Overcoat" Was Made* (*Kak Sdelana*

"Shinel'" Gogolya) the Formalist critic Boris Eikhenbaum explains the built-in grotesque of the narrator's speech as emanating from an intricate system of assonance where mimicry, articulation, and "sound gestures" take precedence over logical meaning.[57] Andrey Bely was torn between his admiration for the poetical images of Gogol's early Ukrainian stories that were "extraordinary in their blended profusion of color, scent, and sound" and the glaring grammatical errors that are threaded through Gogolian prose.[58]

Here rather than in the taboo-lifting usage Gogol strengthens and injects Russian language with fresh energies. He plays havoc with syntax, shifting suffixes and prefixes at will, making adjectives out of adverbs, and arbitrarily changing case endings of irregular nouns. He makes up neologisms, infusing into the *Sorochinsky Fair* numerous Ukrainian idioms and turns of phrase, drawing from a rich personal collection of colorful sayings, local dialects, proverbs, colloquialisms, social euphemisms, and the jargon of the gambler, hunter, bureaucrat, and journalist that filled his notebooks. The result is, lexically, a baroque extravaganza, and from it Gogol constructs a highly complex and unique prose.

The mainsprings of this language are mobility, variety, rhythm. In style, it passes easily from highly pitched lyrical rhetoric which depends on assonance, alliteration, hypnotic repetition of certain sensuous sounds for rhythm and occasionally even rhyme to the pungent comicality of farce or good-natured urbanity. Here, everyday speech crackles with puns, sly drollery, and irrelevant titters used primarily for their auditory appeal, as if Gogol wanted to saturate the page with all the phonic variations in which the Russian language is so rich. This prose read aloud only gains in power and obviously presents almost insurmountable difficulties to the translator. A pithy and unmentionable epithet wrung out of a muzhik during a verbal sparring match with Chichikov's coachman moves Gogol to a rapturous aside on the inimitable quality of Russian wit that "unblemished by German, French, Finnish or any other tribe . . . is never at a loss, doesn't brood over it, and knows how to burst out from the very heart . . ." [59] with an aptly turned Russian word. We know, however, that Gogol worked long and hard over his writing, submitting the highly-charged, far-stretching paragraphs to at least seven or eight thorough revisions before copying them into a final draft.[60] It is tantalizing to speculate how much effort his many verbal victories cost, as for example, the following typically Gogolian sentence, generated, humbly enough, by the sound of Chichikov's light carriage driving into a courtyard at night, and then moving spirally, widening the metaphor with sound gesture, and glance until all these sensations are locked into one illuminating, encapsulating image:

Meanwhile, the dogs were barking in all kinds of voices: one, throwing up his head, howled so long and with such zeal as if he were getting a handsome salary for it; another rapidly clipping his notes like a sexton; in between them, like the jingle bell mail coach tinkled a scrambling soprano, probably a young puppy; and all of these were finally capped by a grandfather bass endowed with a sturdy canine nature, for he was as rumbly in his throat as a basso profundo when the choir recital is in full swing; the tenors rising on tiptoe in their ardor to bring out the high note, all heads flung back and straining upwards while he alone tucking his unshaven chin into his cravat, squatting almost to the floor, lets out a note that makes the window-panes shake and rattle.[61]

VIII *Master of Modern Comic Grotesque*

Dead Souls gave a new dimension to Russian literature and became a supreme example of modern comic grotesque. For over a century critics have grappled with the problem of Gogol's complex satirical art, and he has been variously labeled as a Symbolist, the father of Russian Realism, and a disillusioned Romantic. Romantic he was in his yearning for the Weltanschauung of the German pre-Romantic and Romantic philosophers and poets, feeding his imagination on their esthetics of universal humanism. They grafted themselves on his emotional framework as amorphous and puerile reveries and continued to live in him, abstract, aimless, and sentimental nowhere more vividly than in the startlingly subjective and vehement lyrical interludes that occasionally patch with purple the pithy flow of his comic spirit. The breathlessness and half-anguished pace of these passages are found even earlier in the Ukrainian tales where fantasy, excessively exaggerated, bloated into supernatural horror in *Terrible Vengeance*, and *St. John's Eve* or yet another distortion in *Sorochinsky Fair*, as the excitement of the carnival dance rises to a macabre pitch with the drunken wobbling heads of the old women in a Goya-like flash of traditional medieval iconography.

These were minor literary trappings of pure Romantic grotesque that were on a par with Gogol's marked predilection for the gargoyle-haunted Middle Ages. They became superfluous when he began to draw on the reality of his social milieu which from adolescence he had despised, hated, and feared. There he found a natural climate for his disfiguring genius and created a vision of the world that, once freed of its early Romantic coloration, reached the depths and multi-range sensitivity of a grotesque that adumbrates modern Surrealist perception. It is a world made startling on first contact by absences. No real issues are presented, only scenes; no normalizing factors are present in the ordinary traffic of social exchange, such as attempts at a responsible relationship, understanding, or communication with one another, but a lack of compassion, generosity, friendship, or love that testify to the exile of the heart. Having removed from reality elements that make it tolerable, Gogol proceeds to mutilate it further with a transfiguration of men, animals, and objects that makes the familiar look alien and bizarre: Men are changed into hideous beasts, scurrying insects, or even sausages, cucumbers, and toothbrushes.

A number of principles are operative here. One is the consistent use of hyperbole that inflates actuality to an unrecognizable outsizing of itself and conveys a feeling of dislocation and violence. Another is a systematic breaking up of habitually integrated entities into independent and arbitrary fragments of themselves A nose leaves its owner's face for a week's spree in town; the back of a jacket is writing briskly and even with a flourish; a head sits in a stand-up collar as if it were in a carriage. Still another more subtle alteration of the real world is Gogol's rejection of the particular and individual in favor of generalizations that seem to underline the universality of the chaos that he depicts. The town visited by Chichikov is like all other provincial towns; Akaky Akakievich is one of countless lower ranking civil servants; backward Korobochka is a simplified reflection of more fashionable city matrons. In his major creative effort—that of constructing a gallery of heroes—Gogol reaches the absolute of typification. It was neither within the power, nor was it the purpose of his art to bring to life, as did the pen of Pushkin or

Dead Souls

Tolstoy, such idiosyncratic personalities as Tatyana Larina, Prince Andrey, or Anna Karenina who worked out their destinies to a rhythm distinctly and separately their own. Nor was it for Gogol to capture the fluidity and complexity that mark twentieth-century man, although in certain literary canons he is a direct predecessor of this period.

His perception of the human being was one-sided and caricatural. He elected to extract with a comedian's skill those traits of character that yield most richly to parody, that seemed to him most prevalent among the common lot of men and most loathsome, and he used them as a lever to open up the world of his heroes. We have seen in story after story how Gogol manipulated external objects, organic interconnections of the senses, mannerisms, and verbal idiosyncrasies to enlarge one single aspect of a man until he becomes its very embodiment and his individuality disappears into type. With a kind of neurotic compulsiveness Gogol singles out and fastens upon boneheaded stupidity, avarice, inarticulateness, spongy sentimentalism, soulless acquisitiveness, moral torpor, physical and mental sloth. His reader has no trouble identifying these invariably repelling traits with the names and surnames that blazon through his fiction. For all the apparent aliveness of the Gogolian character, who is put together from a dizzying number of realistic details, he remains immutable, basically passive, constricted to one set of behavior patterns, and unable to break out of the mold in which Gogol had cast him. He is immobilized in the role that is assigned to him. Therefore, we cannot imagine, for instance, Podkolesin doing anything else but jumping out of one or another prospective bride's window in order to regain the security of his bachelor quarters, or Afanasy Ivanovich fortifying himself hourly with rich Ukrainian fare, or Pavel Chichikov engaging again and again in shady deals that are bound to fail.

For sheer inventiveness in creating situations which project dominant behavior patterns in the boldest relief, Gogol has no peers. Clearly for his artistic method which summons separate luminous instances and myriad external objects to produce desired images, the plot is of little importance. In *Viy*, the mounting terror that invades the timid seminarist in the church is more salient to the story than his reason for entering it. Again, the description of a town turning into rumor, in one of Gogol's most

[173]

compelling tropism devices, is given more weight than what actually happens to Chichikov because of that rumor. A truncated world, deformed, feverishly hyperbolic, inhabited by dehumanized images of man, subject to a persistent debasement and denigration by the author's cankerous muse (of the two hundred twenty-one glancing-wit similes in Part I of *Dead Souls* alone, only twenty-seven do not contain a downward metaphor) is what Gogol's appalled and frightened imagination forged on the anvil of his art. It issued on the one hand from the satirist's urge to rip up other people's garments, inspecting and exposing the seamy side, and on the other from the profoundly productive antagonism between an anguished search for beauty and human perfection and a constant discovery of the paltriness of actual life.

Like the grotesque that he conceived, Gogol himself was a mixture of genres. He dreamed of the large, thirsted after the heroic and the sublime, but ironically he was able to only record successfully the mean and the small. He tried to flee into his dream and was bogged down in the reality of the Gogolian world.

In terms of positive human values this is an unredeemable world. Artistically, however, it is a grotesque of genius in its overstatements and deformations, neither tragic nor comic, neither real nor unreal, where logical thought is replaced by an uninhibited association of images that is irrational, absurd, consistently discordant, and—infranatural. Gogol's widened nostrils seem to sniff out with exhiliration the moral pollution in the air, and the society that he depicts basks complacently in its gratification of mean little vices breathing self-interest, venality, shabby ambitions, hypocrisy, inordinate vanity, and outright deceit. The occasional revolt among his characters against the reigning devastation of their existence (Piskarev's suicide, Poproshchin's escape into insanity, the mayor's seizure of rage in the fifth act, the dead wife's voice heard in the garden), pointing to Gogol's awareness of the forces of the unconscious only strengthens the overall impression of the meaninglessness and stagnation of a world led by fools and hobbled by knaves. We sense the anguish of a creator trying to relate the totality of objective and subjective reality that is already a prognosis of the blend of subject and object that was to be sought by twentieth-century writers. This presentation of a Russia resounding to grotesque motifs, which seem to derive as much from social reality as from private nightmare, should lead the reader in an almost Kafkaesque way to a low-keyed state of disquietude as he becomes increasingly aware of the violence done to the principles of harmony and compatibility. But this is not the case. Although Gogol makes his home in a nightmare, he runs it by authority of the comic spirit, and he comes upon us even more compellingly with yet another thrust of his creative power that places his work into a more habitable orbit. He is a sorcerer who, without shedding any tears, knows how to peel terror like an onion and reveal the farce at the heart of it, or conversely—and with the same unruffled urbanity—work the trick backwards and impale the terror lurking within layers of farce. This wizardry is the key to Gogol's comic genius and brings his art to an apogee of comic grotesque.

What are the mainsprings of Gogol's comic genius? This is how he marked the comic elements in his works: first in the Ukrainian Tales "that were easily and frivolously gay when I made people laugh at situations as amusing as possible, just for the fun of it" and then from *The Inspector General* onwards, "when I realized that if one were to laugh, then there is a need to laugh hard especially at that which deserves it." [62] This is a partial and subjective retrospective of his achievement as a great comic writer which he was to transcend consistently and abundantly.

Gogolian humor, palpably omnipresent in all his fiction, is a strategy of intelligence honed by his scalpel-like talent for observation forever moving into action against general stupidity. The world of incongruity is pitted against the world of ideas. The method of activating this comedy is double-edged: on the one hand, the reader is swept into a mobile dynamic of overabundance with the gustatory "mirthologist" barely keeping the sense of the outrageous under control as he creates colossally improbable characters entrapping or being entrapped in preposterous situations; on the other hand, with consummate and self-conscious deliberateness, Gogol selects from his arsenal of satirical weapons travesties of dialogue (Shponka wooing the girl with reflections on summer flies), confrontation (the two Ivans oggling one another at the dinner party), accidental meetings (Chichikov and Nozdrev at the inn)—scenes which charge the narrative and detonate within every two or three pages into lampoon, burlesque, or sheer farce. What heightens the comicality of these turns is the deadly seriousness of the participants and the parochialism and insularity of their speech and behavior. This summons Gogol's Homeric mockery. He also uses an operative technique which is hyperbole in reverse: The prevailing ignorance and distrust of the larger life among his heroes blinds them to the insignificance of the petty and self-contained existence in which they are immersed, and breeds a ludicrous respect expressed in lofty terms for what is essentially vulgar, ordinary, and suffocatingly stupid.

Another device that pays off handsomely in sharpening the absurd is the typical transformation of a small private happening into a repercussive public event involving large segments of the population (crowds of inquisitive spectators in *The Nose,* overzealous neighbors in *Two Ivans,* terrified city dwellers in *Overcoat*) and the ensuing cyclical storm of conjectures, rumors, and near-panic gathers rapid momentum, only to subside very soon in a reverse movement that is just as abrupt and unexpected.

Some fifty years ago A. L. Slonimsky pioneered a detailed and dispassionate analysis of Gogol's comic techniques [63] which continues to illuminate his complex satirical art. He found antecedents for it in the aesthetic theories of Jean Paul Richter and his followers Th. Lipps and Johann Volkelt, who defined humor as a form of the comic which demonstrates the interdependence of the comic and the tragic, preferably projected in sharp and unexpected intrusions upon each other.[64] This juxtaposition is indeed very similar to the virtuoso balancing acts between the comic and the intense which crowd Gogol's works. An early and a later instance: the description of Vakula's bruising passion for Oksana is followed immediately by the erotic tumble-play of the fat burghers (*Christmas Eve*); and in *Dead Souls,* the poet's evocation of a wondrous and strange feeling traversing his soul is interrupted by Chichikov's crudely abusive reprimand to his coachman. Among the most effective devices Slonimsky stresses the pervasiveness of the incredible and the patently improbable "in the deliberate eschewal of logical conclusions" that comes through the wildly disconnected talk and associations of the heroes "who move in a kind of mental fog," unable to express their thoughts—Shponka to his aunt, the Public Prosecutor to his colleagues, Chichikov to Nozdrev, Manilov to anyone at all. This thrumming movement of non-motivated activity and meaningless speech produces in episode after episode a brilliantly comical distortion of the mundane that normally has motivation, articulation, and association.

Gogol proceeds by an endemic system of disassociations, not only in fictive content, as noted by Slonimsky, but also in the structure of the narrative loaded with the author's free-wheeling personal comments to the reader in digressive passages that are moral, lyrical, expository, instructive, anecdotal, and poetically reminiscent, and which by their very profusion become an organic part of the whole. That Gogol is playing games with the reader, taxing his credulity and emotional patience in the manner of Sterne whom he greatly admired is suggested by F. D. Reeves in one of the most sparkling pages of recent Gogolian scholarship.[65] What finally counts is the game itself. Gogol plays it inexhaustibly. Teasing absurdity out of the human act he upsets all traditional writing rules with a turnabout in syntax, plot, and structure with such a plethora of comic inventions that the reader, forgetting the horror lurking underneath gaily rippling surfaces, is captivated by the pace of the game and surrenders to mirth. But we are grateful to him for our liberation from his grimly ironical view of the world in still another way. The risible mood that he creates in us by the deftly constructed and slyly planted comic devices is sustained by a factor of which Gogol himself, who never laughed at his characters, may have been unaware.

The hyperbole at the core of his satirical art—as Valery Bryusov was the first to point out to a shocked audience at the beginning of this century—impelled Gogol, as it did Swift, to a geometric oversimplification of individuals, preventing them from ever becoming complete human beings.[66] We are fascinated by their antics and by Gogol's mocking exposure of their small venal vices, but we remain emotionally uninvolved and do not identify with them any more than we can with Lilliputians or Brobdingnagians. For all their realistic appurtenances, Gogol's men and women remain inhuman, static, and unreal as does their world which consistently is made to appear too trivial, vulgar, and mean to ring alarms on our own experience of reality. In constructing the images of his heroes with the help of locked-up similes, Gogol pushes reality even further and finally denies it. "Sideboard"

Sobakevich, "hurdy-gurdy" Nozdrev, "watermelon-coach" Korobochka are compelling and unforgettable, but comical abstractions. We laugh at them and are indebted to this great comic
inventor for this catharsis of laughter, bringing us back to our
own complex and fluid humanity.

Dead Souls represents the apogee of Gogol's art and immor-
talizes it. It can be stated with impunity that Gogol was writing
Dead Souls during his entire creative life. All the fiction that
preceded it, with the exception of the Ukrainian stories and
Taras Bulba, may be compared to an assortment of small models
in the inventor's workshop built in preparation for the large
perfected machine. Gogol affected to spurn each story upon its
completion up to and until the conception of Chichikov. Then
the grand design of the novel took hold of his imagination and
did not let go. Everything he had learned to use with increasing
ingenuity and skill in his writer's life found its summit in the
novel. Such creative tactics as the dialectic of emotional and
esthetic extremes, comic invention, sharpened satirical instru-
ments, the ravaging of word hoards, verbal jugglery, linguistic
dazzle, and above all the gradual enlargement of archetypal hero-
images become an organized structure of statements and insights
that interpenetrate each other and must be apprehended in their
totality, like different themes in a symphony which gain meaning
by simultaneous interactions.

The spirited finale of the hero's troika speeding away into the
immeasurable vastness of the Russian land, itself transformed
into a symbol of greatness before which "other countries stand
aside," may well have been (borrowing one of Gogol's imaginative tactics) the author's send-off to his masterpiece, projecting
it to readers in Russia and those beyond, to attain greatness in
the annals of world literature.

CHAPTER 8

Disintegration of Creativity

THE last decade of his life marked the slow suicide of the writer by the man, as Gogol labored hard and vainly over the second volume of *Dead Souls.*

The first statement of important volumes to follow—previously only hinted at in a rather grandiose fashion in the novel itself—appeared in a letter to Zhukovsky mailed together with a copy of *Dead Souls*: "Here is the first part . . . I cannot help seeing how insignificant it is compared to the other parts that will follow. In relation to them it seems to me like an entrance to a palace that is planned to be built on a huge scale by a provincial architect. . . ." [1] At the same time Gogol asked the historian Shevyrev, editor of the Slavophile-slanted *Moskvityanin* (*Muscovite*), to write a review of his novel, and was immensely pleased to read at the end of Shevyrev's long and favorable analysis, a comparison of his work to those of Homer, Dante, Shakespeare, and Walter Scott. [2] This was in 1842 when Gogol was making news in both Moscow and Petersburg. *The Wedding* had just completed an unsuccessful run in the two cities, while a first edition of his *Collected Works* focused critical attention on the newly published *Dead Souls.*

A polarity of views was to be expected. As in 1836, the reactionary journalists Bulgarin and Senkovsky banded against the author of *Inspector General* to vilify *Dead Souls* which they considered a bad and vulgar novel, clumsily styled, replete with dishevelled grammar, indecencies, and needless emphasis on detail. An extreme Slavophile view was expressed by Konstantin Aksakov who saw in Gogol's "epic poem" a Homeric rehabilitation of the "act of creation" that in the "fulfillment and complete freedom of its life" had previously been attained only by Homer and Shakespeare. Even the *Muscovite* refused to print these effulgences, and the essay appeared in brochure form. [3] Other less prejudiced appraisals were for the most part positively worded: The novel was true to life (Sorokin in the *St. Petersburg News*), full of social significance (Pletnyov in the *Northern Bee*), admittedly comic in parts with a natural presentation of realistic details (Masalsky in *Son of the Fatherland*). The strongest voice and one of lasting importance was that of Vissarion Belinsky, spokesman for the young radical intelligentsia, who acclaimed the novel as "a completely Russian national work of art that comes from the innermost recesses of a nation's life, is as true as it is patriotic, pitilessly unveils reality . . . a profoundly thoughtful social and historical creation." [4]

During this year of first reactions to his latest work, when what was done was separated from the artist and took on a life of its own, Gogol's letters showed concern about the reception of the novel by the Russian reading public. He worried about the volume of sales; he wrote to one correspondent that what was most precious to him was the opinion of "sensible people, experienced in life, who knew how to draw advantages from it," and he begged his Moscow friends to forward at once all press notices, even the most scurrilous and seemingly unjust. What they attributed to an author's vanity was in fact Gogol's need to come into closer contact with a Russia he now barely knew and to obtain help from comments on his novel for his writing job ahead.

According to Jorge Luis Borges [5], the finished product counts for much less with a writer who has begun a new project and has new expectations; for the critic, however, the given work to be assessed rates as a unique piece. Therefore, communication between writer and critic tends to break down, but in Gogol's case this did not hold true.

Russian critics consistently failed to recognize the unique and inimitable comic spirit that surges through the novel. When its humor was not completely overlooked, it was described as low-class jokes or common rascality, and the fact that no contemporary reviewers were astute enough to discern the irony of ultimate meanings in *Dead Souls* accorded perfectly with Gogol's new resolutions to eschew comicality for its own sake.

I *Toward Spiritual Rehabilitation*

The change in Gogol from an esthetic to a religio-ethical Weltanschauung occurred after his near encounter with death in

Vienna. He had always yearned to be singled out for the fulfillment of a grand design. Early in life he had aspired to serve the
state; much later, when he felt the stirrings of a powerful national epic within his writer's consciousness, he appealed to
divine providence to assist him in that work. In 1840 he became
convinced that God had spared him for the special purpose of
representing truth and goodness to his fellow men through his
writings. He now shuddered at the thought of the novel just
completed. In notes of that period ("Reflections on Some of the
Heroes in Part One of *Dead Souls*") Gogol traces, with evident
disgust, the transformation of a healthy, alive personality into a
kind of putrified object as "he gradually becomes enmeshed in
vulgar, mundane, and trivial life situations that stifle him and
form a hard shell around his soul." He realized that he had
created a host of characters each one more odious than the next
without a single palliating trait. In his new abject attitude of
"standing before God," and renouncing his former esthetic posi-
tions, he became obsessed with the thought that all the shoddy
vices he had described were his very own and that he had attempted to purge himself of them by making them come alive in
his fiction. However, only "a bad soul can envisage a dead one,"
and the artist, in order to create—as the monk painter states in the
revised version of the *Portrait*—"must raise the spirit upward,"
and must himself be liberated of his shortcomings and attain
moral purity before becoming capable of fulfilling a God-given
purpose by means of his works.

Gogol imposed this view of art on his creative life in launch-
ing a program of spiritual self-improvement, typically oversimpli-
fied and excessive, and leading eventually to artistic extinction
and human defeat. The program itself was a complex of vari-
ables related to his daily living, his milieu, and his art. The
perpetual, intimate presence of God pervaded it. There is no
need to doubt the sincerity of Gogol's attempts to probe into
himself, to correct his moral weaknesses, to become ethically
better. He prayed regularly, attended church services, read the
Holy Gospels and the lives of saints, and planned a pilgrimage to
Jerusalem. He worked with the same tenacity in attempting to
achieve spiritual worthiness in order to write in a positive and
moral vein, as he had in blackening his first drafts with corrections for more striking verbal effects. Even his appearance

changed. The older Aksakov noted during the writer's visit to Russia in 1841 that "he is pale, thin, and a quiet submission to God's will is felt in every step replacing his former gluttony, prankishness, and slyness." [6]

A compulsive letter writer, Gogol started subjecting his bewildered friends to the test of his "glowing vision" in a neat blend of Christian humility and pharisaical arrogance concerning the grandeur of his mission. In Biblical terms he admonishes Danilevsky to listen to his words, distributes his blessings lavishly on Zhukovsky and Shevyrev, and even paraphrases Christ's sayings to Sergey Aksakov. Another leitmotif threading through his correspondence is the need for self-vilification and with it numerous requests to his readers for their criticism of his works, no matter how hostile. Does this reflect, as Victor Erlich suggests, yet another aspect of a penitent author seeking deserved punishment, [7] or is it—at least in part—an overt expression of a professional writer's urge to maintain lines of communication with Russians living on Russian soil?

He could have returned to his own country. But he did not. Instead, he wandered about Western Europe, searching from spa to spa a cure for his increasingly uncertain health and staying in places where he could be near friends. Rome no longer charmed him. He preferred to spend a few months in Frankfurt with the Zhukovskys, in Nice with Mme. Smirnova or the Vielgorsky family, and in Paris, visiting Count A. P. Tolstoy.

Meanwhile he was writing. After a three-year silence Gogol broke into print with a review of Zhukovsky's recent translation of the *Odyssey* that had appeared in the *Contemporary* in the summer of 1846. Among his vast reading public, as yet unaware of his new system of religious ideas, and particularly among the younger radicals, who adulated Gogol as the great debunker of the establishment, the article's endorsement of patriarchial Homeric customs and moral and ethical simplicities caused bewilderment and even alarm. So did the preface to the second edition of *Dead Souls* addressed to "Russian people of all ranks and conditions." In an abject, deliberately "self-put-down" manner that now characterized much of his personal correspondence, the author begged his readers to help in the design of the second part of the work by supplying him with detailed information on the area of the country in which they lived. Clearly, Gogol was having trouble as he moiled over the sequel to his novel.

A third flare-up, abruptly snuffed out by the censor before it reached print, was the allegorical ending that Gogol wanted to append to *Inspector General* scheduled for a benefit performance in May 1847. The play that he had composed in an exuberantly comic vein and as an exercise in wit now troubled him for its lack of deeper meaning. He felt that the enigmatic final figure should be given a moral interpretation. The added monologue at the end that begins with "Oh, how I would like everyone to point out my vices and shortcomings," revealed the new Gogol who was about to transform his scintillating masterpiece into a ritual morality play. The actors were to gather around the mayor and, placing a laurel wreath on his head, would allegorize the action. The town was to represent our inner life, the Inspector General— our conscience, the officials—our weaknesses, and Khlestakov—the epitome of mundane frivolity. In angry rebuttal, Shchepkin, the great actor, whose admiration for the creator of the comedy was surpassed only by his own inspired understanding of the mayor's role, wrote to Gogol that he would resist any such changes: "After my death you may even transform the characters into goats if you like, but now I will not even let you have the policeman, Hold-Your-Mug, for he is also precious to me." [8]

The writing of the second part of *Dead Souls* continued fitfully and with great effort. From letters to his closest friends (Aksakov, Shevyrev, Zhukovsky, the poet Yazykov) we glean that an unflagging belief in his ordained mission urged him on. He had moments of joyous certainty and, when he failed, it was not because his genius was forced into unnatural stances, but because he lacked the necessary moral clarity and steadiness. Illness also interfered. How much of the nervous exhaustion and the sudden drying up of creative energies that he had complained about to Mme. Smirnova in April, 1845 was due to physical rather than psychological causes is difficult to determine: "I cannot seem to go on writing *Dead Souls*. Every line is a kind of torture. I am not strong enough to write. . . . The least excitement throws me back into illness." [9] In May and June he was examined by doctors in Baden-Baden, Hamburg, Karlsbad, and Dresden, and when none of the prescribed remedies helped, he had a presentiment of death and went to make his confession at the Russian Orthodox Church in Weimar. In July 1845 he burned all the manuscripts of the second volume that he had been working on for four years. This experience seems to have strengthened and raised his spirits: "Volume II of *Dead Souls* was burned because it was necessary. . . . At a moment when facing death, I wanted to leave at least something which would be the best remembrance of me. I thank God that he gave me the strength to do it." [10]

II *Selected Passages from Correspondence with Friends*

He had reached a creative stalemate. But Gogol was eager to write, and he devised a plan which admirably fitted his attempts to come closer to Russian society and share the "glorious" burden of his spiritual transfiguration with his countrymen. He wanted to show them how his newly acquired spiritual hygiene had brought him back to Christianity. It seemed to him abundantly clear that if he were to define the guidelines that controlled his own conduct, Russia would benefit from his experience and return to the fundamental teachings of Christ. This socio-religious proclamation was couched in epistolary form. Some of the letters were written to fictive persons, others were actual extracts from his correspondence, and a number of set pieces were written as letters to preserve the one-to-one familiarity of the whole work.

Gogol embarked upon this enterprise at a feverish pitch, completing it in a few months. He had rarely felt such peace and fulfillment, his health improved, and the several letters to Pletnyov in October 1846, arranging for the printing of the book, vibrate with confidence in the necessity of such a work and the foregone conclusion of its success. He was so certain of official approval that when the censor deleted five of the letters, he addressed himself directly to the tsar explaining his praiseworthy purpose and begging for imperial intervention. The publication of *Selected Passages* did, as Gogol had predicted, create a great sensation but not for the reasons that he had advanced. The authorities were wary of the author's call for regeneration among lower officials through moral Christian acts that would free the "divinely ordained" Russian state from corruption and mismanagement. The Church considered as dangerous this troublesome idealist who took the tenets of Orthodoxy for granted and assumed that all the clergy lived up to its profession as well. The mass of readers who had savored and clamored for more rascally, Chichikov-inspired, adventures felt betrayed by this serving of socio-religious rules of conduct instead. Had the famous satirist become prey to a mental aberration that he should have found it necessary to draw up a set of specifics as to how a Russian and Christian landowner should run his estate, how his wife should budget their annual income, how a judge was to dispense justice, and how a governor general was to administer his province and make provisions for the poor? All this advice was delivered in pulpit-like tones and further bolstered with pious homilies and devout reflections.

There was little support from the Slavophile Moscow circle. Upon reading the manuscript, Shevyrev had pleaded to have some of the more blatant religious effulgences left out. Sergey Aksakov deemed it a mistake to "drag God into all our affairs," although publicly neither he nor his other close friends ventured to disagree with the essence of Gogol's message which advocated—as they did—the status quo of orthodoxy, autocracy, and serfdom. Precisely this national and religious attitude stung Belinsky into a bitter attack against the author of *St. Petersburg Stories* and *Dead Souls,* whom the critic had extolled as a literary genius and Realist who had understood Russia's sickness and had declared war on the existing social order. He castigated Gogol in *The Contemporary* (No. 1, 1847) as an ignoramus and a barbarian. Safe from censorship in Salzbrunn, Belinsky gave full vent to his outrage and despair in one of the most violent expositions of his stormy polemical career. A passionate three-page letter that became the manifesto of Russian radicalism was sent to Gogol accusing him of being a turncoat to the true Russia and branding him as "a propagandist of the knout, apostle of ignorance, champion of obscurantism, and panegyrist of Tartar morals." [11]

Across the span of more than a century and with the benefit of cumulative scholarship, modern critics with the exception of the Soviets who have continued to endorse the line of Belinsky's choleric attacks, are reassessing *Selected Passages* and are according it a place in the considerable tradition of inspirational literature. Setchkarev views it as Gogol's idealized reconstruction of a divinely ruled social hierarchy where the poet, like the prophet, is chosen by God to interpret his time.[12] In contemporary terms,

Gogol's wish to have his art serve as a means to total knowledge—his fundamental purpose—foreshadowed the absolute commitment of the Surrealists. Predictably, the theologian-philosophers, Zenkovsky and Mochulsky, project Gogol's divinely inspired mission as one that impelled him to maximize for others the privilege of being a Christian.[13] In a recent translation that has at last made *Selected Passages* available in English, Professor Zeldin claims validity for reinterpreting Gogol's artistic production in the light of this controversial volume.[14] The exact place that should be assigned to it is still in dispute.

There are a few gems among the six literary essays: Pushkin's universality underscored by Dostoevsky with such resounding success forty years later is highlighted for the first time, and no one has better assessed Derzhavin as a poet of grandeur or conveyed the sheer delight of reading Krylov, the fabulist. Gogol's "Four Letters to Diverse Persons about *Dead Souls*," is unreliable evidence as to the genesis and the process of making the novel. But it is persuasively quotable, and Gogolian scholars have not resisted culling one or another passage from it to provide needed chapter and verse. The rest of the volume is given over to personal instructions where Gogol takes aim, with the blended zeal and candor of an Old Testament prophet and the practicality of a social worker, at three arch enemies of Russian national life: irreligion, intellectual pride fostered by the social changes and disarray of the West, and indolence that makes a vacuum of life. He counsels Russian landowners to cultivate the Christian purity propagated by the Orthodox Church, to offer their moral resources to the service of the State, and to remain content with whatever place is assigned to them on the hierarchical ladder, united to their countrymen with bonds of brotherhood and love. These prescriptions had for their purpose the introduction of moral harmony into the fragmentation of a religiously declining world. Later they were to become integrated into the spiritual search of Tolstoy and Dostoevsky.

Stylistically, they make difficult reading. It would seem that whenever Gogol is transparently sincere and writing without tongue in cheek, his sentence structure becomes clogged with involuted phrases, awkward wording, and repetitiveness; and the unfailingly righteous tone of this unwieldy prose does not add to the persuasiveness of the ideas expressed. In fact, in his almost desperate clutch at Russia's psyche, in this attempt to breathe life into his failing creative powers, he inescapably revealed his vast ignorance of the vital forces that were at work in his country and his estrangement from the political and social climate of his time.

There are explanations. Soviet commentators blame the small, closed world of the Russian aristocrats whom Gogol frequented at West European resorts for his comatose attitude toward current affairs and point to the aging poet, Zhukovsky and the pious Mme. Smirnova, Gogol's only close woman friend, as the instigators of his religious "aberration." [15] Eikhenbaum believes that Gogol's "deafness" to the social and political change that was ringing alarms all around him in the Europe of the 1840's was related to the historical situation of the Russian writer who had come of literary age in the 1820's, during the Pushkin epoch that was imbued with the spirit of art for art's sake.[16] Gogol's much quoted remark, "We cannot repeat Pushkin," [57] astutely pinpoints his own perception that the drift of literature was now to be freighted with purpose, and for him its loftiest goal was that "the poet must be instructed in a higher, Christian education." [18] This outspoken espousal of didacticism that found its apogee in *Selected Passages* had been given room in *After the Theater* (1836) and had first appeared in *Arabesques* (1835) where the artist was called upon to serve a spiritually worthy purpose. The consistency of Gogol's esthetic views made for a happy marriage with his political views. This was not understood by the Russian liberals who could not forgive the famous writer for turning traitor to his own earlier scathing exposure of the reactionary regime and for favoring, in *Selected Passages,* serfdom and keeping the peasants illiterate, submissive, and hard working. In fact, Gogol had never shifted from his acceptance of serfdom, a centralized bureaucracy, and the unlimited powers of the tsar which shaped the feudal beliefs and mental horizon of the Ukrainian landed gentry into which he had been born. This seemed the more extraordinary because he had left the family manor early, received no income from it, and lived the financially precarious free-lance life of a rootless member of the intelligentsia.

The public censure of *Selected Passages,* Gogol's last published work during his lifetime, shook him badly. Nevertheless, he decided to rally to the defense of the work, and during the summer of 1847 wrote an *Author's Confession* in which he set down the story of his life as a writer, and climaxed it with an apologia of *Selected Passages.* He recounts that the radical transformation from art for art's sake to didactic art had occurred when he was suddenly illuminated "from above" and understood that the source of his imagination was God's will and that was the will to do good. As a writer he could live only in God's service by portraying the good. And since a writer can only create what he knows and what he is, Gogol had to pass through a period of "looking inward" into himself, and he needed a mirror in which to reflect his weaknesses and defects. That mirror was the book that was maligned and misunderstood. This lengthy, soul-searching exegesis calmed the writer's nerves. But he did not venture to publish it any more than *Meditations on the Divine Liturgy* that he had been putting together and had completed by this time. This was a solemnly worded and ornate text of various types of Russian Orthodox rituals, including an ideal mass with priests and congregation reaching together an apogee of spiritual harmony. Both works—published posthumously—were Gogol's last venture in formal nonfictional prose. He had learned that his strength lay in creative art. It was time to return to *Dead Souls.*

III *Penumbra—Volume Two of* Dead Souls

All that remains of the manuscript of the second part that Gogol burned just before his death are reworked drafts of the first four chapters and a fragment of the concluding one. Shevyrev sorted them out and had them published in 1855.

The action opens with Chichikov's visit to the estate of Andrey Tentetnikov, who at thirty has sunk into country torpor, although he still spends long hours in front of a pile of white paper and unread reference books with the intention of writing a vast chronicle of all the Russias and dreams of his university days when he had been steeped in German idealistic philosophy and had joined a philanthropic society of students who hoped to find ways of helping all mankind. Nothing had come of it, nor of his attempts to revitalize the management of his property after he had given up a dull government job at the capital.

This young landowner, prey to lethargy and vacuous day dreaming, resembles Manilov, but is more intelligent and psychologically more complex. He is a forerunner of Goncharov's indolent, indecisive, and well-wishing Oblomov who was to become a major archetype in Russian literature. Chichikov finds out that Tentetnikov has been offended by a retired general whose daughter strongly attracts him, and Chichikov goes off, still in search of dead souls, but ostensibly to heal the breach between the two neighbors.

The second chapter leads into the leisurely existence of General Betrishchev, an aging military man who is at once affable, extremely generous, testy, self-indulgent, willful, and full of picturesque reflections of former glory. Having an aristocratic bearing, and dressed in a splendid royal purple dressing gown, he uses a condescending familiarity of address to everyone around him. The portrait is persuasive, but not as interesting as Gogol could have made it if he had not blunted his satire with such palliative traits as the general's devotion to his daughter. Everyone admires Ulinka, but the reader is not convinced. She is evidently meant to embody that "marvelous Russian girl" poetized in the first part of the novel, but Gogol does not provide any significant action in which her spontaneity, openness, and inner fervor may be brought out, and she remains—like all his other heroines—an idealized abstraction. Several new personalities are introduced: the hugely gluttonous Petukh who lives only to eat and to eat well, languid Platonov carrying about his lack of occupation like a chronic illness, and maniacal Koshkarev bitten by the "efficiency" bug and running his village like a bureaucratic machine with peasants forced to record all their activities in triplicate. These are worthy figments of Gogol's hyperbolic imagination which recall nostalgically the vitriolic crackle of the first part.

Kostanzhoglo represents the ideal landowner. The energy, organizing ability, and love of work that he communicates to his peasants have transformed his estate into a prosperous self-sufficient community, which so impresses Chichikov that he decides to buy the neighboring property of the near-bankrupt Khlobuev and, by using Kostanzhoglo's methods, to restore the neglected estate. With the appearance of Khlobuev in the fourth chapter, a cultivated but vacillating man whose luxurious tastes have brought him to destitution, new elements are brought in: Chichikov manages to falsify the will of Khlobuev's rich aunt that would thereby leave him the larger portion of her wealth. Sporting a splendid new frock coat to celebrate the swindle, he thinks he has succeeded, but at that moment is thrown into prison. A pious old philanthropist, Murazov, visits him there, admonishes him, and touched by his grief decides to intercede with the Governor General. Meanwhile, Chichikov receives unexpected aid from an easily bribable officer of justice who, for the price of 30,000 rubles, will arrange for the destruction of incriminating evidence. Here, the disclosure of wholesale corruption that swamps the province—falsification of records, denunciations, theft of official papers, removal of state witnesses, mass bribery— in its exuberant exaggeration matches the town rumors that in the first part of the novel had whirlwinded around the purchase of dead souls. This page of magnificent comic play is unfortunately interrupted by the speech of the high-principled Governor General to his assembled local officials, placing the guilt on each one of them and adjuring them to take a good look at their duties and obligations since they seem to be unclear to them. . . . And at this point the last chapter breaks off.

The basic theme of the second volume was to be moral regeneration. In 1847, Markov * was explicitly told that "I do not have in mind any virtuous heroes in the second volume; all of them may be called heroes of defects. Only the protagonists will be more significant than the former ones and it is my intention to reach toward a higher meaning of life and show the Russian person from more than one angle." [19] Stated another way, Gogol wanted to redress his lopsided view of human nature by introducing a measure of normalcy into the behavior of his protagonists and endowing them with a more realistic mixture of various and possibly conflicting traits. This attempt to develop a new alchemy of awareness, that is, to trace the path of spiritual regeneration or to create an ambiguous and diverse hero, was to cut against the grain of his satirical talent that functioned best in the projection of isolated, prefixed, exaggerated phenomena. He would have had to become a Realistic, balanced writer interested in the psychological growth of his heroes and their relationship to the milieu during that growth. This was not Gogol's kind of a creative job; he could not achieve such a turnabout in his art, and some one hundred extant pages of the second volume

* K. I. Markov—landowner and minor literary critic.

give full evidence of it. Gogol made desperate efforts to reconcile his natural writing bent with the self-imposed discipline of the "divinely inspired" project and failed.

It was beyond his own artist's perception to change the rascally Chichikov who goes on cheating hard. Whenever he appears, playing a cat-and-mouse game with the general and ingratiating himself with landlords who might be persuaded to part with their dead souls, the action moves into farcical gear. The prison cell scene with the hero rolling on the floor in a paroxysm of sincere grief, clutching at Murazov's feet and begging for mercy while still mouthing the same unctuous hypocrisies that texture all his dealings is masterly grotesque. Delightful and truly in character is Chichikov's hurried visit, immediately after being released from prison and just before leaving town, to the tailor who sits up all night making him another resplendent frock coat to replace the one torn and stained during his confinement. The next day, as Chichikov admires the tautly-modeled fit of the trousers and the coat that agreeably outline his rotundity, he forgets his recent ordeal. These moments, however, rarely lighten a narrative that is bogged down by numerous uplifting or instructive conversations.

Kostanzhoglo leads some of them. He is one of the important, positive heroes who represents the author's views, and he instructs Chichikov in the mystique of the benefits of labor. Not a single cliché is omitted as Kostanzhoglo exposes the utilitarian concept of gain and winds up with a Biblical reference to the sacredness of physical labor by the sweat of the brow. These precepts point the way to substantial material benefits, but despite Chichikov's persistent queries as to how—in effect—this is to be done, the argument swells into rhetorical abstractions about the happiness to be accrued from a busy country existence lived in harmony with the changing seasons and the earth's produce, and independent of the "swinish" urban habits generated by "stupid and useless" refinements imported from the West. Barring his prolixity, this paragon of efficiency and stout defender of patriachial economics is brother to Sobakevich who had impressed Chichikov with the evident prosperity of his well-run estate and his intransigent contempt for his peers who imitated foreigners in their mode of life. But what a pallid version of him. Compare the following description of Kostanzhoglo to the unforgettable one of the house and the man in the earlier volume: "A man about forty, lively-looking, with a dark complexion, was coming up to the porch. He had on a camel's-hair coat and a visored cap. He obviously cared little about what he wore." [20]

The other significant personality is the old Murazov, not a landlord but a leaseholder * who is an entrepreneur par excellence. He is first mentioned by Kostanzhoglo who considers him supremely intelligent because he has over forty million rubles and will soon own half of Russia. It is obvious that the landlord's respect for the immensely wealthy leaseholder is shared by Gogol, and the comment, therefore, is a curious and enlightening one. It would seem that far from mocking the average man's involuntary awe of millions, Gogol is himself fascinated by the idea of really big, acquired money. In creating Murazov who is automatically admired because of his wealth, has access to the highest ranking persons of the realm, and exerts influence in a domain outside of his enterprises, Gogol steps across his century into the middle of ours where the millionaire image has imposed itself on our social consciousness as the embodiment of invulnerability, great social and political power, and a kind of sanctity. Men so rich become philanthropists. So Murazov, like some financial barons of our day, having acquired his first million in unrevealed ways and—as Gogol seems to imply—not in an absolutely aboveboard manner, can now afford to doff his hat to incorruptibility and, haloed by the prestige conferred by forty million rubles, distribute largesse. Gogol does believe in the greatness of Murazov, for he endows him—as befits his own new religious stance—with piety, simple habits, and an evangelical urge to pull up less fortunate men by assisting them with spiritual counsel rather than financial support. He is Gogol's first truly virtuous character—wealthy and good—and in the fourth chapter he is hard at his vocation, injecting some moral fiber into dissolute Khlobuev with a proposal that he set out on a round of travels about Russia collecting funds for the construc-

---

* leaseholder (otkupshchik). An individual who obtained the right to collect state taxes of some specific kind or nature in return for a fee paid to the state. In Gogol's day this was primarily done in a sort of "carpetbagger" fashion with the tax collectors usually trying to collect more than was due the state and pocketing the difference. This term is often translated as "tax farmer."

tion of a church. Murazov feels, as does Gogol at this point, that every man has something "worthy and potentially great in him," even Chichikov, to whom—as a sharp and clever businessman—he had been naturally drawn. But the knave escapes the blandishments of his spiritual mentor; it is not yet time for Chichikov's regeneration to take place.

The four notebooks of fairly clean copy that contain the first four chapters are of heavy white paper, suggesting that the last fragment written in ink of a different color and on glossy thin yellow paper dates from another period. It has not yet been determined whether the extant pages belong to the manuscript destroyed in 1845 or in 1852. The earlier date, however, seems more probable. Gogol was a slow, fastidious writer, copying and recopying drafts with insertions and corrections as many as eight times, and yet, the thirty-three letters of the *Selected Passages* were completed very rapidly, within a few months. Jesse Zeldin shrewdly suggests in the introduction to his translation of the work (p. xv) that the *Selected Passages* constitutes a statement of the basic ideas which were to form the foundation of Part II of *Dead Souls* and, indeed, in tone, temper, and some specific episodes there is a strong resemblance between the two works.

A few examples: Kostanzhoglo's tirades echo the sentiments of thrift, organization, and energy that Gogol deals out to the Russian landowner, even to citations from the Holy Gospel and the conviction that peasants have no time or need for education. The projected tour of Russia to be undertaken by Khlobuev, acquainting him with persons of the most diverse rank and condition and giving him the opportunity to perform Christian actions is an outline of Letter XX, "It is Necessary to Travel Through Russia." Murazov uses the fatherly, self-righteous intonations that vibrate through the prescriptive letters, and both he and the "ideal" landlord favor a practical form of Christianity based on the puritan ethic of work, self-reliance, and an austere way of life. Warnings against the vitiating influence of Western ideas and Western superficiality of conduct are the underlying themes in both works, and the prince's address to his underlings shows Gogol's trust in the efficacy of swaying crowds by personal appeal. One letter instructs a landlord to punish all offenses by bringing peasants in front of him to hear his solemn adjurations. If what remains of the chapters in Part II had been written by 1846, it would account for the speed with which *Selected Passages*—that lean heavily on Part II—were made ready for publication.

IV *The Last Agony*

Gogol had made plans to visit Jerusalem upon publication of the second volume to thank God for his assistance. The writing came slowly and hard, and two blows—Nikolay M. Yazykov's death in 1847 and the disastrous reception of *Selected Passages*—made him postpone the trip for yet another year. He could find no one to accompany him, the impulse had lessened, and he was reluctant to make the sea voyage alone. But he had spoken so often about his need to address the Lord in the land which had witnessed the sacrifice of Christ that at last he embarked in Naples in January 1848. The experience, which started with violent seasickness, was studded with disappointment. In Beirut, he stayed at the house of the Russian Consul General, a former schoolmate, who took him through Syria to Jerusalem where Gogol was dispirited by the barrenness of the landscape and the strange-looking Arab crowds. He received communion in the Church of the Holy Sepulchre and stood near the tomb of Jesus to hear mass. But he could not pray. The service proceeded so quickly that he felt he had no time to pray.

He returned to Russia destined not to leave it again. Stopping for the summer at Vasilevka where he did some fancy gardening, he urged the serfs in the manner of the *Selected Passages* to earn their way to heaven with hard work, endured his mother's agitated adulation and the homespun festivities organized for him by his sisters, and suffered from the heat. In August he went to the capital and came back to Moscow two months later. For the next two years he lived agreeably enough. In Count A. P. Tolstoy's spacious Moscow house a small apartment was set aside for him with all the comforts of the well-to-do. Summers he vacationed at the country villas of the Aksakovs, the Smirnovs, the Vielgorskys and, from the accounts of his friends who were invited to his occasional readings from the work in progress, he was making headway. The 1850–1851 winter spent in Odessa was particularly active: he met the pietist and mystic Alexander Sturdza, read the Church Fathers, studied modern Greek with a vague intent of going to Greece, frequented the opera, helped stage several amateur plays, spent many social evenings with his friends, and wrote. April saw him back in Moscow apparently in good health but prey to alternate moods of buoyancy and deep vacuous depression. He seemed to have reached an impasse in the novel, was torn by doubts as to whether he was advancing in the right spiritual direction, and confided to Father Matthew Konstantinovsky that he had difficulty in composing a single line.

This priest from the Rzhev Church was Count Tolstoy's confessor, and upon the Count's advice Gogol had sent him a copy of *Selected Passages* and asked for spiritual guidance. Father Matthew was a fanatically religious, narrow-minded, and ill-educated churchman, with the looks and manner of a peasant, who at their very first meeting made a strong impression on Gogol with his uncouth appearance and brutal, peremptory utterances. The only path to follow was that of strict Orthodoxy; everything else was suspected of heresy, including literature in which the sinner before him, having been tempted by the devil, was currently entrapped. His expiation could be achieved only through fasting, confession, and prayer. At a time when Gogol was obviously dismayed by his inability to escape some final truth about himself and was often overwhelmed by his weakness and helplessness, the very rigidity of the priest's position seemed to offer needed support. He saw in his confessor the intermediary between his ailing creative power and the God whom he was unable to reach alone. In letter after letter saturated with self-reproach and self-justification, he implored Father Matthew to intervene for him, arguing that since his talent had been God-given, was it not right of him to use it? He also bargained for time, promising to give up writing altogether as soon as he could find a way to salvation by being useful to mankind with some other occupation.

A number of critics have made a Rasputin-like figure of the priest whose evil genius brought Gogol to the verge of insanity and hastened his death. Arguably, he wielded great influence over the writer's faltering will, and his belief in the efficacy of severe fasting may have caused Gogol's final and crucially weakening abstinence from food.

A light that falls differently on this relationship has often been overlooked. The presence of Father Matthew in his life alleviated the utter solitude that was his when he returned to Russia. The biography of his long sojourn abroad that reads like the uneasy

quest of rootless, displaced twentieth-century man, is singularly
uneventful from a private point of view. In the restless moves
along a fixed circuit of acquaintances and places between bouts
of illness and intensive creativity there was the resolution to live
minimally in an alienation of normal human experiences such as
love, marriage, and deep friendships. A twelve-year absence had
estranged Gogol from his former Nezhin school fellows, with
whom as a young man he had enjoyed warm, spontaneous companionship.[21] Of that group Alexander Danilevsky, his ertswhile
traveling comrade and the only person who did not think of him
primarily as an artist, had married and settled on his estate in
the Ukraine. To everyone else he had become a famous Russian
writer and was offered, wherever he stayed, unstinting hospitality
with arrangements made to suit an active writer's life. Receptions
organized for the timid, socially insecure Gogol may have been
something of an ordeal, and it is not surprising that his admirers
would at times complain about his morose and even rude behavior. He probably felt less than comfortable to be placed on
exhibit in their drawing rooms, like a uniformed general on
parade, embarrassingly alone in the starring role. What he hungered for was some happening or person, unaffected by his
public image—relatively insignificant, but personally important
to him—to loosen the intense reciprocity between his obsessive
sense of guilt and the theological intention of his writing, in
short, to grant him an occasional respite from the trauma of his
creative self. He could have used an intelligent, level-headed,
and disinterested friend. Still, there was Father Matthew who
was completely unimpressed by his reputation, and when given
several chapters of Part II of *Dead Souls* to read had derided
them as "trivial scribbling unworthy of a man who wishes to turn
toward God." [22]

It was probably a relief to be treated as an ordinary human
being, a sinner among a multitude of other sinners. In the last
and most painful interview with the priest, Gogol seemed to have
found the strength to rally to the defense of his art—in the name
of Pushkin. It was related that it was then that the man of God
decided to pull out all the stops in an attempt to cleanse his
spiritual charge of moral deviation by drawing terrifying pictures
of eternal damnation, the exhortation for extreme fasting, and the
command that the pagan and sinner Alexander Pushkin be

blotted out of the writer's mind. "No!" cried out Gogol, "Enough, I cannot listen; this is too terrible!" [23] But after the priest's surly departure, he immediately penned several repenting pages to him and started a long final vigil of abstinence from food.

This was in February 1852. A few days before Gogol had been stricken by news of the death of Yazykov's sister, the deeply religious Madame Khomyakova, to whom he had frequently written about his spiritual problems. He stopped writing entirely. Was it the realization that the light generated by the traditional spiritual verities he wished to bring in his novel to shine upon the vagaries of the human condition had failed him? During Lent he hardly touched any food, spent long hours in prayer and suffered hallucinations.

On the night of February 8th, falling asleep on his couch, he heard a voice from the hereafter. He had the impression that he was already dead, uttered a piercing cry, woke his serf-boy Yakim, and sent him to fetch a priest. Three nights later he knelt before the ikons for a long time. Then he called to Yakim to throw a cape around his shoulders, crept out into the other room with his ever-present briefcase, took out of it a sheaf of notebooks and papers tied together, and placing them on the hearth touched them with his lighted candle. "Master, what are you doing? They might still be useful to you." "Mind you own business, be content to pray," [24] Gogol answered, and when everything was burned he began to cry.

It is not certain whether he had meant to destroy seven years of uphill work in its entirety. He had begged Count A. P. Tolstoy the day before to take his manuscript, but the Count had refused, fearing to intensify his guest's morbid state of mind. In the morning Gogol told him, weeping, that "I had only wanted to burn some of the stuff that should have been destroyed long ago . . . and I burned everything! How strong is the Evil One! He made me do it." [25]

He now prepared himself to die. He no longer believed in the sharp contrivance of the spirit against death, and neither the pleas of his friends, nor even those of the Metropolitan Filaret who commanded Gogol in the name of God to break his fast, nor the outrageous methods for reviving his emaciated and defenseless body (clear broth baths, nose leeches, extremely hot and cold body compresses) that the best-known medical specialists applied were successful. To the ailing creative strength that had clouded his brain with darkness he now preferred the absolute darkness of death. The last day he constantly groaned and asked for water. A nervous fever shook him and he began to lose consciousness. His last comprehensible words were: "A ladder, quick, give me a ladder." [26]

He died on the morning of February 21, 1852. He was forty-three years old. His death was an occasion for public mourning, as thousands of people accompanied his coffin to the cemetery of the Saint Daniel Monastery. Someone on the street, watching the procession, asked: "Who is it? He seems to have so many relatives," and was answered: "This is Nikolay Gogol, and all Russia is his relative." [27]

Notes and References

All references to the fourteen-volume edition of Gogol's works published by the Academy of Sciences of the USSR (1940–1952) are abbreviated below as AN SSSR. All translations from Russian were made by the author of this monograph.

Chapter One

1. Gogol', *Sorochinskaia iarmarka*, AN SSSR, I, 112–113.
2. Vsevolod M. Setchkarev, *Gogol, His Life and Works,* (New York, 1965), p. 7.
3. Letter of October 2, 1833, in V. V. Veresaev, *Gogol' v zhizni* (Moscow-Leningrad, 1933), p. 30.
4. *Ibid.*
5. *Ibid.*, p. 29.
6. Letter of March 1, 1823, *loc. cit.*, p. 72.
7. David Magarshak, *Gogol* (New York, 1957), p. 43.
8. Letter to his uncle P. Kosiarovskii, October 3, 1827, in *N. V. Gogol': Sobranie sochinenii* (Moscow, 1967), VIII, 52.
9. Letter of March 15, 1828, in Veresaev, *op. cit.*, p. 61.
10. Letter of October 3, 1827, *loc. cit.*, p. 53.
11. Letter of April 6, 1827, in Veresaev, *op. cit.*, p. 52.
12. Letter of September 8, 1828, *loc. cit.*, p. 74–75.
13. Letter of August 3, 1829, *loc. cit.*, p. 85.
14. Letter of January 3, 1829, *loc. cit.*, p. 77.
15. Letter of March 15, 1828, *loc. cit.*, p. 61.
16. Letter of July 24, 1829, *loc. cit.*, p. 82–84.
17. Alexandra Smirnova, *Zapiski, dnevnik, vospominaniia, pis'ma* (Moscow 1929), p. 186.
18. Maxim Gorkii, *Istoriia russkoi literatury* (Moscow, 1939), I, 136.
19. Letter of February 2, 1830, in Veresaev, *op. cit.*, p. 90.

Chapter Two

1. AN SSSR, I, 135.
2. *Ibid.*, p. 156.
3. *Ibid.*, p. 210.

4. Vasilii Gippius, *Gogol'* (Leningrad, 1924), p. 33.

5. A group of early French Romantics (Eugène Sue, Jules Janin, Frédéric Soulié, Alexandre Dumas père) known as "l'école frénétique" (the Furious School) produced from the 1820's through the 1840's a prolific quantity of sensational pulp fiction distinguished by its swashbuckling, one-dimensional heroes, crowded with incidents and salted with supernatural elements and goriness. The leitmotif of innocent blood shed in payment for dishonestly obtained wealth is a recurrent theme in these works of which the most popular and most widely translated in Russia was Eugène Sue's *Les Mystères de Paris* in which a mysterious prince haunts Paris ghettoes, punishing evil and rewarding virtue, and where the depravity, destitution, and brutality of the underworld is described in graphic, naturalistic detail.

6. AN SSSR, I, 268.

7. *Ibid.*

8. AN SSSR, I, 293–294.

9. *Ibid.*, pp. 300–301.

10. "How to Teach World History," AN SSSR, VIII, 29.

11. Ivan Turgenev, *Sochineniia* (Leningrad, 1967), XIV, 75–76.

12. Letter of December 6, 1835, AN SSSR, X, 378.

13. Letter of January 22, 1835, AN SSSR, X, 348.

14. AN SSSR, VIII, 10.

15. Gogol', *O literature* (Moscow, 1952), p. 43.

Chapter Three

1. The earlier attempt was a novel entitled *Hetman* of which a fragment of the chapter, "The Captive," Gogol included in *Arabesques*. The six other incomplete chapters were published posthumously. *Hetman* bears witness to Gogol's fascination at that time with the "furious" French school of sensational fiction. There is a profusion of gory horrors in the loosely-linked adventures of a young hero fighting in the Ukrainian War of Liberation against the Poles, but a multitude of realistic details scattered throughout the novel does not succeed in bringing to life any of the characters that remain woodenly-drawn stereotypes.

2. AN SSSR, II, 215–216.

3. *Ibid.*, p. 13.

4. *Ibid.*, p. 15.

5. Renato Poggioli, "Gogol's Old Fashioned Landowners, an Inverted Eclogue," *Indiana Slavic Studies*, III (1963), pp. 53–72.

6. Frederick C. Driessen, *Gogol as a Short Story Writer* (The Hague, 1965), p. 123.

7. AN SSSR, II, 16.

8. *Ibid.*, p. 36.
9. *Ibid.*, p. 245.
10. *Ibid.*, p. 261.
11. *Ibid.*, p. 241.
12. *Ibid.*, p. 226.
13. *Ibid.*, p. 244.
14. *Ibid.*, p. 223, 226–228.
15. *Ibid.*, p. 227.
16. *Ibid.*, p. 226.

Chapter Four

1. AN SSSR, IX, 17.
2. AN SSSR, I, 232.
3. See Nils Ake Nilsson, *Gogol et St. Petersbourg* (Stockholm, 1954) for an interesting study of the influence of the French writers— de Jouy and Balzac—on Gogol's vision of St. Petersburg.
4. Faddei Bulgarin, *Sochineniia* (St. Petersburg, 1830) IX, 213 ff.; Nikolai Polevoy, *Moscow Telegraph*, 1829, Nos. 4, 5, and 6.
5. AN SSSR, III, 9.
6. *Ibid.*
7. *Ibid.*, pp. 12–13.
8. *Ibid.*, pp. 45–46.
9. *Ibid.*, p. 45.
10. *Ibid.*, p. 35.
11. *Ibid.*, p. 107.
12. *Ibid.*, p. 117.
13. *Ibid.*, p. 110.
14. *Ibid.*, pp. 87–88.
15. *Ibid.*, p. 134.
16. *Ibid.*, p. 135.
17. *Ibid.*, p. 198.
18. *Ibid.*, p. 193.
19. *Ibid.*, p. 200.
20. See V. V. Ermilov, *Genii Gogolia* (Moscow, 1959), p. 231; Nikolai Stepanov, *N. V. Gogol'* (Moscow, 1955), p. 261; T. N. Pospelov, *Tvorchestvo N. V. Gogolia* (Leningrad-Moscow, 1953), p. 119.
21. AN SSSR, III, 209.
22. *Ibid.*, p. 214.
23. *Ibid.*, p. 51.
24. *Ibid.*, p. 73.
25. See I. Ermakov, *Ocherki po analizu tvorchestva N. V. Gogolia* (Moscow-Petrograd, 1923), for a long and detailed analysis that pioneered in Russia a psychoanalytical approach to Gogol's art, and which

emphasizes the phallic symbolism of *The Nose*. A similar recent interpretation of this story is the subject of Peter C. Spycher's well-documented article, "N. V. Gogol"s 'The Nose': A Satirical Comic Fantasy Born of an Impotence Complex," *Slavic and East European Journal,* VII, 4 (1963), 361–74.

26. The dominating nasal leitmotif in Sterne's widely read *Tristram Shandy* may have instigated this vogue, although as Vinogradov justly comments, nose humor is abundant in the Russian tradition. Its various aspects—frequently obscene—that peppered carnival shows, lower-type journalism, and the oral anecdote were certainly known to Gogol and his fellow writers of the period. V. Vinogradov, *Evoliutsiia russkogo naturalizma* (Leningrad, 1929), pp. 7–89. Gogol's own nose was startlingly long and mobile; he once boasted in an album note to Mlle. E. Chertkova (AN SSSR, IX, 25) that his nose could get into the smallest snuff box without the aid of fingers. Also, see Vladimir Nabokov's rhapsodic page on Gogol's hymn to that organ in *Nikolai Gogol* (Connecticut, 1944), p. 3.

27. Letter of April, 1838, Veresaev, *op. cit.*, p. 184.

28. Pavel V. Annenkov, in *Gogol' v vospominaniakh sovremennikov* (Moscow, 1952), p. 260.

29. AN SSSR, III, 141.

30. *Ibid.*, p. 145.

31. *Ibid.*, p. 168.

32. F. C. Driessen (*Gogol as a Short Story Writer*, p. 194) suggests another source for the story hinging on the hero's name, Akaky, that according to him is derived from Acacius, a saint's name appearing four times in the Orthodox Saints' calendar that Gogol probably consulted to find the outlandish names proposed at his hero's christening. He points out that the hagiographic account of the sixth century Saint Acacius of Sinai, available to Gogol in various compilations, bears a striking resemblance in the extreme meekness of Acacius, the suffering inflicted upon him by his elder and his final martyrdom to the character and situation of Gogol's hero. See John Schillinger's "Gogol's *The Overcoat* as a Travesty of Hagiography" (*Slavic and East European Journal*, Vol. 16, #1, p. 36–40) that uses Driessen's argument as a springboard for an enlarged and detailed treatment of this similarity as to stylistic devices, general tone and subject matter.

33. *Ibid.*, p. 142.

34. *Ibid.*, p. 148.

35. *Ibid.*, p. 145.

36. *Ibid.*, pp. 143–144.

37. Boris Eikhenbaum, "Kak sdelana *Shinel'* Gogolia," *Voprosy poetiki*, #4, (Leningrad, 1924), pp. 172, 182–183.

Notes and References

38. AN SSSR, XII, 135. This viewpoint which is also shared by the Russian emigré critic, Dmitrii Chizhevskii, "O shineli Gogolia," *Sovremennie zapiski*, (Paris, 1938, No. 67, p. 192) differs sharply from the prevailing opinion among Western and Soviet critics that the story treats the hero as a downtrodden victim of Russian bureaucracy and exemplifies Gogol's humanitarian concern for mankind. This opinion may have been in part instigated by a much quoted statement that "we have all come out of Gogol's *Overcoat*" that has been apocryphally attributed to Dostoevskii.

39. AN SSSR, III, 146.
40. *Ibid.*, p. 165.
41. Prof. V. Zenkovskii, *N. V. Gogol'* (Paris, 1961), p. 80.
42. AN SSSR, III, 171.
43. *Ibid.*, p. 178.
44. *Ibid.*, p. 180.

Chapter Five

1. Sergei Aksakov, *Istoriia moego znakomstva s Gogolem* (Moscow, 1960), pp. 11–12.
2. AN SSSR, X, 262.
3. A major Russian playwright (1823–1886) known for his many realistically vigorous comedies, portraying patriachial customs and acquisitive attitudes of the Moscow merchant class.
4. AN SSSR, X, 375.
5. AN SSSR, IV, 11.
6. *Ibid.*, p. 116.
7. *Ibid.*, pp. 48–50.
8. Letter to Zhukovsky, March 6, 1847, AN SSSR, XIII, 243.
9. "Griboedov's *Woe from Wit*," *Otechestvennye zapiski*, Nos. 6 and 7 (1840).
10. AN SSSR, IV, 116.
11. *Literaturnye vospominaniia* (Leningrad, 1960), p. 81.
12. *Ibid.*, p. 82.
13. Letter of April 29, 1836, Veresaev, *op. cit.*, p. 163.
14. AN SSSR, XI, 45.
15. "On the Development of Journalistic Writing in 1834 and 1835," in which Gogol pointed out the literary ignorance, colorlessness, and trivial judgments of Russian literary critics. Singling out for primary attack Osip Senkovskii, editor of *Library for Reading*, the biggest journal in bulk and circulation, Gogol' accused him of a lack of esthetic perception and the "unseemly" habit of using pages of the journal to lavish praise on his own fiction pieces which came out under various pseudonyms. Gogol's subjective, emotionally-charged tone clearly

revealed his irritation at earlier unfavorable criticism of the Ukrainian tales and the *Arabesques* from the conservative press. Pushkin, embarrassed by the personal tone of the essay, added—editorially—that the lively and provocative article did not reflect the general attitude of *The Contemporary*. For a detailed account of the skirmish between Gogol and Senkowskii see, Paul Debreczeny, *Nikolay Gogol and His Contemporary Critics* (Philadelphia, 1966), pp. 14–15.

16. AN SSSR, V, 142.

17. *Ibid.*, p. 144.

18. *Ibid.*, p. 146.

19. *Ibid.*, p. 169.

20. AN SSSR, VIII, 186.

21. *Ibid.*, p. 187.

22. See Nikolai Stepanov, *Poety i prozaiki* (Moscow, 1966), p. 225.

23. June 28, 1836, AN SSSR, XI, 50. Gogol was extremely sensitive to any derogatory comment regarding his work, and the coolness between the two writers must be attributed to Pushkin's evident disapproval of the acerbity and bias contained in Gogol's article on the Petersburg press. See note 15, above.

Chapter Six

1. Letter of June 28, 1836, AN SSSR, XI, 49.

2. Letter to Zhukovskii, November 12, 1836, *loc. cit.*, p. 74.

3. Letter to Prokopovich, January 25, 1837, *loc. cit.*, p. 81.

4. Letter of March 30, 1837, AN SSSR, XI, 91.

5. Letter to Danilevskii, April 15, 1837, *loc. cit.*, p. 95.

6. Annenkov, *loc. cit.*, p. 276.

7. Letter to Danilevskii, April 15, 1837, AN SSSR, XI, 95.

8. *Rome*, AN SSSR, III, 234.

9. For a brief but persuasive defense of this argument, see Leonard J. Kent's "Introduction" to *Gogol's Collected Tales and Plays* (New York, 1964), pp. xxi–xxii.

10. Aksakov, *op. cit.*, p. 222.

11. Magarshak, *op. cit.*, p. 168.

12. AN SSSR, III, 324.

13. Aksakov, *op. cit.*, pp. 31– 32.

14. AN SSSR, XI, 330.

15. Annenkov, *loc. cit.*, p. 271.

16. Aksakov, *op. cit.*, pp. 69–70.

Chapter Seven

1. *Avtorskaia ispoved'* (*Author's Confession*) 1847, AN SSSR, VIII, 440.

2. Letter to Zhukovskii, November 28, 1836. AN SSSR, XI, 77.

3. *Uchebnaia kniga slovesnosti dlia russkogo iunoshestva* (*A Manual of Literature for Russian Youth*) (1845–1846), AN SSSR, VIII, 478–479.

4. AN SSSR, VI, 7.

5. *Ibid.*, p. 8.

6. Ibid., p. 10.

7. *Ibid.*, p. 11.

8. *Ibid.*, p. 12.

9. *Ibid.*, p. 26.

10. *Ibid.*, p. 45.

11. *Ibid.*, p. 53.

12. *Ibid.*, p. 70.

13. *Ibid.*, p. 94.

14. *Ibid.*, pp. 112–113.

15. *Ibid.*, p. 116.

16. *Ibid.*, p. 119.

17. *Ibid.*, p. 115.

18. *Ibid.*, p. 224.

19. *Ibid.*, p. 242.

20. *Ibid.*, p. 53.

21. *Ibid.*, p. 176.

22. Ibid., p. 693.

23. *Ibid.*, p. 157.

24. V. Ermilov, *Genii Gogolia*, p. 375; N. Stepanov, *Gogol'*, p. 444.

25. AN SSSR, VI, 220.

26. For a thorough and interesting treatment of the development of Belinskii's thought see: Herbert E. Bowman, *Vissarion Belinskii* (Cambridge, 1954).

27. Vissarion Belinskii, "Dead Souls" (critical article), *N. V. Gogol' v russkoi kritike* (Moscow, 1953), p. 121.

28. Bulgarin considered that the unadorned exposure of substandard conditions of life in the St. Petersburg ghettos found in the writings of the new school were comparable in their eschewal of "pruderie" to the excessive Naturalism of underworld scenes that shocked and thrilled the French readers of the *Mystères de Paris* by Eugène Sue. See note 5 in Chapter Two.

29. For a careful and erudite analysis of the influence of Gogol's stylistic mannerisms on the language of Dostoevskii, see: V. V. Vinogradov, *Evolutsiia russkogo naturalizma* (Leningrad, 1929).

30. D. S. Mirskii, *A History of Russian Literature* (New York, 1949), p. 171.

31. Vladimir Lenin, *Polnoe sobranie sochinenii,* Vol. XXV: March–June 1914, p. 94.

32. "Four letters to Diverse Persons about *Dead Souls,*" AN SSSR, VIII, 294.

33. Andrei Belyi (1880–1934), Symbolist poet, novelist, critic, original theorist on Russian prosody. Poetry distinguished for intricate musical patterns, linguistic experimentation; the novels (*Silver Dove,* 1910, *Petersburg,* 1913, *Kotik Letaev,* 1918) bear traces of Gogol and Dostoevskii, where reality is replaced or distorted by a grotesque world of his imagination.

34. Vasilii Rozanov (1856–1919), critic and philosopher who stressed the sexual principle as the generative creative spirit of the universe, and whose reputation rests chiefly on his collection of maxims, aphorisms, essays (*Solitaria,* 1912, *Fallen Leaves,* 1915), and a penetrating critical study of Dostoevskii.

35. Valerii Briusov (1873–1924), a leading Symbolist poet, one of the best known critics and verse theorizers of his day. In 1904 he founded the *Scales (Vesy),* the most important literary publication of the Symbolist movement.

36. Dmitrii Merezhkovskii (1866–1941), writer, critic, moralist, a leading figure in the Decadent movement; prominent member of the Religious and Philosophical Society where he presented his view of European history as a struggle between paganism and Christianity, popularized in a trilogy of historical novels—*Death of the Gods,* 1893; *Leonardo da Vinci,* 1896; *Peter and Alexis,* 1902—which brought him fame in Russia and abroad.

37. Nabokov, *op. cit.,* p. 70.

38. AN SSSR, VI, 21–22.

39. *Ibid.,* p. 103.

40. *Ibid.,* p. 98.

41. Letter of November 12, 1836, AN SSSR, XI, 75.

42. AN SSSR, VI, 134.

43. *Ibid.*

44. *Ibid.,* p. 243.

45. Professor Carl Proffer makes a strong case for this conjecture in *The Simile and Gogol's Dead Souls* (The Hague, 1967), pp. 193–194.

46. "Four Letters to Diverse Persons about *Dead Souls,*" p. 293.

47. Nabokov, *op. cit.,* pp. 63–66.

48. "Four Letters to Diverse Persons . . . ," p. 293.

49. AN SSSR, VI, 134.

50. *Ibid.,* pp. 134–135.

51. *Ibid.,* p. 221.

52. *Ibid.,* p. 247.

53. For an exhaustive and scholarly review of Gogol's liberal use of similes see Carl Proffer, *op. cit.*, in Note 45, above.

54. AN SSSR, VI, 126.

55. *Ibid.*, p. 94.

56. V. Vinogradov, *Evolutsiia russkogo naturalizma* (Leningrad, 1929), pp. 154–155.

57. Eikhenbaum, "Kak sdelana shinel' Gogolia," *loc. cit.*, pp. 152–155.

58. Andrei Belyi, *Masterstvo Gogolia* (Moscow-Leningrad, 1934), pp. 196–197.

59. AN SSSR, VI, 109.

60. In an unusual mood of professional frankness, Gogol described his laborious method of work in a conversation with Nikolai Berg, poet, translator, and ertswhile contributor to the *Muscovite*, at Shevarev's house in 1848: *Gogol' v vospominaniiakh sovremennikov* (Moscow-Leningrad, 1952), p. 506.

61. AN SSSR, VI, 44.

62. Letter to Zhukovskii, January 10, 1848, in Veresaev, *Gogol' v zhizni*, p. 165.

63. A. L. Slonimskii, *Tekhnika komicheskogo u Gogolia* (Petrograd, 1923).

64. Johann Paul Friedrich Richter, known as Jean Paul (1763–1825); Th. Lipps, (1851–1914); Johann Volkelt, (1848–1930).

65. F. D. Reeves *The Russian Novel* (New York, 1966), p. 86.

66. In a brilliant address entitled "Ispepel'nyi" ("The Burned-Out One"), delivered on the occasion of Gogol's Centenary at the Russian Literary Society of St. Petersburg, in April 1909.

Chapter Eight

1. Letter of June 26, 1842, AN SSSR, XII, 69–70.

2. *Muscovite*, 1842, Nos. 7 and 8.

3. Konstantin Aksakov, *Neskol'ko slov o poeme Gogolia "Pokhozhdeniia Chichikova ili Mertvye Dushi"* (Moscow, 1842).

4. Belinskii, *Otechestvennye zapiski*, St. Petersburg, 1842, No. 1.

5. Jorge Luis Borges, "Secret Miracle," *Labyrinths* (New York, 1964), p. 90.

6. Aksakov, *op. cit.*, p. 54.

7. Victor Erlich, *Gogol* (New Haven, 1969), p. 169.

8. Letter of May 22, 1847, in *N. V. Gogol' v pis'makh i vospominaniiakh*, edited by Vasilii Gippius (Moscow, 1931), p. 344.

9. Letter of April, 1845, AN SSSR, p. 477.

10. "Four Letters to Diverse Persons about *Dead Souls*," AN SSSR, VII, 297.

11. Belinskii, first published by Alexander Herzen in *Poliarnaia zvezda*, 1855, pp. 65–75.

12. Setchkarev, *op. cit.*, p. 237.

13. Konstantin Mochulskii, *Dukhovnyi put' Gogolia* (Paris, 1934), pp. 106–109; Zenkovskii, *op. cit.*, pp. 178–185.

14. *Selected Passages from Correspondence with Friends* by Nikolai Gogol, translated by Jesse Zeldin (Nashville, 1969), pp. xv–xvi.

15. Ermilov, *op. cit.*, p. 397; M. Khrapchenko, *Tvorchestvo Gogolia* (Moscow, 1956), pp. 496–497; Stepanov, *N. V. Gogol'*, pp. 518–522.

16. Eikhenbaum, "Gogol' i delo literatury" *Voprosy poetiki*, pp. 160–161.

17. *Selected Passages* . . . , letter No. 31, "What is the Essence of Russian Poetry and its Originality?" AN SSSR, VIII, 407.

18. *Ibid.*, p. 408.

19. Letter of December 3, 1849. AN SSSR, XIV, 152.

20. AN SSSR, VII, 59.

21. Three years before his final return to Russia, Gogol had expressed his dread of remaining a stranger in his native land even if he were to settle there for good. Letter to Mme. Smirnova, April 2, 1845, AN SSSR, XII, 473.

22. F. Obraztsov Archpriest of Tver, recorded these words as they were spoken to him by Father Matthew; in "Otets Matvey Konstantinovskii po moim vospominaniiam," *Tverskie Eparkhial'nye Novosti*, No. 5 (1902), pp. 137–138.

23. A. Tarasenkov, "Poslednie dni zhizni Gogolia, *Gogol' v vospominaniiakh sovremennikov*, p. 514. Dr. Tarasenkov was a friend of Gogol and one of the doctors in attendance during his last illness. He has provided a detailed and orderly account of Gogol's last few weeks before his death.

24. *Ibid.*, p. 516.

25. *Ibid.*, p. 517.

26. *Ibid.*, p. 524.

27. N. V. Zhdanov, *N. V. Gogol'* (Moscow, 1933), p. 90.

Selected Bibliography

PRIMARY SOURCES

The Collected Tales and Plays of Nikolai Gogol. Ed. by L. J. Kent. New York: Random House, 1964.

Dead Souls. Tr. by Bernard G. Guerney. New York: Holt, Rinehart and Winston 1962.

Dead Souls. Tr. by George Reavey. London: McGraw-Hill, 1957.

Letters of Nikolai Gogol. Selected and edited by Carl Proffer. The Hague: Mouton, 1967.

O literature. Izbrannye stat'i i pis'ma. Moscow: Goslitizdat, 1952.

Oeuvres Complètes. Edition de la Pléiade, sous la direction de G. Aucouturier. Paris: Bibliothèque de la Pléiade, 1966.

Polnoe sobranie sochinenii, 10th edition. Ed. by N. S. Tikhonravov and V. Shenrok. St. Petersburg, 1889–1896.

Polnoe sobranie sochinenii. 14 vols. Moscow-Leningrad: AN SSSR, 1940–1952.

Selected Passages from Correspondence with Friends. Tr. by Jesse Zelden. Nashville: Vanderbilt U. Press, 1969.

Sobranie sochinenii v shesti tomakh. Moscow: Goslitizdat, 1953.

SECONDARY SOURCES

AKSAKOV, SERGEI T. *Istoriia moego znakomstva s Gogolem.* Moscow: AN SSSR, 1960. Despite its somewhat emotional tone, this personal and detailed memoir gives much authentic and interesting firsthand information about Gogol's long and close contacts with his Moscow circle of friends.

DEBRECZENY, PAUL. *Nikolay Gogol and His Contemporary Critics.* Philadelphia: American Philosophical Society, 1966. Detailed summaries of all the criticism written on Gogol's works up to 1848 form this thoroughly documented study which also contains an author-title index and a bibliography of about 100 reviews. Valuable guide.

DRIESSEN, FREDERICK C. *Gogol as a Short Story Writer.* The Hague: Mouton, 1965. A complete handbook of all the stories with a genesis for each, detailed plot summaries, listing of major themes, and a painstaking study of the evolution of character portrayal. A solid, basic interpretation, but pedestrian in style and inclined to be indiscriminate in overall admiration of the writer. Extensive bibliography.

ERLICH, VICTOR. *Gogol.* New Haven: Yale Univ. Press, 1969. A number of fresh and persuasive insights into the nature of Gogol's distorted art, his own kind of realism, and his insistence on recurring themes and images is offered in an erudite, but disorganized review of Gogol's works. Many topics are provocatively suggested and referentially supported, but seldom fully developed. Many passages of excellent theoretical interpretation, but lacking sufficient confirming illustrations from the text.

ERMILOV, V. V. *Genii Gogolia.* Moscow: *Sovetskii pisatel'*, 1959. A strongly Belinskii-influenced study, poorly structured, which omits in characteristic Soviet fashion any mention of Gogol's borrowings from literary sources common to the West. Nevertheless, despite the deliberate emphasis on Gogol's humanitarianism and realism, there remains a powerful impression of his uneasy confrontation with his world and his time.

GIPPIUS, VASILII. *Ot Pushkina do Bloka.* Leningrad: Nauka, 1966. The best annotated critical survey of Gogol's works, admirably terse, factual, unprejudiced. An indispensable reference.

GOURFINKEL, N. *Nicolas Gogol, dramaturge.* Paris: L'Arche, 1956. A brief, but most informative account of Gogol's theater, its fortunes in Russia and abroad. Lucid style vies with punctilious scholarship.

GUKOVSKII, G. A. *Realizm Gogolia.* Moscow: Goslitizdat, 1959. One of the most dependable Soviet studies of Gogol, but too inclined to support the official view of predominating realism in the mature works.

KHRAPCHENKO, M. B. *Tvorchestvo Gogolia.* Moscow: AN SSSR, 1954. A scholarly and exhaustive survey of the literary climate in Gogol's day and a painstaking analysis of his fiction, but marred by an overemphasis on sociological factors.

KOTLIAREVSKII, N. A. *Nikolai Vasil'evich Gogol'.* 4th rev. ed. Petrograd, 1915. This study, by the Russian Dean of Gogol scholars, situates the writer and his works within the Russian literary world of his day, and carefully traces native and foreign influences on his art. Although obsolete in places, still remains basic and important.

KHLESHOV, V. I. *Natural'naia shkola v russkoi literature XIX veka.* Moscow: "Prosveshchenie," 1965.

Selected Bibliography

MAGARSHAK, DAVID. *Gogol.* New York: Grove Press, 1957. Gogol's artistic development is examined in a sober, matter-of-fact way with abundant quotations from Gogol's own writings, and the memoirs and impressions of his contemporaries. Mundane, lively, interesting.

MOCHUL'SKII, KONSTANTIN. *Dukhovnyi put' Gogolia.* Paris: YMCA Press, 1934. A searching examination Gogol's "angst" from a Christian, theological point of view, defined as a pathological fear of death. The last two chapters, dealing with the growth of an obsessive and tortured religiosity are extremely well done.

NABOKOV, VLADIMIR. *Nikolai Gogol.* Norfolk: New Directions Books, Conn. 1944). A brief, brilliant essay in the Formalist manner with emphasis on the symbolic quality and the universality of Gogol's mature work. Clever, consciously brittle in tone.

SCHLOEZER, DE B. *Gogol.* Paris: J. B. Janin, 1946. A highly sensitive and probing evocation of Gogol's inner life. The fatal split in his nature is shown as a key to his personal tragedy and how it is reflected in the apogee and decline of his art.

SETCHKAREV, VSEVOLOD M. New York: New York University Press, 1965. A comprehensive account which separates biography from critical analysis. Much canny and astute detection shows up Gogol's borrowings in plot and themes from Western European writers and each piece of fiction is thoroughly summarized for plot. No footnotes and little bibliography.

STEPANOV, NIKOLAI L. *N. V. Gogol'.* Moscow: Goslitizdat, 1955. An orderly chronicle of Gogol's life, literary production, and professional associations. Strongly tinctured with nationalistic bias in the Soviet manner. Valuable comments on Gogol's dramatic art.

TROYAT, HENRI. *Gogol.* Paris: Flammarion, 1971. An ambitious, dramatically written documentary, exhaustive, but insensitive. Helpful appendix of bibliographical and biographical information.

VERESAEV, V. V. *Gogol' v zhizni.* Moscow-Leningrad: "Academia," 1933. The largest collection in a single volume of Gogol's letters interspersed with pertinent background material and comments by contemporaries. An indispensable biographical aid.

VINOGRADOV, V. V. *Etiudy o stile Gogolia.* Leningrad: "Academia," 1926. A pioneer work in the diagnosis of Gogol's language and style which still leads in the punctilious linguistic research of discovering the various components of the Gogolian idiom and his innovation of the Russian literary language. Splendid piece of linguistic scholarship.

Index

Index

Shchepkin, Mikhail, 45, 46, 105, 116, 122, 183
Shevyrev, Stepan, 179, 182, 183, 185, 188
Slonimsky, A. L., 176, 177
Sollogub, Vladimir, 158
Sorokin, M. P., 180
Stanislavsky, Konstantin, 116
Stendhal (pseudonym of Henri Beyle), 73
Sterne, Laurence, 168, 177
Sturdza, Alexander, 194
Swift, Jonathan, 177

Tasso, Torquato, 136
Teryaev, Ivan, 25
Tieck, Johann Ludwig, 39
Tolstoy, A. P., 182, 194, 195, 197
Tolstoy, Leo, 159, 173, 186
Troshchinsky, Andrey, 30
Troshchinsky, Dmitry, 17, 19, 23, 30
Turgenev, Ivan, 8, 47, 124

Uvarov, S. S., 47

Vasilevka, 19, 22, 24, 27, 45, 131, 194
Venevitinov, Dmitry, 49
Vielgorsky, Joseph, 129-30, 132
Vielgorsky, M. J., 129, 133, 182, 194
Vinogradov, V. V., 169
Volkelt, Johann, 176
Volkonskaya, Zinaida, 126
Voss, Johann Heinrich, 25
Vyazemsky, Peter A., 117
Vysotsky, Gerasim, 22, 28

Yakim, 27, 28, 46, 197
Yazykov, Nikolay, 131, 132, 183, 194, 197

Zagoskin, Mikhail, 45, 102
Zeldin, Jesse, 186, 193
Zenkovsky, V., 98, 186
Zhukovsky, Vasily, 20, 25, 31, 32, 47, 49, 122, 123, 125, 126, 131, 164, 179, 182, 183, 187
Zolotarev, Ivan, 122, 126